ATOMS, ENERGY and MACHINES

an introduction to chemistry and physics

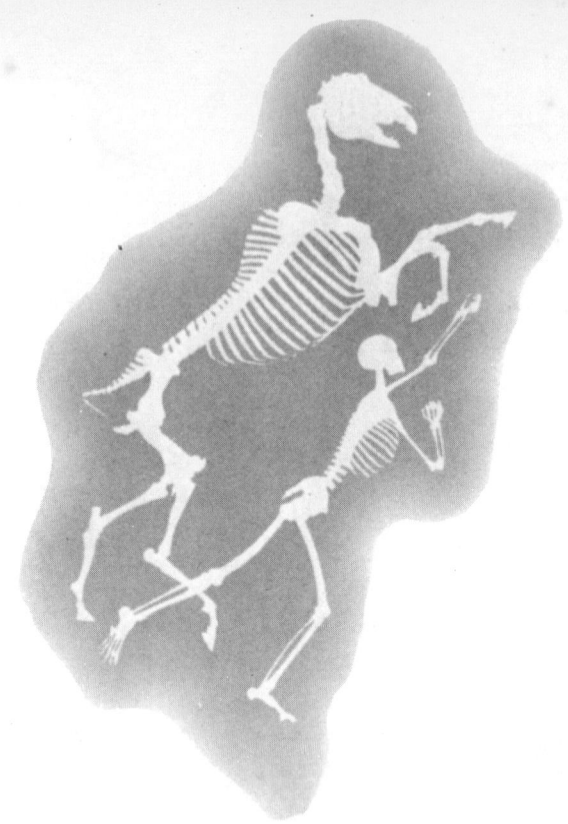

CREATIVE SCIENCE SERIES
Etta Schneider Ress, Ed.D., *editor-in-chief*
Gerhard Ramberg, *art editor*   Bueford D. Smith, *art editor*

PLANETS, STARS AND SPACE
Joseph Miles Chamberlain, Ed.D.
Assistant Director, The American Museum of Natural History
Kenneth L. Franklin, Ph.D.,
Astronomer, American Museum — Hayden Planetarium
Thomas D. Nicholson, Ph.D.,
Chairman and Astronomer, American Museum — Hayden Planetarium

THE EARTH'S STORY
Gerald Ames and Rose Wyler
Authors, *The Golden Book of Astronomy, The Story of the Ice Age, The Golden Book of Biology, Planet Earth, Food and Life*

THE WAY OF THE WEATHER
Jerome Spar, Ph.D., Professor
Department of Meteorology and Oceanography
New York University, N.Y.

ATOMS, ENERGY AND MACHINES
Jack McCormick, Ph.D., Curator
The Academy of Natural Sciences of Philadelphia, Pennsylvania

THE LIVES OF ANIMALS
Sydney Anderson, Ph.D., Associate Curator, American Museum of Natural History, New York

MAN FROM THE BEGINNING
Stanley A. Freed, Ph.D., Associate Curator, American Museum of Natural History, New York
Ruth S. Freed, Ph.D., Assistant Professor of Anthropology, New York University, New York

THE OCEAN LABORATORY
Athelstan Spilhaus, D.Sc.
Formerly Dean, Institute of Technology,
University of Minnesota

FOOD AND LIFE
Gerald Ames and Rose Wyler
Authors, *The Golden Book of Astronomy, The Story of the Ice Age, The Golden Book of Biology, Planet Earth, The Earth's Story*

The four books above are also available in Spanish.

ATOMS, ENERGY and MACHINES

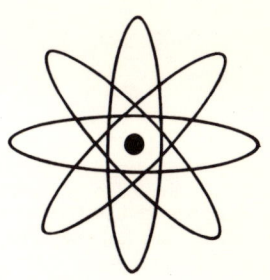

by

Jack McCormick

The Academy of Natural Sciences
of Philadelphia

Published by

CREATIVE
EDUCATIONAL
SOCIETY, INC.

In Co-operation with
THE AMERICAN MUSEUM OF NATURAL HISTORY
NEW YORK

ATOMS, ENERGY AND MACHINES

Copyright 1957, 1962, 1967
Creative Educational Society, Inc.
Mankato, Minnesota

*International copyrights
reserved in all countries*

PRINTED IN THE U.S.A.

Library of Congress Catalog Card Number 66-30642

PICTURE ACKNOWLEDGMENTS

Aero Service Corp. 128
Allied Chemical and Dye Corp. 132
Allis-Chalmers 160
American Forest Products Industries, Inc. . . . 23, 100
American Iron & Steel Institute 188, 189
A.T.&T. (Lazarnick) . . . . 172 (bottom), 173
Atlas Chemical Industries. 65
Barnett, Bud 34
Battelle Memorial Institute . . . . 219 (bottom), (right, left)
Bell Aerosystems Co. 164
Bell Helicopter Corp. 167
Bell Telephone Co. 168
Black Star . . . . 139 (top), 142 (Jesse Lunger)
Boeing Airplane Co. 149
Borden Company . . . . 126 (top left)
Brahms, Dr. Jack P. 171
Brookhaven National Laboratory 217
Bureau of Reclamation (A. E. McCloud) 74
Caterpillar Tractor Co. . . . . 69 (bottom)
Chicago, Rock Island & Pacific Railroad 156
Columbia Broadcasting System 174, 175
Corning Glass Works 171
Chrysler Corp. 154, 163
D. C. Heath and Co. . . . . 71 (top)
Diamond Match Co. 64
Dupont 204
Eastman Kodak 206
Ebco Manufacturing Co. . . . . 32 (top right)
Educational Services, Inc. 43, 72
Elgin Watch Co. 88, 89, 108
F.P.G. (A. W. Blakesley) 48
F. P. G. (D. L. Hunsberger) 107
Galloway, Ewing . . . . 17, 20, 31, 44, 52, 62, 71 (bottom), 90, 105 (top left), 117 (right), 120, 125, 126 (left center, bottom left), 139 (bottom), 161 (top), 172 (top), 182, 184, 186
General Electric 99, 178
General Motors . . . . 202 (left)
Goodyear Tire and Rubber Co. . . . . 151 (top)
Glenbrook Laboratories 95
H. Armstrong Roberts . . . . 55, 63 (right), 113
Hawaii Press Bureau . . . . 126 (top right), 145
Hoffman Electronics Corp. 57
Howard, Dick . . . . 28 (left), 33, 36, 39, 41, 47 (bottom), 49, 50, 69 (top), 85, 104 (bottom), 105 (top right, bottom left), 114, 115 (right), 118, 121, 122, 123, 133, 201 (right)
Information Service of South Africa 124
International News 130
Johns-Manville 58
Ken Bell Photography Ltd. 141
Kinkead, Harvey A. III . . . . 29 (bottom)
Lever Brothers Co. 200
Libbey-Owens-Ford Glass Co. 196, 197
Lockheed-California Co. . . . . 165 (bottom)
Marquardt Corp. . . . . . . 161 (bottom), 162 (top)
McCormick, Jack . . . . . 21, 25, 28 (right), 30, 37, 80, 111
Meisel from Monkmeyer . . . . 104 (top)
Mobil Oil Co. . . . . 63 (right)
NASA . . . . 165 (top), 195
National Board of Fire Underwriters . . . 32 (top left)
National Broadcasting Co. 177
National Bureau of Standards 79, 96
National Dairy Council 146
National Institutes of Health . . . . 219 (top)
New Departure . . . . 63 (left)
Ohaus Scale Corp. 84
Old Town Canoe Co. . . 47 (top), 105 (bottom right)
O'Rourke, J. Barry, from
   Playboy Magazine . . . . 207 (left)
Pennsylvania Railroad 158
Picner X-Ray 217
Popular Science 98
Remington Arms 45
Reynolds Metal Co. 190, 191
Seabrook Farms Co. . . . . 32 (bottom left), 147 (bottom)
Sherwin-Williams Co. . . . . 202 (right), 203
Siebert, Dick 42
Squibb Division of Olin . . . . 147 (top)
Standard Oil Co. . . . . 68, 126 (top center), 180, 193
Sugar Inf., Inc. 22
Tokheim Corp. 81
Toledo Scale Corp. 76
Trane Co. 169
Union Carbide . . . . 194 (right), 218
Union Pacific Railroad 10, 153
U.S. Air Force . . . . 83, 94, 194 (left)
U.S. Forest Service . . . . 115 (left), 183
United States Lines Co. 150
U.S. Navy . . . . 151 (bottom)
U.S. Weather Bureau . . . . 131 (Killian)
Van de Poll from Monkmeyer . . . . 126 (right center, bottom right)
Westinghouse 87
Weyerhaeuser Timber Co., The 24
Wm. S. Merrel Co. . . . . 219 (bottom)

Illustrated by

**Helmut Wimmer, American Museum-Hayden Planetarium, New York, N. Y.
and H. William Paulson**

Foreword

SCIENCE has come to be recognized as one of the dominant forces of our time. Because of its leading role in shaping our civilization, science must be brought to people everywhere.

There are many ways of practicing the dissemination of science, and several media through which this process can operate. As long as it remains accurate, sincere, and interesting, each approach to public education in this field has its legitimate place.

The printed word, aided and augmented by appropriate pictorial illustration, remains one of the best ways of carrying science to the public. In this book Dr. McCormick, through the medium of a hundred brief texts and numerous photographs and diagrams, presents a concise yet far-ranging survey of many aspects of our physical environment.

People want direct, simple answers to the many questions that arise in their minds as a result of the unprecedented scientific development and technical wizardry of the age in which they are living. *Atoms, Energy and Machines* will meet this need admirably as far as the physical world is concerned. It might be thought of as a first, informal introduction to physics and chemistry. As such, it treats many developments that are on the frontiers of these mushrooming sciences, yet it pays due attention to the more basic, if somewhat less spectacular topics which are fundamental to the later developments.

Clear, simple and forthright in method of presentation, this book should do much toward bringing science down to earth and thereby open new vistas of pleasurable enlightenment for the average person.

IRA M. FREEMAN
Rutgers, The State University
New Brunswick, N. J.

Contents

Picture Acknowledgments 4
Foreword 5
Introduction 9

Chapter I
MATTER AND ITS BUILDING BLOCKS...10-11

The World of the Atom...**12-19**
Compounds, Mixtures, and Dispersions...**20-23**
Change: Physical and Chemical...**24-25**
Four Kinds of Chemical Reactions...**26-27**
Matter and Its Forms: Gases, Liquids, Solids...**28-35**
Changes of Phase...**36-39**
Matter in Motion: Newton's Laws...**40-47**
How We Recognize Things...**48-49**

Chapter II
ENERGY EVERYWHERE...50-51

Two Forms of Energy: Potential and Kinetic...**52-55**
Radiant Energy...**56-57**
Heat Energy...**58-59**
Friction...**60-63**
Chemical Energy...**64-65**
Electrical Energy...**66-67**
Force...**68-69**
Magnetic Force...**70-71**
Gravitation...**72-73**
The Conversion and Conservation of Energy...**74-75**

Chapter III
HOW WE MEASURE...76-77

Linear Measures and Standards of Measurement...**78-79**
Area and Volume...**80-81**
Mass and Weight...**82-85**
Density and Specific Gravity...**86-87**
Time...**88-89**
Speed, Velocity, and Acceleration...**90-91**
Work and Power...**92-93**
Temperature, Total Heat, and Specific Heat...**94-97**
Electricity...**98-99**

Chapter IV
THE PHYSICS OF SIMPLE MACHINES...100-101

The Lever...**102-105**
The Wheel and Axle...**106-109**
The Pulley...**110-111**
The Inclined Plane, Wedge, and Screw...**112-117**

Chapter V

A WORLD OF LIFE...118-119

Air and Air Pressure...**120-123**
Carbon...**124-125**
The Carbon Cycle...**126-127**
Oxygen...**128-129**
Hydrogen...**130-131**
Acids and Bases...**132-133**

Water...**134-137**
The Nitrogen Cycle...**138-139**
What Makes a Man?...**140-141**
The Chemistry of a Plant...**142-143**
Photosynthesis...**144-145**
Vitamins...**146-147**

Chapter VI

PHYSICS IN EVERYDAY LIFE...148-149

Boats, Balloons, and Submarines...**150-151**
The Steam Engine...**152-153**
The Gas Engine...**154-155**
The Diesel Engine...**156-157**
The Electric Motor...**158-159**
The Turbine...**160**
The Jet Engine...**161-163**
Rockets...**164-165**
The Airplane...**166-167**

Sound...**168-169**
Bending Light...**170-171**
The Telephone...**172-173**
Radio...**174-175**
Television...**176-177**
Refrigeration...**178-179**
Putting Air Pressure to Work...**180-181**
Microscopes and Telescopes...**182-183**
Electrolysis and Electroplating...**184-185**

Chapter VII

CHEMISTRY IN EVERYDAY LIFE...186-187

The Chemistry of Iron and Steel...**188-189**
The Chemistry of Aluminum...**190-191**
The Chemistry of Petroleum...**192-193**
Plastics...**194-195**
Glass...**196-197**

Extinguishing Fires...**198-199**
Soap...**200-201**
Paint...**202-203**
Chemistry on the Farm...**204-205**
Photography...**206-207**

Chapter VIII

TOMORROW'S WORLD: POWER FROM THE ATOM...208-209

Nuclear Fission, Nuclear Fusion, and Nuclear Reactors...**210-216**

Plants, Animals and the Atom......**217-219**

Appendix...**220-221**

Index...**222-224**

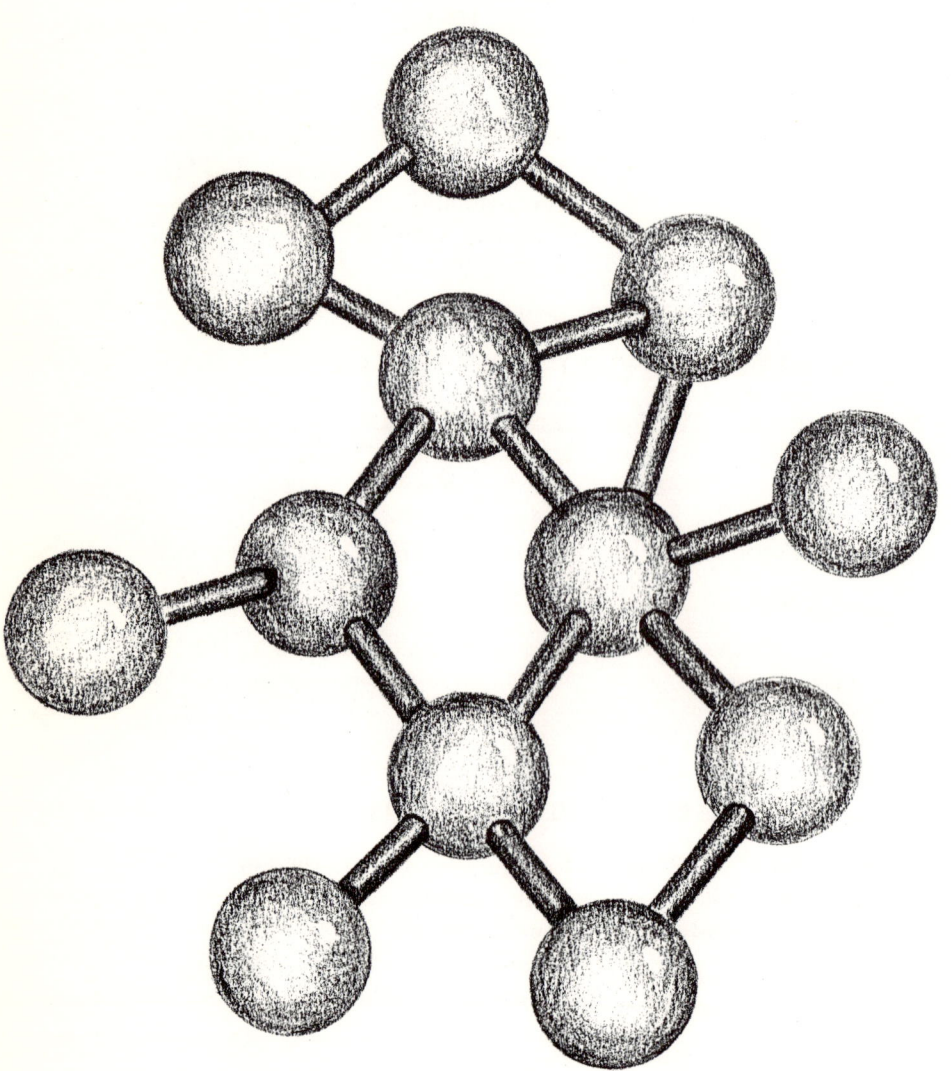

Introduction

THIS IS A book about *science*. This word, "science," is used so commonly today that many people have forgotten its real meaning. It should be used only to describe man's orderly search for knowledge by methods of precise observation and measurement, by controlled experiments, and by careful reasoning based upon these observations, measurements and experiments.

Two main divisions of science generally are recognized. *Biological science* deals with living things, their functions, and their histories. In contrast, *physical science,* which includes astronomy, meteorology, geology, chemistry, and physics, is concerned with non-living things. These two divisions of science actually are related closely, for many of the principles discovered by physical scientists apply to living things.

Chemistry and physics both are concerned with the variety and structure of matter. *Chemistry,* however, is concerned primarily with the basic kinds of matter — the elements, the changes which occur when different kinds of matter are brought together, and the energy that is released or absorbed during these changes. *Physics,* in comparison, considers the motions of bodies, the ultimate structure of matter, the various forms of energy, and concepts of space and time.

I have written this book about chemistry and physics with the hope that you young men and women who read it will find in it the inspiration that will lead you to seek further into science. This search will prepare you for your role as citizens of a new scientific age in which you will be expected to guide our nation and our world by your votes and by your participation in government. Should you choose a career in science, you will find it to be exciting, stimulating, and, perhaps, supremely beneficial to all mankind.

Humbly, this book is dedicated to my children, Jim and Wendy, and to the other young citizens of our world who will inherit the power to destroy and the responsibility to protect man and nature.

JACK MCCORMICK

CHAPTER I

MATTER AND ITS BUILDING BLOCKS

Three phases of matter
Solid, Liquid, Gas

Ordinarily, we think of matter as something we can touch — rocks, liquids, cloth, flesh, paper, wood. Scientists, however, must deal with things which are so small that we would not be aware of them if we were to touch them or things which are so far away we may never touch them. To provide a definition of matter which will apply anywhere and to any substance, scientists say that matter is something which has mass and inertia and occupies space. You probably do not understand the words "mass" and "inertia" now, but you will learn about them in the following pages.

For centuries, man has been seeking to understand the workings of nature. When he learned the principles of the behavior of matter and, much later, how matter is constructed, he was able to understand many things which had been mysteries before — how two substances can join to make a third, different substance; how a solid can melt and form a liquid which can later change to a gas or back to a solid; why some things float and others do not; why a rock falls to earth, but a gas-filled balloon will rise. This understanding has developed largely since 1600 and its effect on our lives is almost unbelievable. Civilization has changed more in the 370 years since 1600 than it had during the previous 2000 years. Distances which were unknown before the voyage of Columbus now are spanned in a split second by radio, in a few minutes by an orbiting satellite, and in a few hours by a jet airplane.

In this chapter, you will see many objects which are familiar to you, but they will appear in a new light — as matter behaving according to the principles of chemistry and physics. You will learn how matter is put together and that all things are basically alike.

THE WORLD OF THE ATOM

About 2,000 years ago, some philosophers reasoned that because things burn, are juicy, or leave an ash when burned, everything must be composed of four "elements" — earth, air, fire, and water. Others argued that if a substance were cut into smaller and smaller pieces, at last only solid particles, exactly alike and which could not be cut again, would remain. They called these particles *atoms* (Greek for "uncut"). Atoms of each substance were believed to be shaped differently from atoms of any other substance.

Some Greek philosophers believed matter to be composed of atoms which differed only in size and shape.

Other philosophers believed all things were made of these four elements.

The atomic theory was almost forgotten, but the belief in four "elements" persisted until about 300 years ago. However, observations accumulated that could not be explained in terms of four elements. In 1804, John Dalton proposed a *modern atomic theory*. By Dalton's time, it was known that most substances (*compounds*) can be separated into simpler ones called *elements*. Elements cannot be separated by ordinary means. Scientists found that when elements combine and form a compound, the amount of each element that enters into the reaction always is proportional to the amount of the other element or elements. This fact is termed the *Law of Definite Proportions*. For example, when hydrogen (H) and oxygen (O) form water, eight times more oxygen (by weight) than hydrogen is used. If the amounts of the two elements are not in this proportion (8:1), some oxygen or hydrogen remains uncombined.

Some elements combine in different proportions and form different compounds. For example, if sixteen times as much oxygen as hydrogen is present, they form hydrogen peroxide rather than water. This fact is expressed by the *Law of Multiple Proportions*.

Knowledge that elements always combine in definite proportions convinced John Dalton that: 1) Matter is formed of atoms; 2) The variety of atoms is limited. Atoms of a given element are alike in size, shape, and weight, and differ from atoms of all other elements. 3) Chemical changes involve joining or separating of entire atoms and do not alter the atoms; 4) Each compound has basic units, called *molecules*, composed of atoms of elements which formed the compound. If molecules are divided, the compound is destroyed — reduced to its elements.

Dalton believed atoms were the smallest particles of matter. This belief continued until 1895 when Sir Joseph J. Thompson discovered the *electron*, a part of an atom. Electrons have a negative electric charge (see page 66). Because the atom is electrically neutral, the discovery of one charged atomic particle suggested the presence of a second particle with an opposite electric charge. A positively-charged particle, named the *proton*, was found in 1911. A third particle, the electrically neutral *neutron*, was discovered in 1932. Thus, our understanding of the minute structure of matter has developed only recently. It has been only 160 years since the atomic structure of matter was proved and about 75 years since we learned that each atom has several parts. This knowledge has allowed us to develop methods by which we can split and change atoms — and release tremendous amounts of energy. (Chapter VIII.)

After the parts of an atom were known, scientists learned how they fit together. Protons and neutrons form the center or *nucleus* of the atom. They are called *nuclear particles*, or *nucleons*. Electrons orbit around the nucleus and are so far from it that the atom consists largely of empty space. For example, if the nucleus of a hydrogen atom were basketball-size, its electron would be whirling more than a mile away.

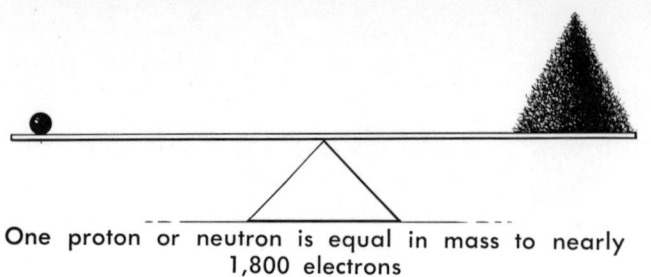
One proton or neutron is equal in mass to nearly 1,800 electrons

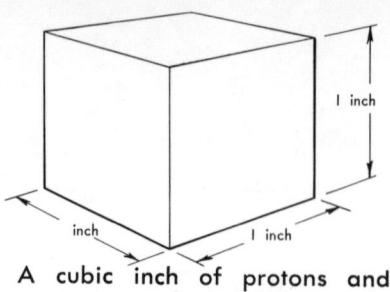
A cubic inch of protons and neutrons, packed tightly together, would weigh more than a billion tons.

In addition, scientists have found that the parts of an atom are very different in size and mass (mass is explained on page 82). Practically all of the mass of an atom is contained in its nucleus. The reason for this is that the mass of a single proton or neutron is equal to the combined mass of nearly 1800 electrons. But even the nuclear particles are unbelievably light. If we could weigh a single proton or neutron, it would tip the scales at less than a million-billion-billionth of a pound. However, nuclear particles are so tiny that one cubic inch packed full of protons and neutrons would weigh more than a billion tons!

The electrons of one atom are identical to the electrons of any other atom. This is true also of protons and neutrons. This fact has led to the present concept that atoms differ chiefly in the numbers of electrons, protons, and neutrons they contain.

A substance formed entirely of similar atoms is known as an *element*. An element cannot be changed into another element, nor can an element be made from some other substance by ordinary chemical methods. Carbon, copper, gold, iron, lead, mercury, silver, sulfur, and tin are elements which were known before the Christian era. The tenth element, arsenic, was not discovered until 1250 years after the birth of Christ. But by 1925, 88

A particle from one atom is identical to the same part from any other atom

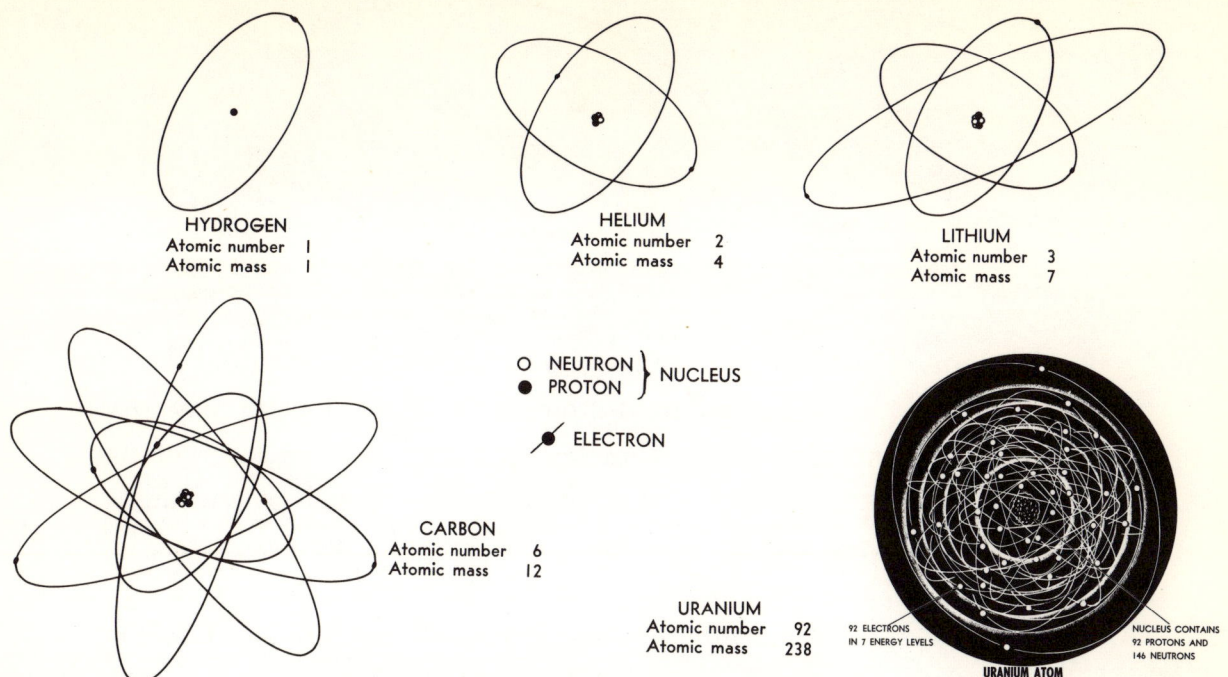

ATOMS OF THE ELEMENTS DIFFER CHIEFLY IN THE NUMBERS OF THE PROTONS, NEUTRONS AND ELECTRONS THEY CONTAIN.

elements were known. Then, as research with atom smashers began and work on the development of the first atomic bomb progressed, four new elements — technetium, promethium, astatine, and Francium — were made in the laboratory. During the post war years, eleven more elements have been produced, so that we now know *103 elements*. The 15 man-made elements are so unstable that their atoms break apart or "decay" very rapidly — some of them in just a few seconds — and form simpler elements. Although these short-lived elements may have occurred in our earth during its formation, they disappeared within a short time. However, evidence of their presence has been found in stars.

The atoms of different elements have different masses. Hydrogen, for example, is very light, but uranium is very heavy. These differences in mass are due to the fact that the various elements have different numbers of particles in their atoms. Hydrogen has only one proton in its nucleus and one electron in orbit. But uranium has 92 protons and 143 neutrons in its nucleus and 92 electrons in orbit around the nucleus. Thus, you would expect uranium, which has 235 nuclear particles, to have a mass many times as great as that of hydrogen, which has only one nuclear particle.

ISOTOPES OF HYDROGEN

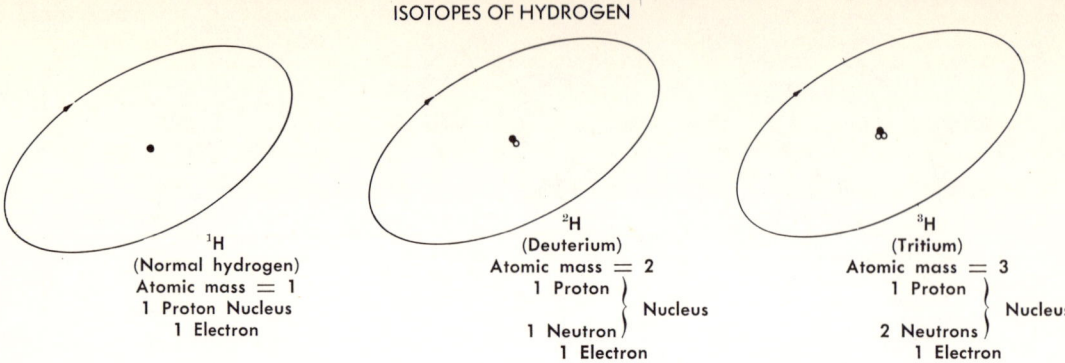

^{1}H
(Normal hydrogen)
Atomic mass = 1
1 Proton Nucleus
1 Electron

^{2}H
(Deuterium)
Atomic mass = 2
1 Proton ⎫
1 Neutron ⎬ Nucleus
1 Electron

^{3}H
(Tritium)
Atomic mass = 3
1 Proton ⎫
2 Neutrons ⎬ Nucleus
1 Electron

All atoms of an element have the same number of protons and the same number of electrons, but different atoms of the same element may vary in the number of neutrons in their nuclei. As a result, various kinds of atoms of an element — its *isotopes* — have slightly different masses and differ in stability. Hydrogen has at least three isotopes. The normal isotope (^{1}H) has one proton and one electron. Its atomic mass is 1. The second isotope (^{2}H, or D), called deuterium, has one additional neutron. Its atomic mass is 2. Tritium, the third isotope of hydrogen (^{3}H), has two neutrons, which brings its atomic mass to 3. Chemically, all isotopes of an element behave similarly. For example, any isotope of hydrogen can combine with oxygen and form water (H_2O). Water with ^{1}H is common in living things. But "heavy water" made with deuterium (D_2O) produces change in the appearance and activities of plants and animals. Several kinds of algae and fungi have grown in nearly pure (99.7%) heavy water. So far, no higher animal or plant has been reared entirely on deuterated water. No mammal, for example, has survived when 40 per cent or more of the hydrogen in its food and water was deuterium.

In the table, all elements are listed numerically by their *atomic numbers*. The atomic number tells how many protons are in the nucleus of the atom and how many electrons rotate around the nucleus, for these two kinds of particles are present in equal quantities. The table also shows the abbreviation, or *symbol* for the *atomic mass*, or *atomic weight* for each element. The atomic mass indicates the mass of the element in relation to the masses of other elements when the atomic (nucleic) mass of the principal isotope of carbon is set equal to 12. Notice that the mass of carbon listed (atomic number 6) is not 12, but is 12.01115. The reason for this is that the mass of each isotope of an element is different from that of the other isotopes. The atomic mass in the table is the average for all the isotopes of the element in the proportions in which they occur in nature.

	Atomic Number	Symbol	Atomic Mass		Atomic Number	Symbol	Atomic Mass
Hydrogen	1	H	1.00797	Iodine	53	I	126.9044
Helium	2	He	4.0026	Xenon	54	Xe	131.30
Lithium	3	Li	6.939	Cesium	55	Cs	132.905
Beryllium	4	Be	9.0122	Barium	56	Ba	137.34
Boron	5	B	10.811	Lanthanum	57	La	138.91
Carbon	6	C	12.01115	Cerium	58	Ce	140.12
Nitrogen	7	N	14.0067	Praseodymium	59	Pr	140.907
Oxygen	8	O	15.9994	Neodymium	60	Nd	144.24
Fluorine	9	F	18.9984	Promethium	61	Pm	(145)
Neon	10	Ne	20.183	Samarium	62	Sm	150.35
Sodium	11	Na	22.9898	Europium	63	Eu	151.96
Magnesium	12	Mg	24.312	Gadolinium	64	Gd	157.25
Aluminum	13	Al	26.9815	Terbium	65	Tb	158.924
Silicon	14	Si	28.086	Dysprosium	66	Dy	162.50
Phosphorus	15	P	30.9738	Holmium	67	Ho	164.930
Sulfur	16	S	32.064	Erbium	68	Er	167.26
Chlorine	17	Cl	35.453	Thulium	69	Tm	168.934
Argon	18	Ar	39.948	Ytterbium	70	Yb	173.04
Potassium	19	K	39.102	Lutetium	71	Lu	174.97
Calcium	20	Ca	40.08	Hafnium	72	Hf	178.49
Scandium	21	Sc	44.956	Tantalum	73	Ta	180.948
Titanium	22	Ti	47.90	Tungsten*	74	W	183.85
Vanadium	23	V	50.942	Rhenium	75	Re	186.2
Chromium	24	Cr	51.996	Osmium	76	Os	190.2
Manganese	25	Mn	54.9380	Iridium	77	Ir	192.2
Iron	26	Fe	55.847	Platinum	78	Pt	195.09
Cobalt	27	Co	58.9332	Gold	79	Au	196.967
Nickel	28	Ni	58.71	Mercury	80	Hg	200.59
Copper	29	Cu	63.54	Thallium	81	Tl	204.37
Zinc	30	Zn	65.37	Lead**	82	Pb	207.19
Gallium	31	Ga	69.72	Bismuth	83	Bi	208.980
Germanium	32	Ge	72.59	Polonium	84	Po	(210)
Arsenic	33	As	74.9216	Astatine	85	At	(210)
Selenium	34	Se	78.96	Radon	86	Rn	(222)
Bromine	35	Br	79.909	Francium	87	Fr	(223)
Krypton	36	Kr	83.80	Radium	88	Ra	(227)
Rubidium	37	Rb	85.47	Actinium	89	Ac	(227)
Strontium	38	Sr	87.62	Thorium	90	Th	232.038
Yttrium	39	Y	88.905	Protactinium	91	Pa	(231)
Zirconium	40	Zr	91.22	Uranium	92	U	238.03
Niobium	41	Nb	92.906	Neptunium	93	Np	(237)
Molybdenum	42	Mo	95.94	Plutonium	94	Pu	(242)
Technetium	43	Tc	(99)	Americium	95	Am	(243)
Ruthenium	44	Ru	101.07	Curium	96	Cm	(245)
Rhodium	45	Rh	102.905	Berkelium	97	Bk	(249)
Palladium	46	Pd	106.4	Californium	98	Cf	(249)
Silver	47	Ag	107.870	Einsteinium	99	Es	(254)
Cadmium	48	Cd	112.40	Fermium	100	Fm	(252)
Indium	49	In	114.82	Mendelevium	101	Md	(256)
Tin	50	Sn	118.69	(Unnamed)	102	—	(254)
Antimony	51	Sb	121.75	Lawrencium	103	Lw	(257)
Tellurium	52	Te	127.60				

Elements 84–92 (Polonium through Uranium): NATURALLY RADIOACTIVE
Elements 93–103 (Neptunium through Lawrencium): NOT FOUND IN NATURE — INCREASINGLY UNSTABLE

*Also known as Wolfram
**Also known as Plumbum

Parentheses indicate radioactive elements which have no fixed atomic mass. Mass given is for the most stable isotope.

The elliptical paths in which the electrons orbit around the nucleus of an atom are not haphazard — they form several *electron shells* or *energy levels* at more or less fixed distances from the nucleus. The orbits of the electrons in any given energy level cross over one another so that in a complex atom their paths trace a net-like sphere which completely envelops the nucleus (see diagrams on page 15).

There may be from one to seven energy levels in an atom, depending upon the number of electrons it contains. The energy level closest to the nucleus can hold 2 electrons. The second level can hold 8 electrons; the third level 18; and the fourth 32. The fifth and sixth energy levels never have more than 32 electrons, although they may be able to hold more. The seventh level probably never contains more than two electrons. But regardless of its capacity, when an energy level is the outermost one of the atom, it can hold no more than 8 electrons.

The number of electrons in the outermost energy level determines the chemical behavior of an atom. If it contains fewer than 8 electrons, the atom is chemically unstable and will add electrons to complete the group of 8 or lose them so that the last complete energy level is exposed. The number of electrons an atom can add or lose is known as its *valence*.

When an atom which can add electrons contacts an atom that can lose them, electrons may pass from one atom to the other. The atom that loses a negatively charged electron is left with a surplus positive electrical charge. By adding an electron, the second atom will have a surplus negative electrical charge. These charged atoms are called *ions* to distinguish them from normal, electrically neutral atoms. Because opposite charges attract one another, the ions are electrically joined or bonded together and form a *molecule*.

The process by which molecules are formed after the transfer of electrons from the atoms of one element to those of another is known as *electrovalence*. Sodium, a soft, silvery-white, poisonous metal, and chlorine, a poisonous greenish-yellow gas, are examples of elements which form an electrovanelt molecule — sodium chloride, more familiar to us as salt. This

THE FORMATION OF MOLECULES

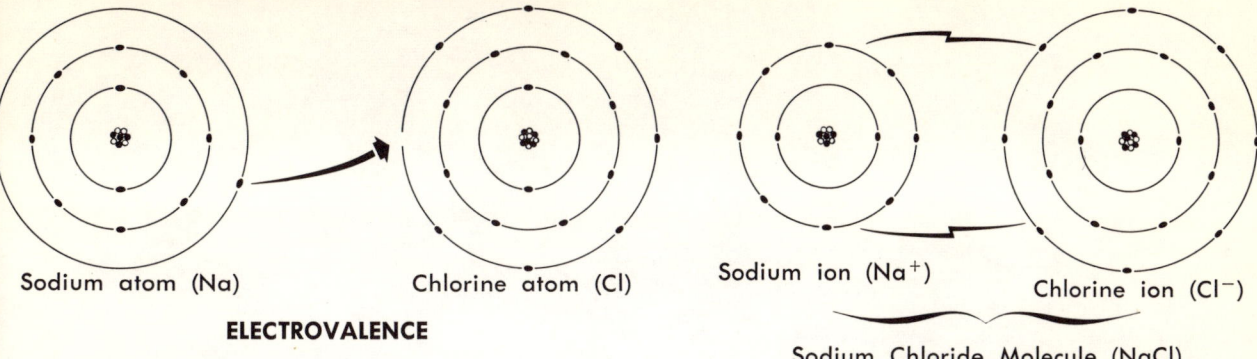

ELECTROVALENCE

also demonstrates a surprising thing — when elements combine to form a molecule they usually become unrecognizable and the molecule has properties which are totally different from those of the elements which form it.

Another way in which molecules are formed is illustrated by two gases, hydrogen and oxygen, which combine to make water. Hydrogen has a single electron, whereas oxygen has 8 electrons, of which 2 fill the innermost electron shell and 6 orbit in the second shell which thus has space for 2 more electrons. Instead of surrendering electrons to the oxygen and becoming ions, two hydrogen atoms become attached to each oxygen atom and share their electrons with it. Such a molecule is said to be *covalent*.

A molecule is the smallest particle of a substance that can exist alone and each of more than half a million substances has its own distinctive molecule. A few elements which have 8 electrons in the outermost shell, such as helium, xenon, radon, and argon are very inactive and were believed not to combine with other atoms. But in 1962 scientists at Argonne National Laboratory demonstrated stable compounds of xenon and radon, and others doubtless exist. However, the molecules of these inactive elements are single atoms. Other molecules may contain hundreds of atoms, but all are small. A glass of water, for example, contains about 10 trillion trillion molecules (10,000,000,000,000,000,000,000,000 or 10^{24}).

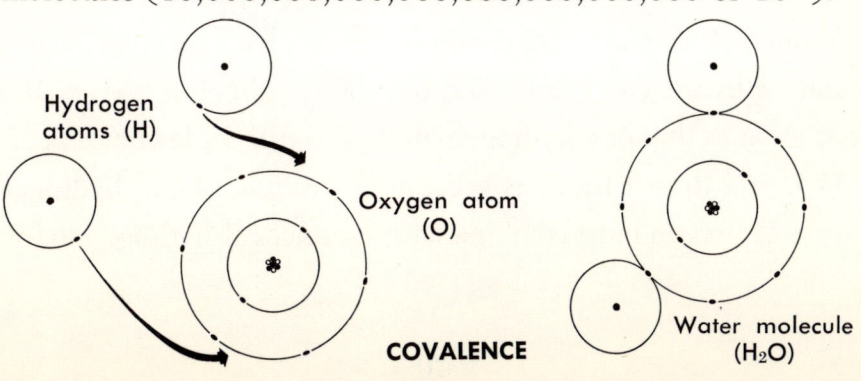

COVALENCE

COMPOUNDS, MIXTURES, AND DISPERSIONS

Although they may not be aware of it, these people are breathing a mixture (air), have compounds (salt and water) contained in a mixture (glass) before them, and are eating a mixture (soup). There are several other mixtures around them.

If the molecules of a substance are composed of atoms of two or more elements, the substance is known as a *compound*. Because each compound has its own characteristic molecule, it also has a definite chemical composition. A molecule of water, for example, always has one atom of oxygen and two atoms of hydrogen (H_2O). Because the weight of an oxygen atom is 16 times as great as that of a hydrogen atom (See the table of atomic masses on page 17), and thus 8 times as great as the weight of two hydrogen atoms, 16 ounces of oxygen must combine with 2 ounces of hydrogen to form every

18 ounces of water. The same proportions could be used even if the weights were measured in pounds or tons.

The molecules of compounds are the products of chemical reactions. During their formation energy in the form of heat, light, or electricity may be given off or absorbed. Compounds also must be broken down by chemical means. For instance, the hydrogen and oxygen atoms in a molecule of water cannot be separated by pulling them apart. They separate easily, however, when an electric current is passed through the water.

A *mixture* is composed of two or more compounds or elements. These compounds or elements may be thoroughly intermixed, but each retains its own properties. No chemical reaction occurs during the formation of a mixture to create a characteristic structural unit, such as a molecule. The ingredients of a mixture, therefore, can be present in any proportion. And because their ingredients are not bonded together by chemical forces, mixtures often can be separated by mechanical means. You could easily sort a mixture of licorice sticks, cinnamon balls, and peppermint patties.

Many substances which we see or use every day are mixtures. Air is a mixture composed almost entirely of elements. Paper, milk, soil, gasoline,

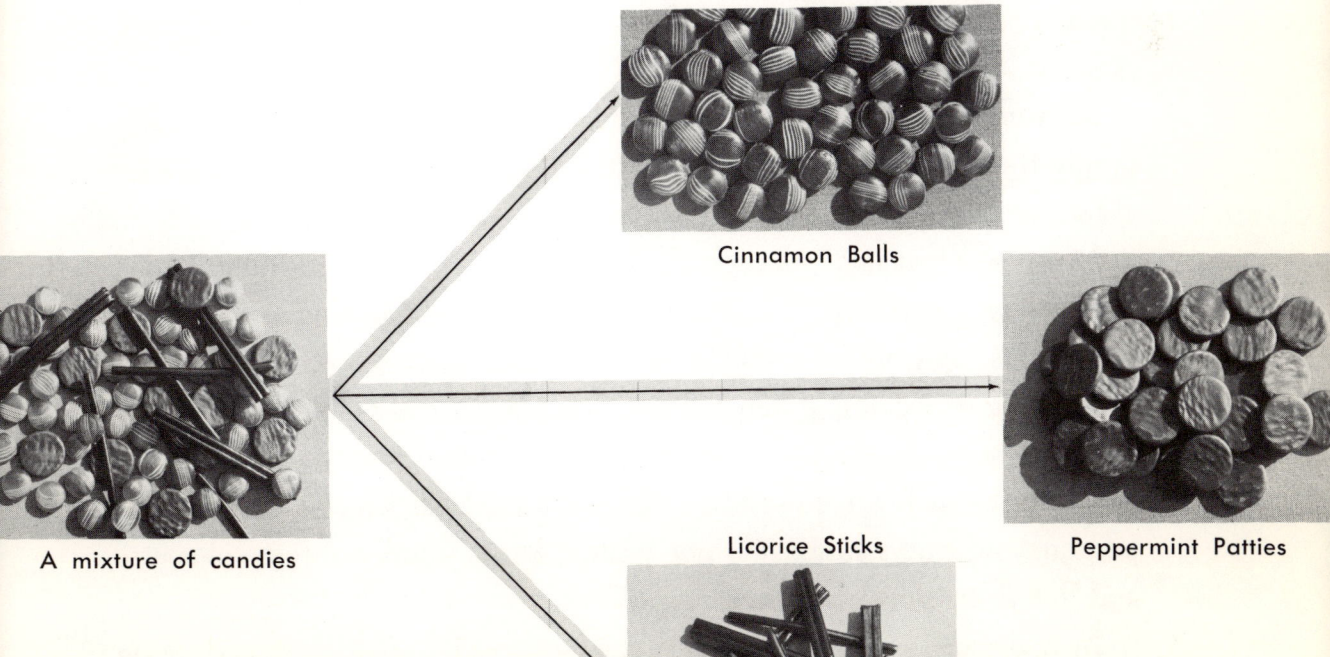

Cinnamon Balls

A mixture of candies

Licorice Sticks

Peppermint Patties

THE INGREDIENTS OF A MIXTURE OFTEN CAN BE SEPARATED MECHANICALLY

concrete, steel, glass, blood, and many other materials are mixtures of compounds.

Mixtures in which particles of one substance are scattered more or less evenly through a second substance are called *dispersions*. There are four classes of dispersions, based on the size of the scattered particles.

In *coarse dispersions*, the scattered particles are visible with the unaided eye. In *fine dispersions*, they can be seen with a microscope. In *colloidal* dispersions, they are too small to be seen with a microscope, but are larger than single molecules. When the scattered particles are molecules or ions, the dispersion is called a *true solution*. Sugar dissolved in water or coffee forms such a true solution. The scattered particles in colloidal dispersions and true solutions do not settle if left to stand, but those of coarse and fine dispersions will settle out.

In a dispersion, the material that is scattered — such as insect poison sprayed from an airplane — is called the *dispersed* or *inner phase*. The other material, in this example the air, is called the *dispersion medium*, or *outer phase*. The following table lists eight kinds of dispersions. The ninth possibility, the dispersion of a gas in a gas, always results in a true solution.

Solutions are mixtures which are homogeneous or exactly the same throughout. The scattered substance (solute), such as sugar, is said to be dissolved in the second substance (the solvent), such as coffee. Even though liquid solutions are the most familiar, there are several other kinds. A soft drink, such as root beer or cola, contains carbonated water — a solution of a gas in a liquid.

Solutions are vital to every living thing on earth. The air around us is a mixture of gases. The vast oceans, lakes, and rivers of the earth are liquid solutions. And liquid solutions fill the bodies of all plants and animals.

TYPES OF DISPERSIONS

Dispersion Medium	Dispersed Phase	General Name	Examples
Gas	Liquid	Fog	Insect sprays, clouds, fog
Gas	Solid	Smoke	Smoke
Liquid	Gas	Foam	Whipped cream
Liquid	Liquid	Emulsion	Milk
Liquid	Solid	Suspension	Muddy water, India jnk
Solid	Gas		White hair, pumice stone
Solid	Liquid		Jelly, cheese
Solid	Solid		Metal alloys

TYPES OF SOLUTIONS

Solvent	Solute	Examples	Solvent	Solute	Examples
Liquid	Gas	Carbonated water	Solid	Gas	Hydrogen in platinum
Liquid	Liquid	Rubbing alcohol	Solid	Liquid	Mercury in copper
Liquid	Solid	Sugar in coffee	Solid	Solid	Gold in copper

CHANGE:
PHYSICAL AND CHEMICAL

A PAPER IS TORN; a lump of sugar dissolves and disappears in a cup of coffee; a log is sawed into lumber; water boils, steams, and disappears—in each instance something changes. But in none of these changes does the substance involved lose its identity. A small piece of paper differs only in size from a large piece. If coffee evaporates, the sugar it contains can be recovered. Lumber is made of the same wood that once formed the log. And water vapor from the air may condense in small drops of water on the window pane. A change of this kind, in which the structure of the molecule is not altered, although its position relative to other molecules is altered, is called a physical change.

If the paper is burned, the lump of sugar is charred, the log is burned, or the water is split into hydrogen and oxygen, another type of change takes place. The substance undergoing the change disappears and one or more different substances appear. In this kind of change the molecules of the substance involved are not simply torn apart from one another. Their structures are completely altered. We call this kind of alteration a chemical change.

Chemical and physical changes are usually well-marked and readily defined. However, many changes which occur in nature, in industry, in the home, and in the laboratory are complicated combinations of both chemical and physical changes which occur simultaneously or nearly so. These combined changes can be analyzed only after careful study.

FOUR KINDS OF CHEMICAL REACTIONS

IN A CHEMICAL REACTION, such as those which occur in the laboratory, the atoms of the reacting substances are rearranged to form an entirely different substance or substances. These reactions may release energy in the form of heat, light, or electrical energy. In this case, the reaction is said to be *exothermic* (from Greek words meaning "heat" and "out of"). Or, they may absorb energy. These are known as an *endothermic* reaction (from Greek words meaning "heat" and "within"). Or, there may be no apparent change in the energy levels of the substances involved.

There are four main types of chemical reactions:

(1) *Combination.* Two or more elements or simple compounds combine to form a single complex substance.

Example: Iron plus oxygen yields iron oxide (rust).

(2) *Decomposition.* A compound splits into two or more simple compounds or elements. Heat and electricity are the agents most commonly used to decompose substances.

Example: Water when an electric current passes through it yields oxygen and hydrogen. (Acid is added to water to make an electrolyte. See p. 85.)

(3) *Replacement.* One element takes the place of another element in a compound.

Example: Aluminum plus iron oxide yields aluminum oxide plus iron.

(4) *Double Replacement.* Two compounds interchange parts to produce two new compounds. Each of the original compounds separates into two parts, called positive and negative ions. The positive ion of one compound joins with the negative ion of the other, and vice versa, forming new compounds.

Example: Silver nitrate plus sodium chloride (table salt) yields silver chloride plus sodium nitrate.

1 COMBINATION REACTION

$$4Fe + 3O_2 \longrightarrow 2Fe_2O_3$$

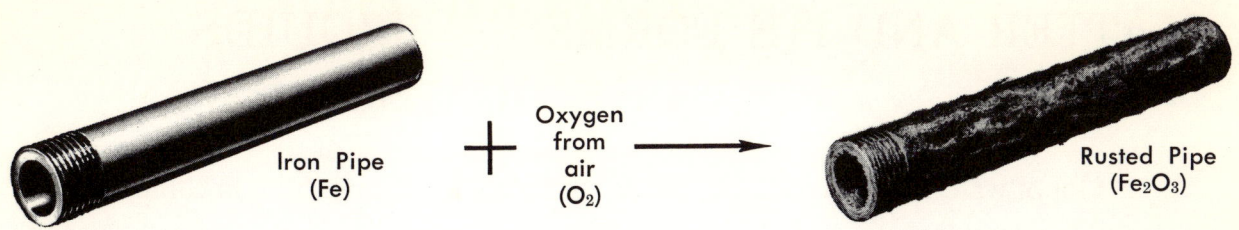

2 DECOMPOSITION

$$2H_2O \longrightarrow 2H_2 + O_2$$

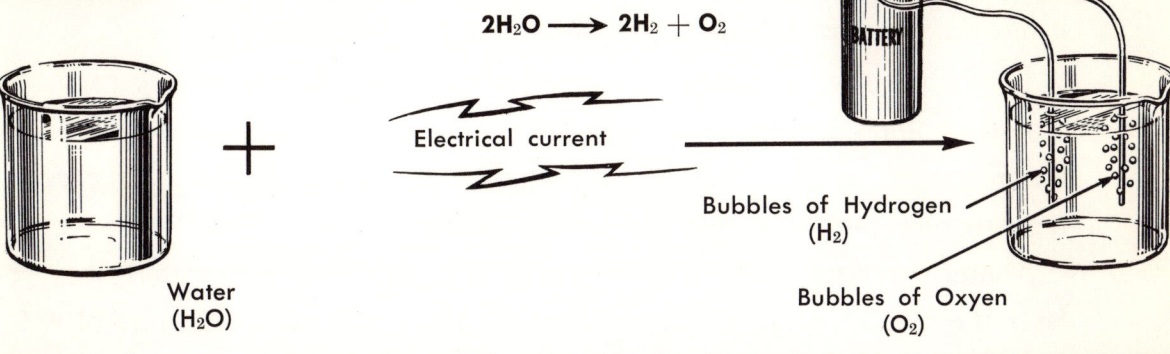

3 REPLACEMENT

Colorless solution of Sodium Bromide (NaBr) in Water

$$Cl_2 + 2NaBr \longrightarrow 2NaCl + Br_2$$

Chlorine Gas (Yellowish Green) (Cl_2)

Mix

Red solution of Bromine (Br_2) in Water and colorless solution of Table Salt (NaCl)

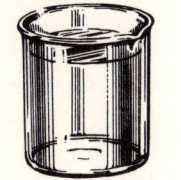
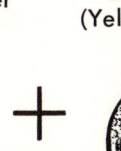

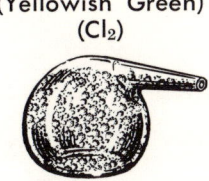
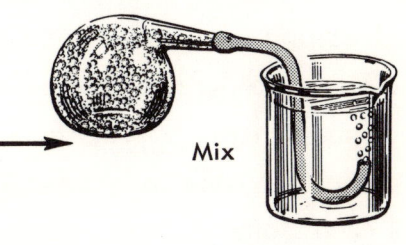
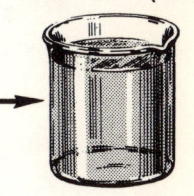

4 DOUBLE REPLACEMENT

$$Na_2CO_3 + CaCl_2 \longrightarrow CaCO_3 + 2NaCl$$

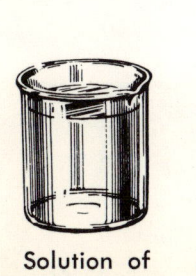
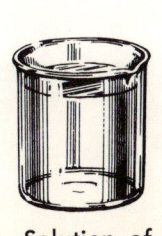
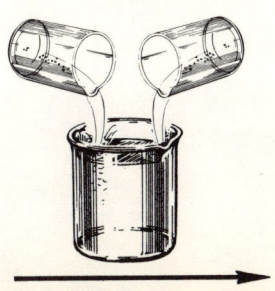
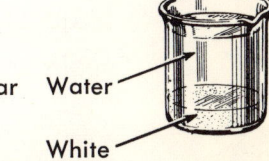

Solution of Washing Soda (Na_2CO_3)

Solution of Calcium Chloride ($CaCl_2$)

Mix, dissolve in water

Clear Water
White

Table Salt (NaCl) (dissolved in water) and Calcium Carbonate ($CaCO_3$) White precipitate

MATTER AND ITS FORMS: GASES LIQUIDS SOLIDS

GOLD, water, iron, wood, air, paper, and glass have something in common. They are all composed of *matter*. One characteristic of matter is that it occupies space exclusively. No two portions of matter, therefore, can occupy the same space at the same time. A second characteristic of matter is that it has mass and, in a gravitational field, weight (see page 82).

Fundamentally, all matter is composed of atoms. As we have learned, groups of atoms are electrically bonded together to form molecules. And the molecules, in turn, may be held together by forces of mutual attraction, thereby joining to produce visible matter.

Matter may assume the form of a solid, like gold, a rock, or iron. It may be in the form of a liquid, like water or oil. Or it may be in the form of a gas, like air or helium. These forms — solid, liquid, and gas — are known as the three *states or phases of matter*. You can undoubtedly see several examples of each of the states of matter about you now. In your school, you are sitting and writing on a solid (your chair — your desk), breathing a gas (air), and you write with a liquid (ink).

Even though most matter appears to be static or motionless, the particles which form matter are constantly moving. Electrons are speeding around the nucleus of each atom in a never-ending journey. Atoms are continually varying their positions within the structure of each molecule. And molecules may constantly vibrate in rather fixed positions, as in solids; they may slip and slide one over the other, as in liquids; or they may move about, frequently colliding with one another, only to bound away and collide again, as in gases.

THE GASEOUS PHASE: Gas molecules combine the talents of daredevil racers and expert tumblers. At room temperature they travel about 1200 miles per hour — 1 mile every 3 seconds. But even a thimbleful of gas contains nearly 200 billion times as many molecules as there are people in the United States. During a single second each gas molecule has about 5 thousand million collisions with other molecules — a number about equal to the times your heart will beat during your entire lifetime.

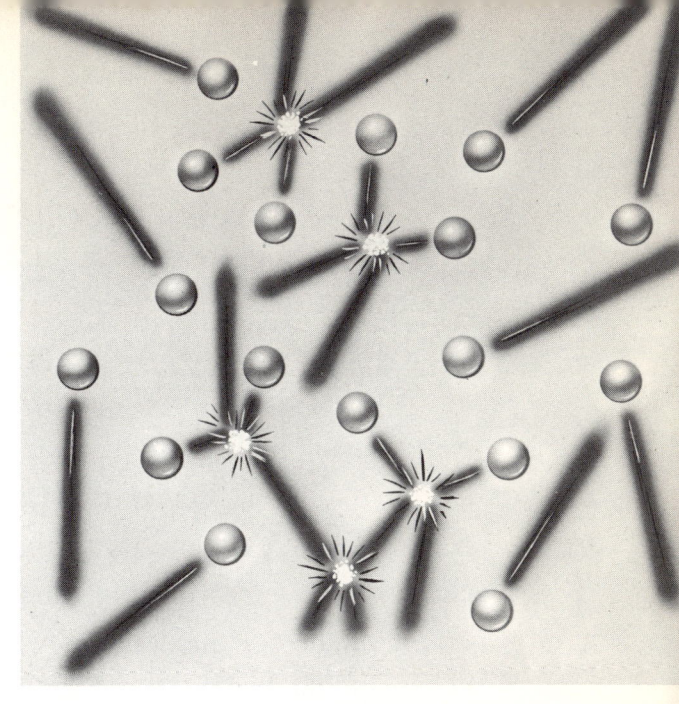

Under normal conditions, gas molecules are widely spaced. By the application of pressure, however, the molecules are forced together and the volume of the gas is reduced. The air in your living room would fit into a suitcase if it were subjected to sufficiently high pressure. In addition, every gas can expand infinitely. Regardless of the size of the container in which a sample of gas is placed, its molecules will scatter until the entire space is occupied. If the container is not closed, the gas will continue to spread indefinitely. You can see these things for yourself by opening a bottle of strong perfume or spraying an air freshener in a room. Very soon, the odor can be detected all over the room. If you open a window or a door, the fragrance — which indicates the presence of molecules of the perfumed gas — can be detected outside the room.

Countless gas molecules continuously bombard the walls of their container, imparting some force with each impact. The sum of these impacts results in a continuous pressure upon the walls. It is the collision of billions of gas molecules that keeps a toy balloon from collapsing. If the gas is compressed, the same number of molecules bombard a smaller area of wall space. The pressure exerted by a gas consequently increases as the gas is compressed. Remember, when you blow air into a balloon, you are compressing a gas. The more air you blow into the balloon, the more you compress the air. If you blow too much, the gas exerts too much pressure and the balloon explodes! We use the pressure of compressed air in tires to support the weight of our bodies and our bicycles or automobiles. What happens when a tire is punctured and some of the air escapes?

If a gas in a closed container is heated, its molecules are supplied with additional energy, they move more rapidly, and they strike the walls more often and with greater force. The pressure exerted by a gas increases, therefore, as its temperature rises. We make use of this principle in steam engines and internal combustion engines where the pressure of a gas is used to push a piston which turns wheels and other machinery (see pages 152 and 154).

Like other forms of matter, gases have mass (page 82) and occupy space. Therefore, air — a gas — can support this parachute and float its passenger gently to the ground. When they are in a gravitational field (page 72), gases also have weight. You can see this for yourself by weighting an empty inner tube or balloon, then weighing it again after it is filled with compressed air (see page 121). But the

weight of a gas is considerably less, volume for volume, than that of either a liquid or solid in which the molecules are much more closely packed.

When gases meet, their rapidly bouncing molecules intermingle freely. Because the molecules of a gas are so far apart, the molecules of other gases easily fit into spaces between them. There is no limit to the volume of one gas that can mix or diffuse into another gas.

Water for
fighting fires

Water for
drinking

THE LIQUID PHASE: Nature has few liquids. Water is the only common one. But man has learned to make many new liquids, although he uses none of these in such volume nor for so many purposes as water.

When a substance changes from liquid to gas — as water into vapor — the volume of the gas is about 1,650 times that of the liquid. The number and size of the molecules in the gas and liquid, however, are the same. The difference between the two states is that distances between molecules are great in gases, but very small in liquids.

Because their molecules are so close, liquids can be compressed only slightly. A pressure 12,000 times greater than normal reduces the volume of water only 20 percent. Temperature changes also have slight effect on the volume of a liquid in contrast to effects they produce in a gas.

Distribution of
molecules in a liquid

Water for plant growth

The nearness of molecules in a liquid allows them to attract one another strongly. Therefore, the molecules stick together. But their mutual attraction is not great enough to prevent them from moving about freely and rapidly, allowing the liquid to flow and assume the shape of its container. If the capacity of the container exceeds the volume of the liquid, the molecules of the liquid do not scatter and fill the space uniformly. They stick together much too tightly to allow that. The liquid, therefore, will have a definite upper surface and will always occupy the same volume, regardless of the shape of its container.

The forces operating on a molecule within a liquid are the same in all directions. But in the surface layer of the liquid the forces are not balanced. Molecules within the liquid tend to pull a molecule of the surface layer into the liquid; other surface molecules tend to pull it sideways. But there are no molecules to pull it upward. This unbalance produces *surface tension*. The liquid surface behaves like a tightly-stretched elastic film. The strength of this film depends upon the kind of liquid. A razor blade or needle will "float" on water but not on the weaker surface film of alcohol.

Surface film of water supports blade

Surface film of alcohol does not support blade

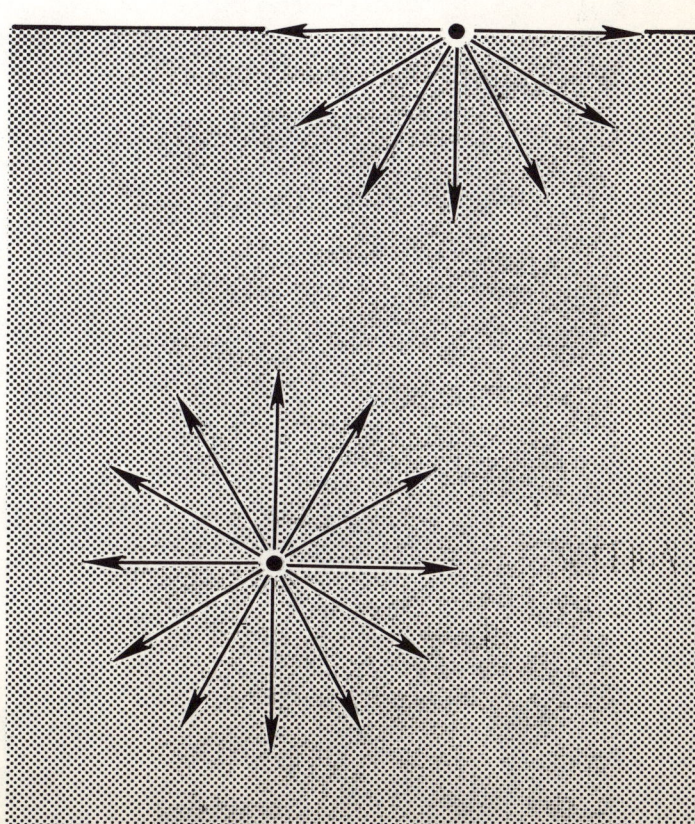

THE SOLID PHASE: A solid is matter in its most compact form. Solids are virtually incompressible because their molecules are so tightly packed. And unlike liquids and gases, solids cannot flow. You would not expect this ice to cascade over Niagara Falls as liquid water does. The forces of attraction between the molecules of a solid are so great that they do not tumble and rebound from place to place like those of gases and liquids. Instead, they merely vibrate in more or less fixed positions. This stability of structure causes a solid to maintain a definite shape which is independent of the shape of the container in which it is placed.

There are three general classes of solids: crystalline, plastic, and vitreous solids. *Crystalline solids* are the most important. They occur as particles, called crystals, which have a shape that is characteristic for each substance. Each crystal has four or more flat faces which meet in straight edges. Salt, sugar, quartz, and diamonds are a few crystallines which have crystals that are easily seen. A great many other solids have crystals which are not ordinarily seen, but which are visible under a microscope. The

Only frost can mute the thundering voice of Niagara Falls.

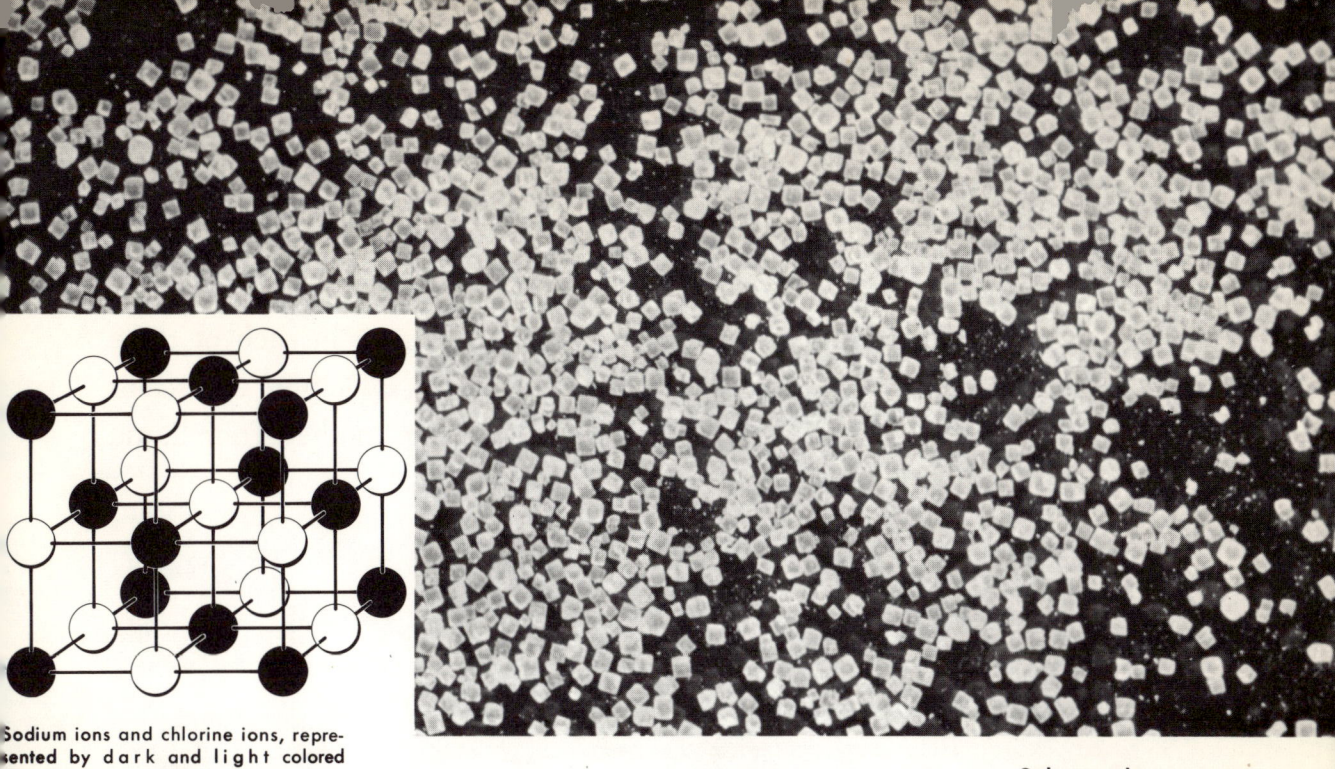

Sodium ions and chlorine ions, represented by dark and light colored spheres, are arranged alternately in crystal of common table salt.

Salt crystals

structure of the crystals of a given substance is so constant, crystals are often used by chemists to identify compounds. Physicists have learned that electrical forces bond the molecules of a solid together to form a crystal.

Plastic and vitreous solids do not have a crystalline structure. *Plastic solids,* such as clay, can be deformed permanently by pressure to any desired degree. *Vitreous or glassy solids* are actually supercooled liquids. They behave as solids at lower temperatures, but when heated they gradually soften rather than melting at a definite temperature. Asphalt, glass, candle wax, and tar are vitreous solids.

Crystalline solids possess several properties not exhibited by matter in other states. *Tenacity* is the ability of a solid to resist forces which tend to pull it apart. (Tensile strength is the measured degree of tenacity.) *Malleability* is the property which allows some metals, such as gold and tin, to be rolled or hammered into very thin sheets. *Ductility* is the capacity for a substance to be drawn out to form fine wires. Some solids, such as platinum, can be drawn into a wire so thin it can be threaded lengthwise through a human hair. *Hardness* is probably the most familiar property restricted to solids. The degree of hardness is measured by the ability of an object to scratch other substances.

CHANGES OF PHASE

DRYING CLOTHES, making ice cubes, melting paraffin — in each of these common activities something disappears and perhaps something else seems to take its place. Matter is changed from one phase to another: from liquid to gas, liquid to solid, or solid to liquid.

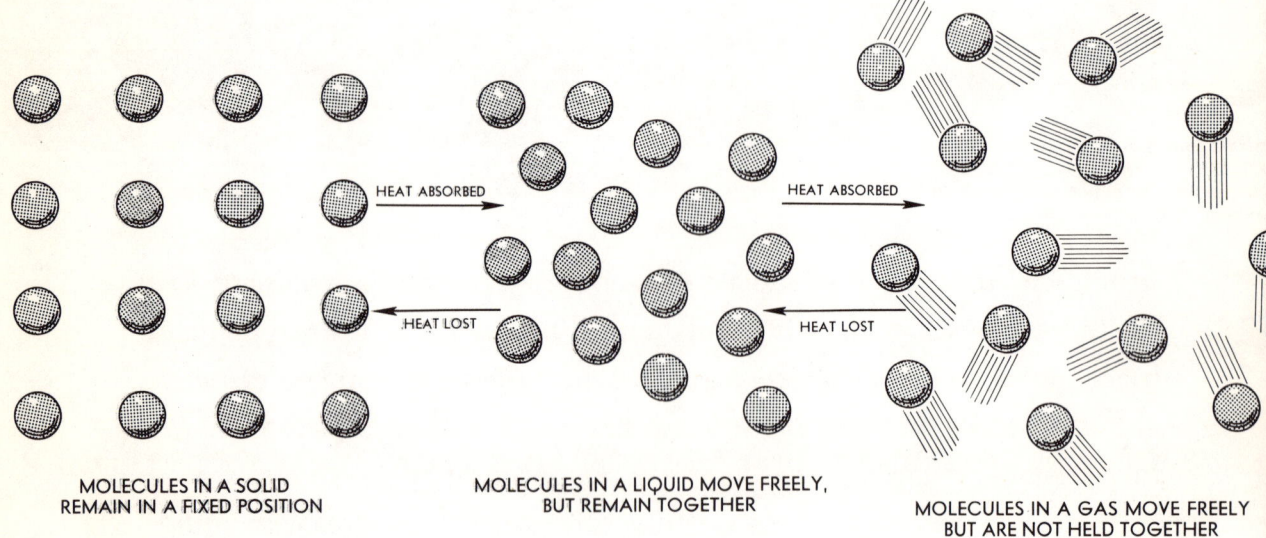

MOLECULES IN A SOLID REMAIN IN A FIXED POSITION

MOLECULES IN A LIQUID MOVE FREELY, BUT REMAIN TOGETHER

MOLECULES IN A GAS MOVE FREELY BUT ARE NOT HELD TOGETHER

Whether a particular group of molecules forms a solid, a liquid, or a gas depends upon the strength of the cohesive forces which tend to hold the molecules together and upon the temperature of the substance formed by the molecules. Temperature is a measure of the average amount of kinetic energy (see page 52) possessed by the molecules. If the force of attraction between the molecules is much stronger than the kinetic or "break-away" energy of the molecules, the molecules will be held in rather fixed positions and will form a solid. However, if the break-away energy of the molecules is nearly as great as the forces of attraction between the molecules, a liquid will be formed. In a liquid, the molecules do not remain in fixed positions, but the force of attraction between them is still great enough to hold them together. When the break-away energy exceeds the forces of attraction between the molecules of a substance, the molecules are no longer held together, but move about freely and at relatively large distances from one another. In this state, they form a gas.

In every change of phase, energy in the form of heat either is absorbed or released. Heat is absorbed when a solid melts. At first, the heat added to a solid raises the temperature of the substance, but at a certain temperature, called the *melting point,* additional heat will not raise the temperature. Instead, the heat energy serves to overcome the cohesive forces between molecules so that they move about more freely and form a liquid. The amount of heat required to change a solid to a liquid after the melting point has been reached is known as the *latent heat of fusion.* The absorption of heat by a melting solid is put to use in the cooling of food by ice.

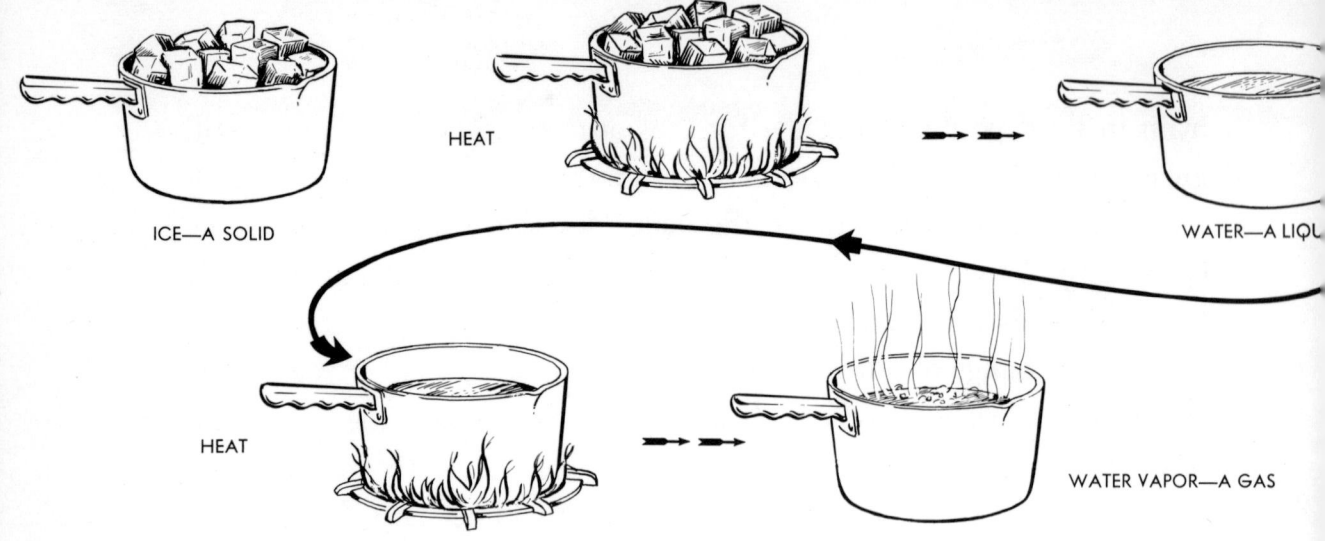

Some of the molecules of a liquid move more rapidly than others — their break-away energy is greater. Those which reach the surface of the liquid with sufficient energy escape from the attractive forces of their neighbors and mix with the molecules of the air, thus the liquid will slowly disappear or *evaporate*. This happens when clothes are hung to dry or when you stand on the beach with your skin and bathing suit wet. You feel cold because the water evaporating from your body is absorbing heat. Heating imparts greater energy to the molecules of a liquid and allows many more to break through the surface in a given time. That is why clothes dry faster on a warm day or in a clothes dryer.

If sufficient heat is applied to a liquid, its temperature will rise until the *boiling point* of the liquid is reached. The boiling point of water is 100° C (212° F). Additional heat applied to a liquid at its boiling point will not raise its temperature. This heat energy is used to overcome the forces of attraction between the molecules so that the molecules can move more rapidly and escape from the liquid and form a gas. The amount of heat absorbed when a liquid changes to a gas is known as the *latent heat of evaporation*. At the boiling point, all of the molecules within the liquid, as well as those at its surface, have sufficient energy to escape as a gas or vapor. Bubbles of vapor form throughout the liquid, rise to the surface, and burst — an action we call *boiling*.

In each of these examples, heat energy was absorbed — to change a solid to a liquid and to change a liquid to a gas. Heat energy is released when the reverse changes occur — when a gas changes to a liquid or when a liquid changes to a solid. The quantity of heat released is equal to the quantity absorbed by the opposite change of phase.

Life as we know it is possible because of the temperature of our earth and the heat relations of the substances which compose it. This unique temperature range is particularly important to the existence of liquid water, upon which all forms of earthly life are dependent. If the earth's temperature were slightly higher, all the water would be a vapor. If its temperature were lower, all water would be a solid (ice).

MATTER IN MOTION: NEWTON'S LAWS

THREE LAWS which describe the motions of all matter were formulated by Sir Isaac Newton, an English mathematician. They first appeared in his monumental book, *Principia,* or *Principles of Natural Philosophy,* which was published in 1687. These laws have become the foundation of the modern branch of physics known as *mechanics.*

Newton's first law of motion states that: *A body at rest tends to remain at rest and a body in motion tends to remain in motion in a straight line and at a constant speed when left alone* (that is, when it is not acted upon by some unbalanced force).

The characteristic of matter that causes it to resist any change in motion is called *inertia.* Inertia is related to the quantity of matter present in an object — the number and kinds of atoms or parts of atoms. Scientists do not know why matter has inertia, but you can show that a coin, such as a nickel, does possess inertia. Put a playing card on your finger, then balance a nickel on the card above your finger. Now, flip the card with the index finger of your other hand. The card will fly out into the air, but the inertia of the coin will keep it on your finger.

A ball, a rock, or any other non-living object cannot begin to move of its own accord. If movement is to occur, the object must be acted upon by

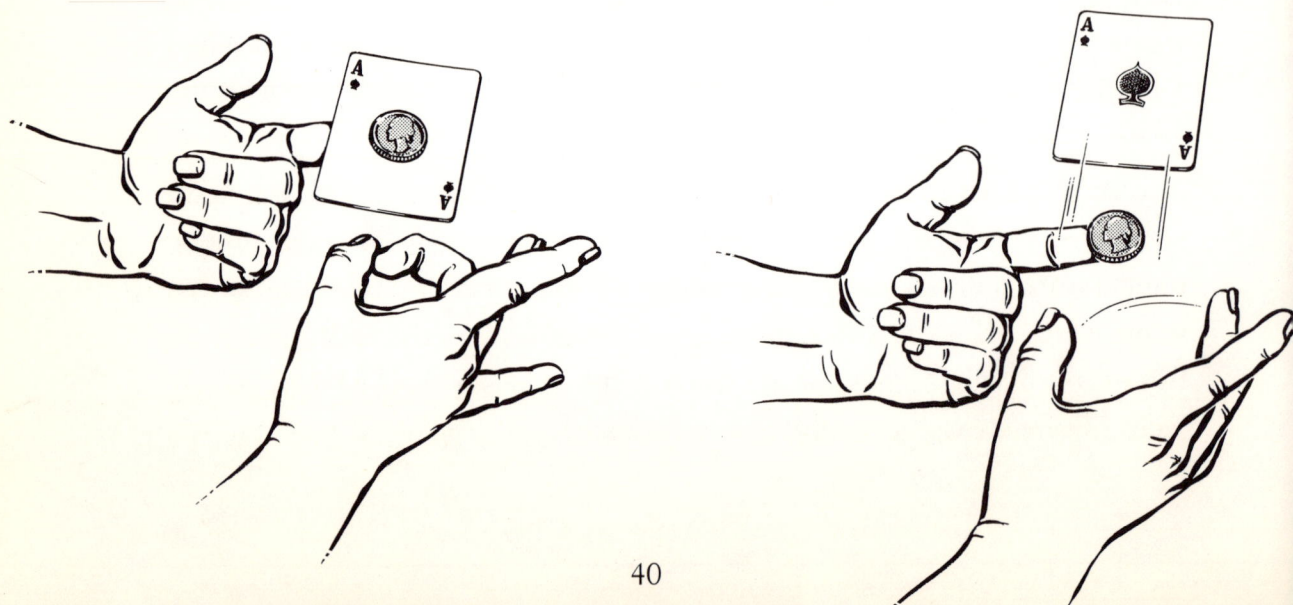

some unbalanced, outside force that is large enough to overcome the inertia of the object. Two equal forces acting from opposite directions, of course, will balance one another and will cause no motion.

Until we launched satellites that escaped from the dense layers of air that surround the earth, we had no real observation of a freely moving body because every moving body on earth is retarded by the force of friction (see page 60). The friction may be from the air (air resistance), from the ground, or from some other substance which an object moves through or over. Thus, a force equal and opposite to that of friction must be applied to keep an earthly body moving at a constant speed. In our automobiles, a gasoline or diesel engine supplies this force. To oppose the inertia of a moving automobile and bring it to a stop, we let up on the gas pedal, thereby halting the force supplied by the engine, and apply the brakes, an action that quickly increases friction by preventing the car's wheels from turning.

The first law of motion describes what happens when no outside force acts upon a body. In a second law, Sir Isaac Newton described the change in motion when an outside force does act upon a body. This second law states that, *when an unbalanced force acts upon a body it will change the velocity of the body in the direction of the force. The change of velocity will be in direct proportion to the size of the force and to the time during which*

it acts on the body, and in inverse proportion to the mass of the body. (Velocity is explained on page 91.)

A small force, thus, will not produce as great a change in the velocity of a body as a larger force will produce. Put a ball on the floor. Which makes the ball roll farther, a gentle nudge with your toe or a hard kick?

A force will produce a greater change in velocity if it acts upon a body for a longer time. The explosion of gunpowder lasts but a split second, but it can accelerate a bullet from rest, or 0 miles per hour, to more than 400 miles per hour. An arrow may attain a speed very close to that of a bullet. Its speed, however, is the result of a much smaller force — the recoil of a bow string — acting on the arrow for a longer time than the powder explosion acts upon the bullet. A baseball player makes use of this principle when he "follows through" on his swing and thus keeps his bat in contact with the ball for as long as possible. By extending the length of time the force of his bat acts on the ball, the player may stretch a two-base hit into a home-run.

Another part of the second law also is easy to demonstrate: the effect produced by a force acting on a body is reduced to one half if the mass of the body is doubled. If you had one regular football, made of a rubber bladder inflated with air, and a second football made of iron, which ball could you kick the farthest? Another demonstration is shown in the accompanying photograph. If two balls of different mass are pushed apart by equal forces, such as the force of a spring, the ball with the smaller mass will move faster (accelerate more) than the ball with the larger mass. This photograph was taken with a stroboscopic flash gun that "stopped" the balls at intervals of a split second. Which ball travelled farther between the flashes? Which ball has the smaller mass?

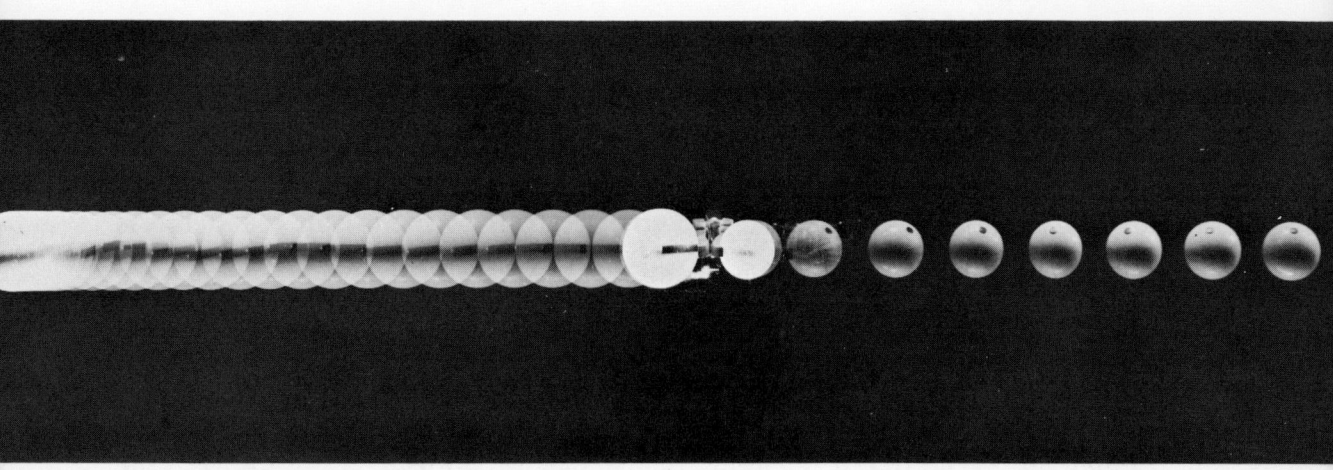

A body moving in a circular path, or orbit, is acted upon by an unbalanced outside force which has its point of origin, or focus, at the center of the orbit. This force, called *centripetal force,* is an inward pull that tends to cause the orbiting body to fall to the center of its orbit. The inertia of the body, however, tends to cause the body to move in a straight line course. Inertia, thus, exerts a force opposite to the centripetal force, one we call *centrifugal force.* As a satellite, such as the huge United States Echo I, circles the earth, the "pull" of the earth, or gravity, is the centripetal force.

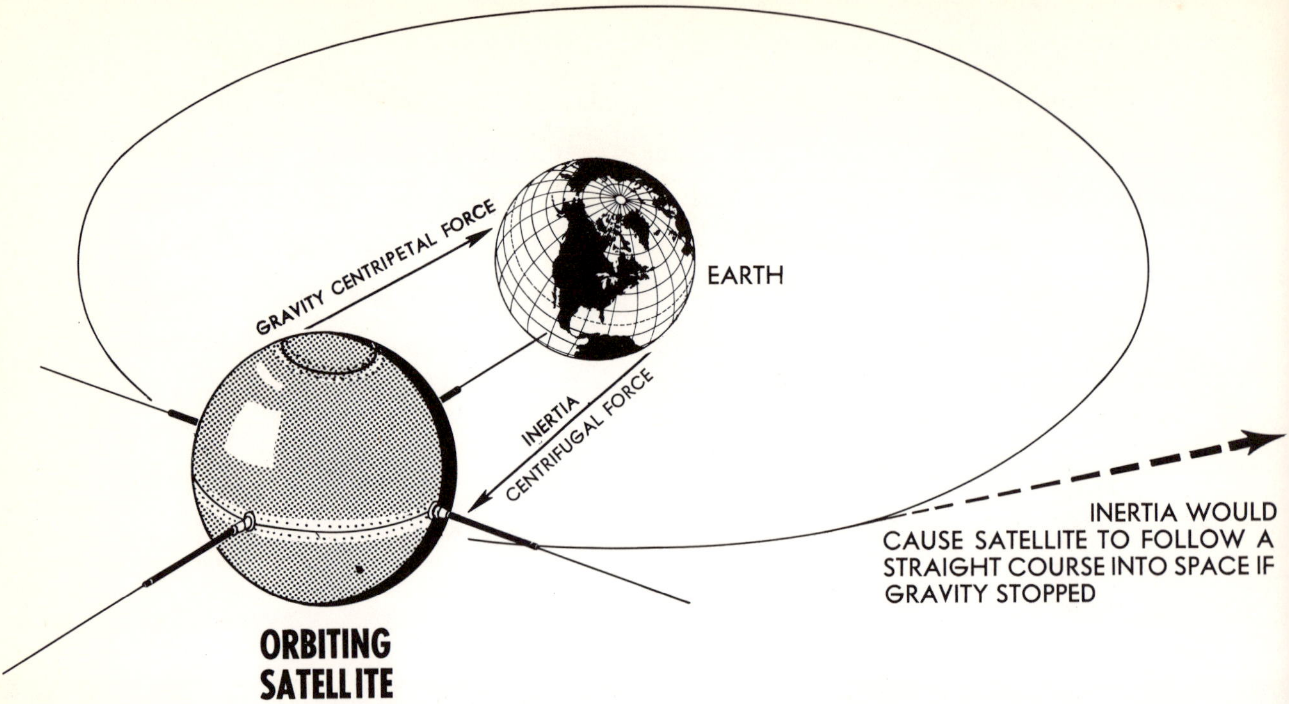

![Diagram of orbiting satellite showing GRAVITY CENTRIPETAL FORCE, INERTIA CENTRIFUGAL FORCE, EARTH, ORBITING SATELLITE, and a dashed arrow labeled "INERTIA WOULD CAUSE SATELLITE TO FOLLOW A STRAIGHT COURSE INTO SPACE IF GRAVITY STOPPED"]

The centripetal force holds the satellite in orbit. If it were removed, the satellite would at once veer outward into space. You can demonstrate this by twirling a ball on the end of a string. Your own pull on the string is centripetal force. The opposite pull you can feel is the centrifugal force exerted by the inertia of the ball. Now, let go of the string. Does the ball continue to orbit around your hand?

Centrifugal force is the force that causes water to fly off a dog's back when he shakes, or out of clothes when they are whirled around during the spin-dry cycle of your washing machine. It is the force that thrills you on the whirling "octopus" or "crack-the-whip" ride at a carnival.

44

"Kick" of a shotgun is a reaction

Newton's third law of motion is a very simple statement that describes an occurrence associated with every application of force: *for every action there is an equal and opposite reaction.*

When a gun or cannon is fired, a force released by the explosion of a charge of powder causes a bullet or shell to accelerate very rapidly forward. An equal force is directed against the gun and causes it to accelerate backward. We say that the gun recoils, or "kicks." The gun, of course, does not accelerate as much as the bullet or shell, because it has a much greater mass.

Our newspapers, radios, and television sets bring us frequent news of another application of Newton's third law — in the rockets that launch scientific instruments and military warheads on journeys of a few hundred miles, several thousand miles, into orbits around the earth, or into space. The action in these cases is the blast of hot exhaust gases from the rear of the rocket engines. The reaction is the movement of the rocket and its nose cone in the opposite direction. The speed of the rocket at the time all of the fuel is burned depends chiefly on the ratio between the weight of the rocket and the weight of the fuel. This is in accord with Newton's second law and is similar to the experiment with the two balls which were accelerated by the same spring. The larger the mass of the fuel is in comparison to the mass of the rocket, the faster the rocket will accelerate.

U.S. Saturn super-booster rocket at lift off.

The third law also governs situations in which the action occurs at a distance from the point of origin of the force, such as when the earth's gravity attracts an airplane or a magnet attracts a compass needle. The earth's gravity exerts a downward force, or pull, on a flying airplane and the plane exerts an equal, upward force upon the earth. The force of the earth on the plane is very important, of course, for if the wings of the plane were suddenly removed, the machine would plunge to earth and crash. However, the force of the plane on the earth produces no noticeable effect.

Some other examples of direct actions and reactions are given below.

ACTION	REACTION
Man jumps from rowboat to dock	Rowboat lurches away from dock
Stretch rubber band between thumbs, pull with left thumb	Must also pull with right thumb to stretch band
Water squirts out of garden sprinkler	Garden sprinkler turns
Man paddling canoe pushes backward against water	Canoe moves forward
Man pulls on a spring scale hooked to a second scale which is fastened to wall	Wall exerts an equal and opposite "pull" on the second scale.

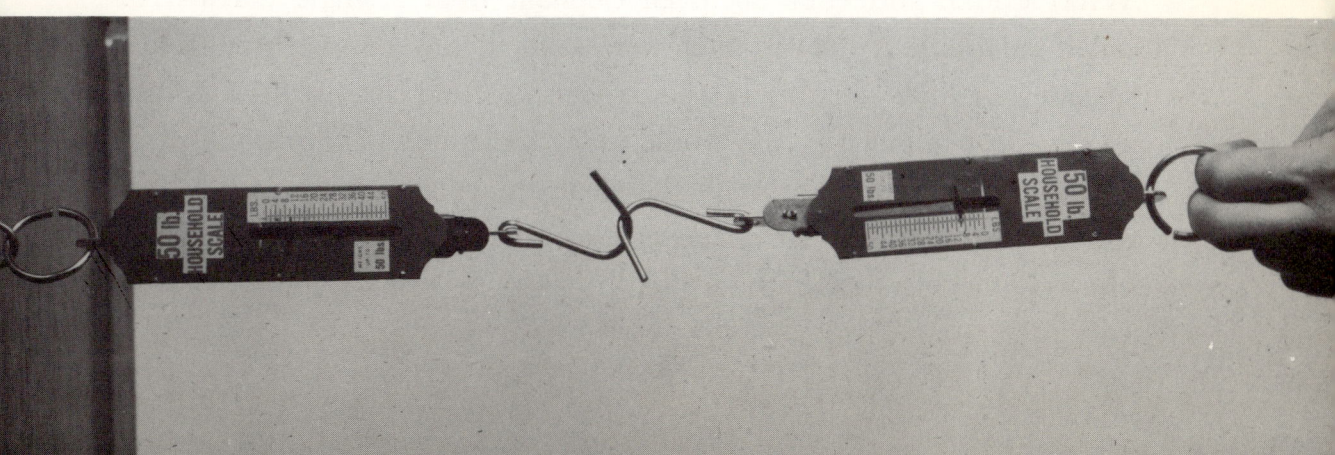

HOW WE RECOGNIZE THINGS

WHAT COULD YOU TELL about an elephant from a single touch? You might determine if the elephant were solid, liquid, or gas; firm or soft; smooth, rough, or hairy; moist or dry; warm or cold. By reaching as high as you could to touch it, you would know something of the height of an elephant. And you might smell the elephant while touching it. All the things you would learn are characteristic of the elephant you touched, and of every other elephant in the world.

An elephant always looks like an elephant. It never appears in any other form. But compounds and elements and the substances which they comprise can appear in a variety of forms. Glass, for instance, can be found in the form of a bottle, mirror, statue, window pane, drinking glass, door knob, television tube, vase, or other object. Each of the hundreds of thousands of substances in our world, however, has certain characteristics, called specific properties, by which it can be identified and described. These properties describe the substance regardless of the form in which it may appear.

In the column below the most important specific properties of substances are listed.

SOME SPECIFIC PROPERTIES OF A SUBSTANCE

Physical state—At room temperature is it solid, liquid, or gas?

Color—What color is it?

Odor—Does it have an odor?

Taste—Does it have any taste?

Solubility—Does it dissolve in water or some other solvent?

Hardness—If it is a solid, what substances will it scratch? Which will scratch it?

Elasticity—Is it brittle, inelastic, or flexible?

Boiling point—At what temperature will it change from a liquid to a gas?

Melting point—At what temperature will it change from a solid to a liquid?

Inflammability—Does it burn easily?

Magnetism—Is it attracted by a magnet?

Density—What is its wt. per unit of volume?

Compressibility—What volume changes occur when the substance is subjected to increased pressure?

Electrical conductivity—How easily will an electric current pass through it?

Viscosity—If it is a liquid, does it pour easily?

Thermal expansion—How much does it expand when heated?

Attracted by magnet

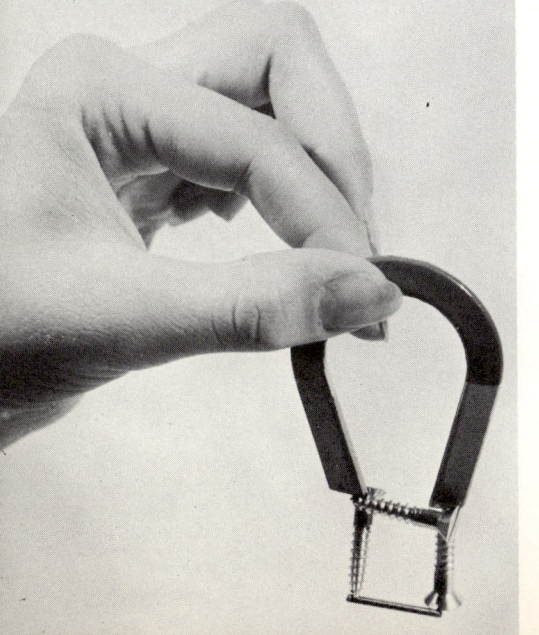

Inflammable

CHAPTER II

ENERGY EVERYWHERE

WE OFTEN SAY that a friend who can run fast, play ball well, or who joins in a variety of school activities has lots of energy. In a way, we are using the word "energy" in its scientific sense, for energy is the term scientists use to describe *the capacity to do work.*

Each month, your family buys energy from the supermarket, electric power company, oil dealer, service station, and other businesses. Each of them sells energy in a form that can be used by your body, your home appliances, your furnace, or your automobile. You probably can think of many other ways we obtain and use energy.

Our world's appetite for energy is increasing rapidly as machinery is substituted for human muscle on a greater number of jobs, as more and larger automobiles, trucks, airplanes, and other vehicles are made to transport people and materials, and as people demand more comfort in their daily lives in the form of heat in winter, air-conditioning in summer, more intense and uniform lighting, television sets, and many other modern devices. Although we are not faced with immediate exhaustion of any major energy source, our supplies of some fuels, particularly petroleum, are dwindling. For normal uses, however, it is not the amount of fuel that remains in the earth that is limiting. It is the cost of obtaining the energy contained in those fuels at the time, the place, and in the form we desire. Oil shale, for example, contains vast amounts of petroleum, but the present cost of separating petroleum from the shale is too high. There are many other examples of the need for research to find new sources of energy or new ways to utilize sources already known. One source of free energy in almost unlimited amounts is the sun, but we have not yet devised economical ways to use solar energy on an industrial scale.

This chapter is an introduction to the forms of energy, the ways by which energy can be changed from one form to another, and certain principles which describe the behavior of energy.

TWO FORMS OF ENERGY:

POTENTIAL AND KINETIC

POTENTIAL ENERGY is the energy stored in an object — the capacity of an object to do work because of its *position*, its *condition*, or its *composition*. In the picture above, the boy climbing the tree and the apples dangling from the twigs possess energy because of their position high above the ground. The tightly wound spring in your watch and the compressed gas in an air rifle possess energy because of their condition. And the fuel in a giant rocket and a stick of dynamite possess energy because of their chemical composition (see page 64).

Potential energy is measured in terms of the amount of work that could be done by an object (see page 93 for measures of work). But such a measurement is only relative. For example, a rock resting on a table is pulled downward by gravity and could fall. Therefore, it has potential energy. This energy is equal to the weight of the rock times the vertical distance through which the rock could fall. We could calculate the rock's potential energy by multiplying its weight by its distance above the floor. However, we would obtain a considerably different value if the potential energy of the rock were calculated on the basis of the rock's height above the ground, especially if the table were in a room at the top of a tall building.

If a suspended object, such as a boy in a tree, begins to fall, it loses potential energy as it gets closer to the ground. As its velocity increases, however, the object gains energy of motion, or *kinetic energy*. When the object reaches the bottom of its fall, all of its potential energy will have been changed to kinetic energy. If the body comes to rest when it strikes the ground, that is, if it does not bounce as a rubber ball would, the kinetic energy it possesses will be changed into heat energy in the ground and in the body.

Weights that drive the machinery of some clocks work on the same principle of energy change, but the velocity of the fall is kept uniform and slow by the clock mechanism. As the weights drop, their potential energy is transformed to kinetic energy which is used immediately to operate the clock machinery. When they reach their lowest positions, the useable potential energy in the weights has been converted entirely into kinetic energy. Someone must use his arm muscle and energy derived from his food to raise the clock weights back to the top again.

Kinetic energy is a characteristic of any moving mass — expanding gases, running water, flying birds, whirling electrons, orbiting satellites, speeding racecars. The action of this baseball game, right, was stopped as the second baseman threw the ball to first base for a double play. The speeding ball, caught in mid-air by the camera, possesses kinetic energy due to its forward motion and potential energy due to its height above the ground.

Kinetic energy is proportional to the mass of the moving object and the square of its velocity (see page 91). The mathematical equation for kinetic energy is:

$$E_k = \frac{\text{mass} \times (\text{velocity})^2}{2}.$$

This equation is merely a simplified statement of easily observed facts. You know that two objects traveling at the same speed may have very different energy levels, depending upon their masses. For example, you would run to get out of the path of a bus traveling 20 miles per hour, but a leaf carried along by the wind at the same speed might not even cause you to dodge. You also know that the energy level of an object increases with the velocity of the

object. If someone dropped a pebble in your hand, you would not be injured by the rock. However, if the same pebble were thrown at you, it could cause a painful cut or bruise.

The fact that kinetic energy increases as the velocity of an object increases is of great importance to an automobile driver. He must allow about four times as much distance to stop his car each time its speed is doubled. The brakes can stop a car in a distance of 84 feet at 30 miles per hour, but they require a distance of 300 feet at 60 miles per hour. The distance a car travels between the time its driver sees danger and the time he applies the brake also lengthens as the car's speed increases.

RADIANT ENERGY

RADIANT ENERGY is familiar to us as light, radiant heat, x-rays, radar waves, and the carrier waves that bring radio and television programs into our homes (see pages 174 and 176). The exact nature of radiant energy, however, is one of the greatest unknowns of modern science. Physicists believe that it is composed of minute energy packages called *quanta* (singular, *quantum*). Quanta seem to travel in waves, known as *electromagnetic waves*, which are similar in form to the ripples produced when a pebble is dropped into the water of a quiet pond. The distance between the crests of two successive electromagnetic waves is known as the length of the wave.

The wave length of radiant energy determines its effects on matter, on the human senses, and on living things. The chart below shows the lengths of different waves, from those of radio waves 30,000 meters long (nearly 2 miles) to gamma rays only one trillionth of an inch long.

Electromagnetic waves travel at 186,320.69 miles per second, or 670,754,520 miles per hour. Physicists refer to this as the *speed of light,* and consider it the fastest speed obtainable. Words spoken by a man in the General Electric laboratory at Schenectady, New York, were carried by wire to the Bell Telephone laboratories at Holmdel, New Jersey, and then transmitted by radio to the moon. These radio waves were reflected from the moon and received back at Schenectady only 2½ seconds after

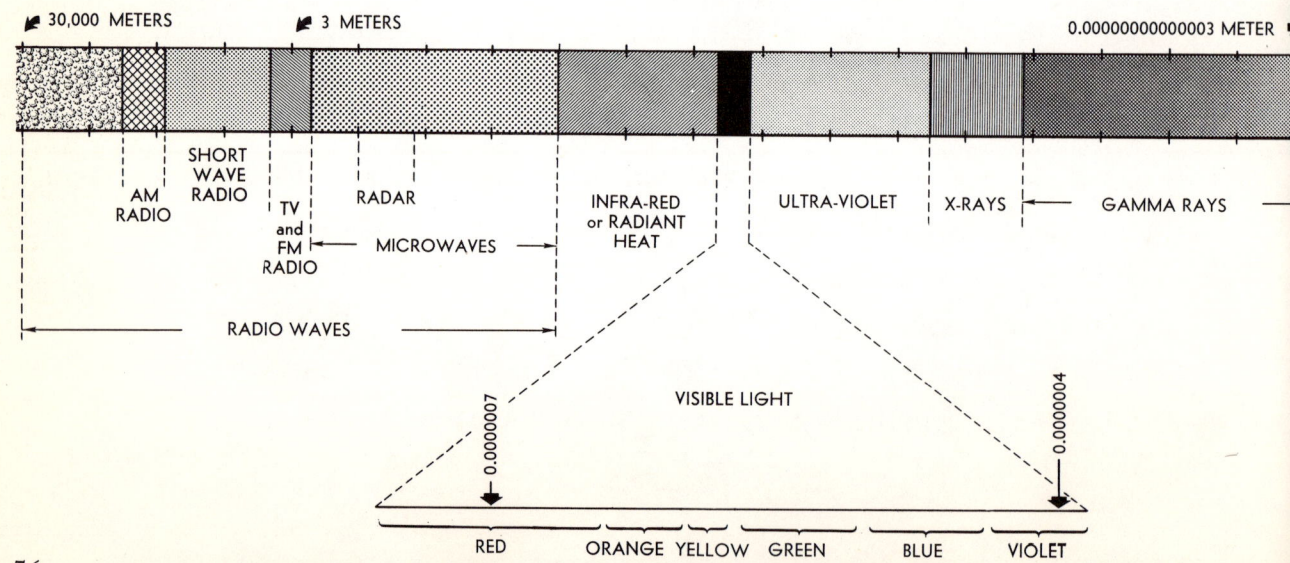

they were spoken. They traveled a distance of **nearly 466,000 miles** in those 2½ seconds!

Electromagnetic waves of intermediate length, between the lengths of infra-red and ultra-violet rays, are light waves and affect our eyes in such a way that we see light. Color is produced by the reaction of our eyes to light waves of different lengths, as you can see in the diagram. Light is produced by extremely hot, or *incandescent* substances, such as the sun and other stars, the filament of a light-bulb, and burning fuels. But it also may be produced from relatively cool bodies. For example, the neon lights used in advertising signs radiate light when electricity passes through the rare gas, neon. Slow oxidation of some substances also produces light — a good example is the eerie flicker of a firefly or lightning bug.

Recently, man has begun to change radiant energy directly into electrical power by means of small cells made of the elements silicon or caesium. Radiant energy with waves in the light and ultra-violet lengths which falls on these *solar cells* disturbs electrons in the material and creates an electric current. The four paddlewheels of the Pioneer V space probe, now in orbit around the sun, carry 4,800 solar cells and the Courier I-B earth satellite is covered by 19,152 solar cells which supply power to operate recorders and radios.

Courier Satellite

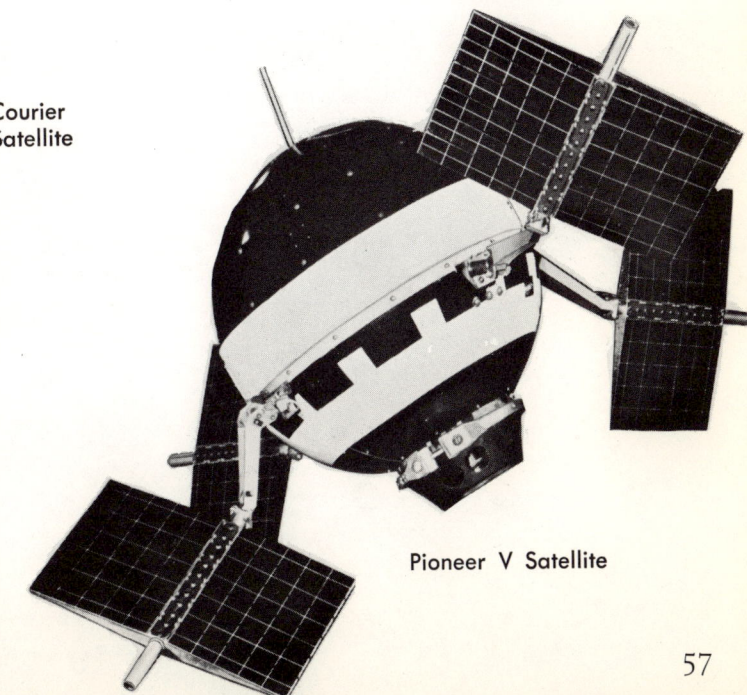

Pioneer V Satellite

HEAT ENERGY

THE MOLECULES of every substance are in constant motion — vibrating in place, or slipping and sliding over one another. *The kinetic energy of molecules is known as heat.* As the velocity of its molecules increases, the temperature of a body increases. As their velocity decreases, the temperature of the body decreases.

The earth's most important source of heat is the sun. But many earthly reactions also release heat. For instance, the oxidation of coal, fuel oil, or gas releases sufficient energy to increase the velocity of the air molecules in your home and to keep you warm through the winter.

Heat is transferred from place to place by conduction, convection, and radiation. *Conduction* is the transfer of energy from more-rapidly moving (hotter) molecules to more sluggish (colder) ones by collisions. It occurs between molecules of gases, liquids, and solids, and is the only method by which heat is transferred through an opaque solid, such as steel, lead, or compact, dry soil. Some matter conducts heat much better than other matter. For example, if a steel kitchen spoon is used to stir hot soup, heat conducted through its shaft may make its handle too hot to touch. If a wood handle is used, however, the spoon can be used without discomfort because wood does not conduct heat well. Good conductors are used in cooking

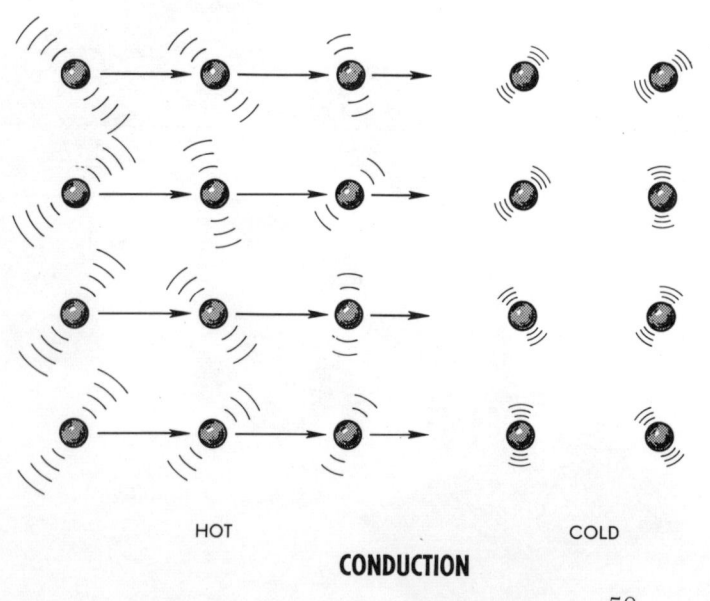

CONDUCTION

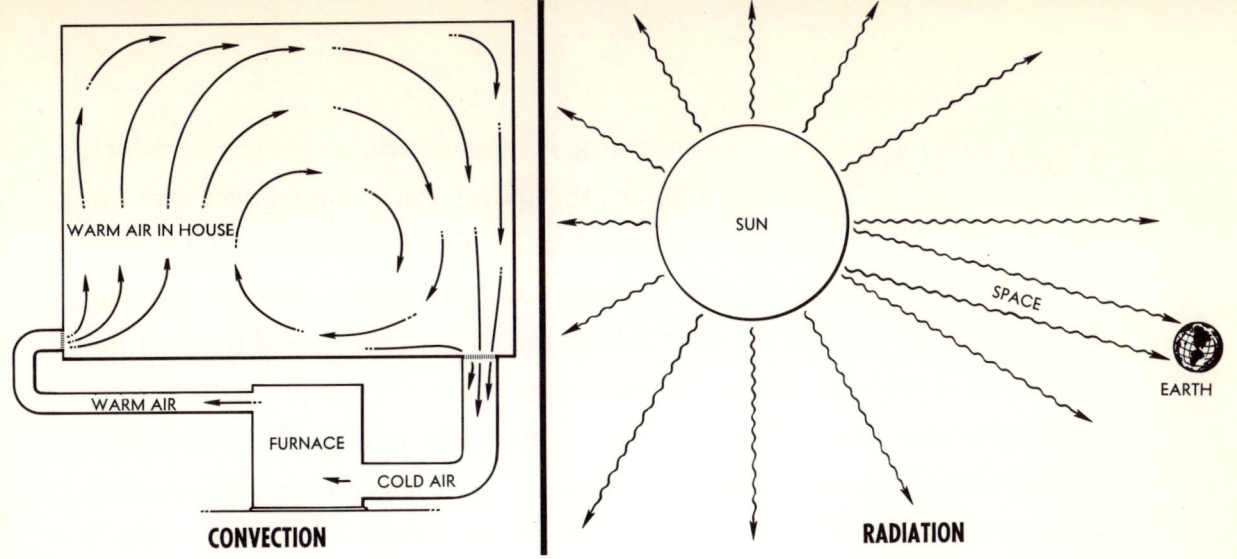

utensils, heating equipment, engines, and other items. Poor conductors are used to reduce the transfer of heat. Asbestos, for example, is made into protective covering for fire fighters and others who must work around open flames, such as the man in the photograph. Several kinds of poor conductors, such as rock wool, glass wool, and asbestos, are used to insulate homes against heat loss in winter and overheating in summer.

Convection is the movement of heated portions of a substance due to expansion and reduction of density that accompany heating. Therefore, convection occurs only in liquids and gases and usually is of greater importance in them than is conduction. Air heated by the furnace rises, flows out through the registers, and warms your home by convection.

Radiation is the transfer of heat in the form of electromagnetic energy of long wave lengths (infra-red waves). These waves produce the sensation of warmth. Unlike other methods, radiation does not require the presence of matter to effect an energy transfer. Electromagnetic waves can pass through a vacuum — as do those emitted by the sun which reach the earth. Infra-red waves are continually emitted from a body and may be absorbed, reflected from, or transmitted through other bodies. If they are absorbed, the body is heated. Some physicists believe that the term "heat" should be used only to describe energy in transit in the form of electromagnetic waves. The kinetic energy of molecules would be called "internal" or microscopic kinetic energy.

FRICTION

FRICTION IS THE FORCE or resistance which opposes the movement of one object over another object or through another substance. It always acts opposite to the direction in which the object is moving and parallel to the surface over which the object moves, and tends either to slow or to stop the motion of the object.

Friction converts mechanical energy into heat energy. You may have noticed this when you rubbed your hands together during cold weather to warm them by the heat produced by friction. And when you strike a match, the heat of friction causes it to burst into flame. The amount of heat produced by friction is proportional to the amount of work done against the force of friction. This proportion is known as the *mechanical equivalent of heat*.

There are three general types of friction: sliding, rolling, and fluid. Sliding friction is caused primarily by the pits and ridges of one surface interlocking with those of another surface and by the attraction of the molecules of one object for those of another. Friction increases as the contacting surfaces become rougher, as the force pressing the surfaces together becomes greater, and as the attraction between the molecules of the two bodies increases.

Rolling friction is much smaller than sliding friction. For example, a wheeled vehicle, such as a scooter or automobile, will move rapidly along a sidewalk or highway until we apply the brake. The brake presses against the wheel to stop it from turning. When a wheel stops rolling, the friction between its tire and the pavement becomes sliding friction and is so much greater than rolling friction that the vehicle skids to a stop.

Rolling friction is produced by two occurrences: 1) A rolling object is temporarily flattened at the

MAGNIFIED VIEW OF APPARENTLY SMOOTH SURFACES SHOWING IRREGULARITIES

point where it contacts the surface upon which it is moving. 2) The surface beneath the rolling object is pushed into a small ridge which the rolling object is always forced to climb.

Fluid friction is the internal friction between the layers of a liquid or gas. It is most commonly known as *viscosity*. Differences in viscosity of liquids are most easily seen when the liquids are poured. A highly viscous liquid, such as oil or molasses, pours slowly. Less viscous liquids, such as water or alcohol, pour easily.

Friction is essential to many of our activities, but to others it is a serious handicap. Without friction, your feet would slide out from under you as if you were continually walking on ice. Wheels would not drive cars, trucks, buses, trains, or machine parts because they would only spin on the surfaces they touch. Nails, screws, and pins would drop from their holes. The threads that make up a piece of cloth, string, or rope would slide apart. Knots and bows would come untied. Zippers would unzip, snaps would unsnap,

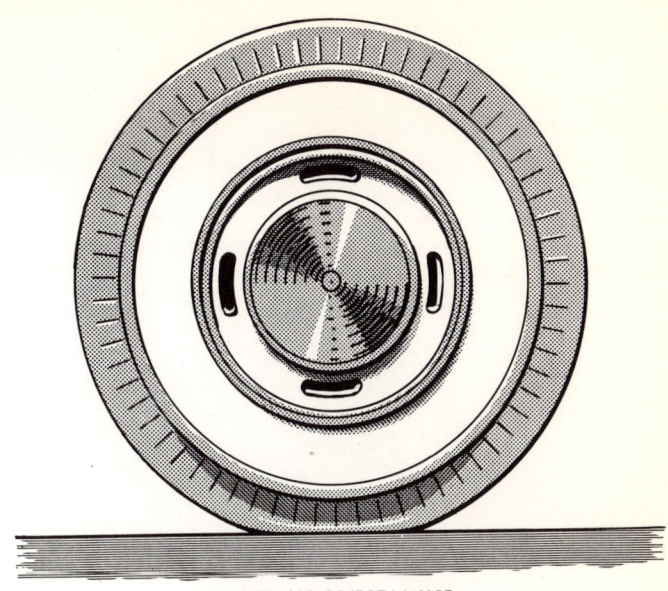

A ROLLING OBJECT MAY BE FLATTENED AT ITS POINT OF CONTACT

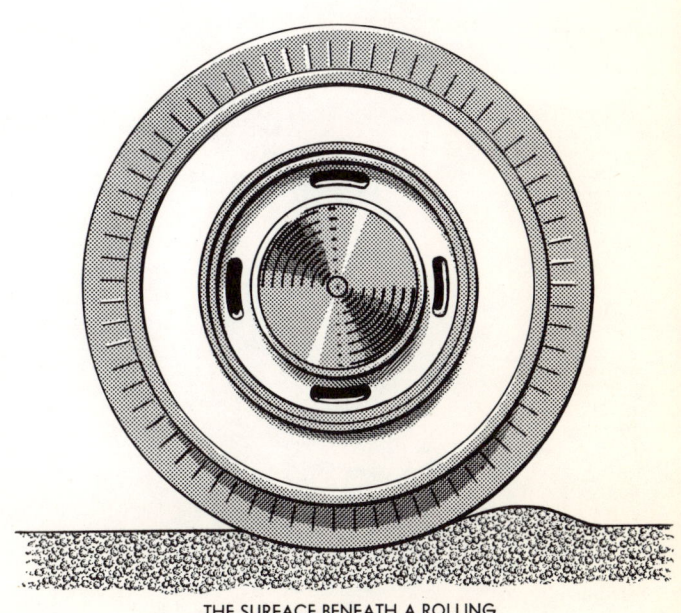

THE SURFACE BENEATH A ROLLING OBJECT MAY BE PUSHED INTO A RIDGE

and adjustable buckles would not hold belts or straps. This girl could not push her scooter. And no object, once in motion, could stop.

Except in places where it is needed, as between a belt and the wheel it turns, friction is a handicap in machinery. Regardless of the kind of machine, its complexity, or its size, the work a machine does is always less than the work done on it because of frictional losses. Engineers, therefore, are searching for new ways to reduce friction and to increase the efficiency of our machines.

One way to reduce friction is to make the surfaces of any parts that rub together as smooth as possible. Airplanes and rockets are streamlined to reduce air resistance, the friction between their bodies and the air.

The first man to use a wheel learned that rolling friction is less than sliding friction. In modern machinery, balls or rollers often are inserted between an object and the surface over which it moves to convert a sliding motion to a rolling one and thus to reduce friction.

The discovery that friction between layers of a fluid is much less than that between the surfaces of two solids led to the development of lubricants, such as oils and greases. Lubricants are used to coat contacting surfaces of solids. Friction then occurs partly between the layers of the liquid lubricant and partly between the solids. The lubricant further reduces friction by filling small surface irregularities in the solids.

Today, all three methods of combating friction are used. Surfaces are smoothed, ball and roller bearings are used freely, and all moving parts (including the bearings) are lubricated. These pictures show ball bearings from a machine and a mechanic greasing an automobile.

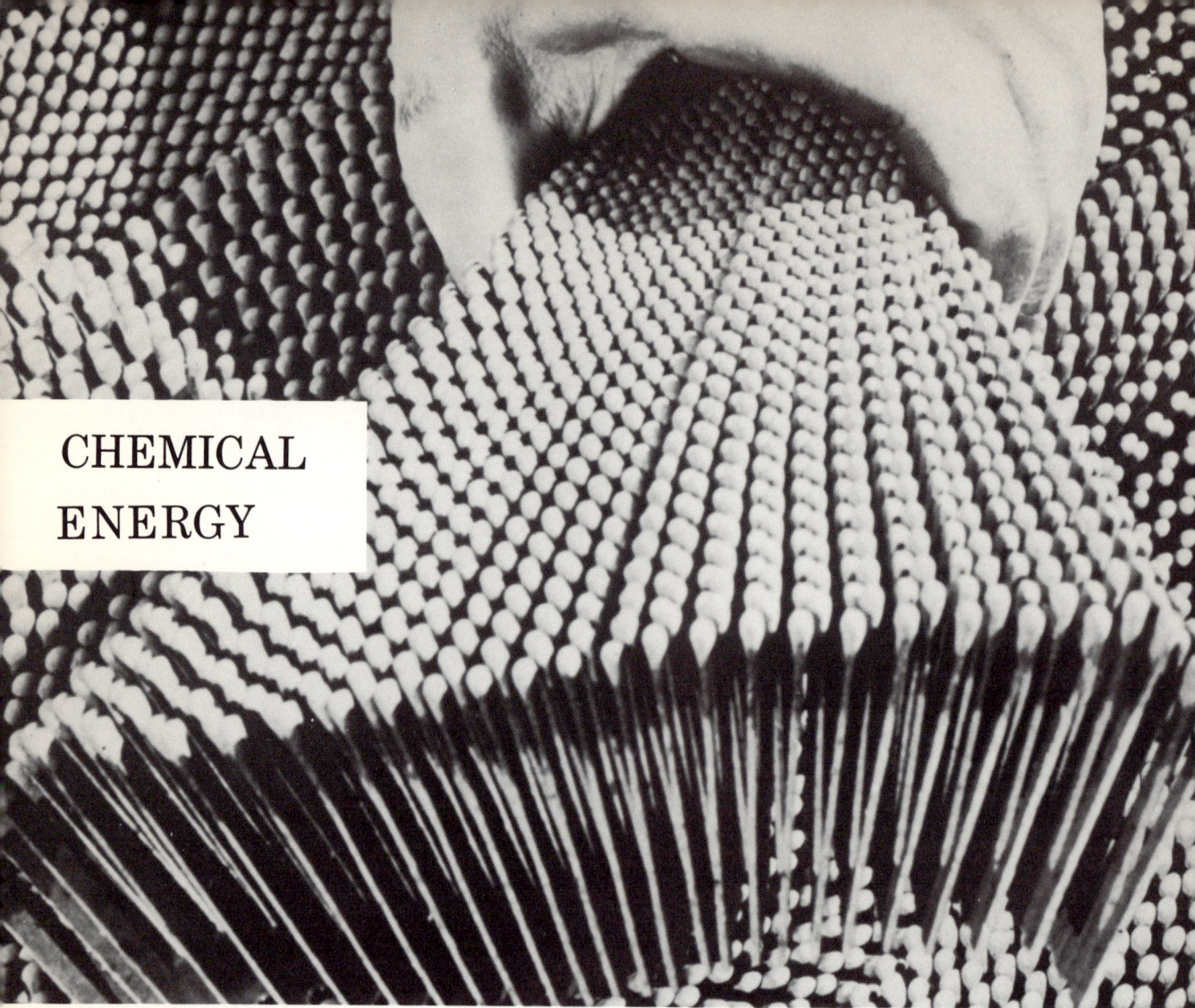

CHEMICAL ENERGY

WE DO NOT PURCHASE gasoline merely to manufacture water vapor, carbon dioxide, and other exhaust gases. Nor do we burn wood or fuel oil just to produce gases and smoke which rise up through the chimney. We are interested instead in the energy that these fuels will release when they are burned.

All substances possess chemical energy — internal energy in a potential form. This energy can be transformed to a usable, kinetic form through a chemical reaction. Coal, gasoline, and fuel oil are burned to release their chemical energy. The chemical energy of food is released by slow oxidation. The matches in the photograph above will release their store of chemical energy almost instantly when they are struck.

Most chemical reactions either absorb heat energy (*endothermic reactions*) or release heat energy (*exothermic reactions*). When absorbed, this heat energy becomes chemical energy which may be used to bind atoms of the resulting compounds into molecules. Heat energy released by a chemical reaction usually is chemical energy freed when the molecules of a compound are decomposed into their atoms or into simpler molecules.

The release of chemical energy is of primary importance to our world. During the process of photosynthesis (see page 144), green plants transform radiant energy of sunlight into chemical energy in simple sugars. These sugars are used to build new plant tissues. When we eat the plants, or other animals that have eaten plants, our bodies oxidize the substances derived from the simple sugars and obtain the energy for our own use. Most of the world's industries, transportation systems, and homes are powered and heated by the chemical energy of coal, petroleum, and gas. Mining, excavation, and warfare rely heavily upon the chemical energy of dynamite and other explosive compounds which can be released in an instant to move large obstacles, great masses of earth, or fire bullets or shells.

1.7 million pounds of nitrocarbonitrate blasting agent and dynamite detonated in a quarry operation near Great Salt Lake, Utah shattered approximately 3 million tons of rock.

ELECTRICAL ENERGY

Pieces of paper will jump toward a comb that has been passed through your hair. A glass rod stroked with silk also attracts light objects. In this condition, the comb and glass are said to be electrically charged.

Charged glass will attract a charged comb, but will repel other charged glass. Charged combs also repel one another. Thus, there are two kinds of electrical charges. *Unlike charges attract; like charges repel.* A charge which behaves like that on glass is called a positive charge. One which behaves like that on a comb is called a negative charge.

Static electricity is electricity residing in an object. When objects with opposite charges are connected, electrons flow between them. These moving electrons form an electric current. The energy of moving electricity is used to light cities, to power industry, and to run thousands of machines which ease our daily chores. The plight of a modern family deprived of electricity is humorously shown in this cartoon.

There are two kinds of electric currents. A direct current (D.C.) flows only in one direction. An alternating current (A.C.) flows first in one direction and then in the other. One complete back-and-forth movement is known as a cycle. Ordinary house current is 60-cycle A.C., that is, the direction of flow is reversed 120 times each second.

Substances through which an electric current can flow are called conductors. The atoms of a conductor have electrons or ions which can move about. When they move in the same direction, due to a "push" supplied by a battery or generator, an electric current flows through the conductor. Non-conducting substances, called insulators, are comprised of atoms whose electrons are immobile, or compounds which do not ionize.

When you use a comb, electrons pass to it from your hair. The comb, oversupplied with electrons, becomes negatively charged. Your hair is left with a positive charge. A similar exchange takes place between glass and silk, except that electrons are transferred to the cloth and the glass is left with a positive charge.

FORCE

A pulling force

A FORCE IS A PUSH OR A PULL that acts or could act upon an object. A force may tend to cause a resting object to move. It may accelerate a moving object or cause it to slow or stop. It may change the direction of a moving object. Or it may produce distortion in an object, just as a rubber ball is distorted when it is pinched. Gravity and friction are common forces. All bodily movements are the result of forces exerted by muscles. These horses are exerting a force on the wagon they are pulling and the bulldozer pictured on the facing page is exerting a very large force on the material it is moving.

The scientific definition of a force and the formula for determining the size of a force are obtained from the second law of motion (page 41). This law states that an unbalanced force acting upon a body will change the velocity of the body and that this change will be in direct proportion to the size of the force and in inverse proportion to the mass of the body. This can be summarized by an equation: velocity $= \frac{\text{force}}{\text{mass}}$. A law, or an equation, can be restated in several ways. So long as the correct relationship between the factors in such a law or equation is kept the same, the law or equation will be equally true in whatever form it is stated. Thus, we can say that *a force is something which, when it acts upon a body,*

Force producing distortion

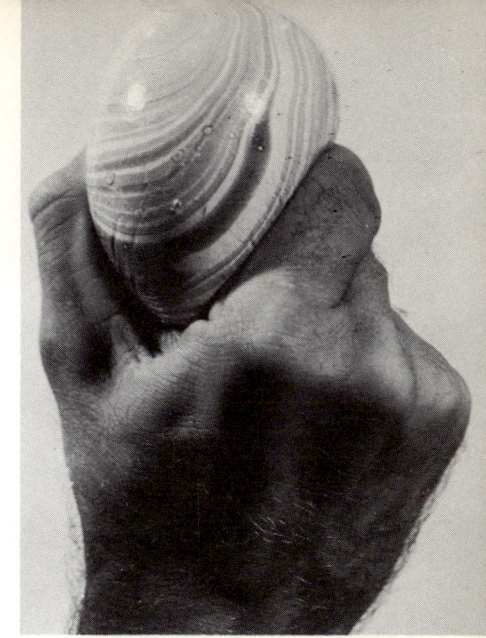

changes the velocity of the body and this change in velocity is related directly to the size of the force and the mass of the body (force = change of velocity × mass).

In the metric system, the unit of force is the *newton*. A newton is the force which gives a mass of 1 kilogram an acceleration of 1 meter per second per second. A much smaller unit of force, the *dyne,* is the force which produces an acceleration of 1 centimeter per second per second in a 1 gram mass. A newton is equal to 100,000 dynes.

The unit of force in the English system is the *poundal*. It is the force required to give a mass of 1 pound an acceleration of 1 foot per second per second.

The newton, the dyne, and the poundal are known as *absolute units of force* because they can be used at any place on earth or at any point in space. However, the English system also employs a second kind of force unit, a *gravitational unit of force*. This unit, called the *pound,* is the force of attraction which a standard gravity (32 feet per second per second) exerts upon a 1 pound mass. Thus, a pound force is equal to about 32 poundals. Gravity, as we have learned, varies slightly from place to place on earth and is reduced rapidly as a body travels into space away from the earth's center. Therefore, the pound force is meaningful only under certain limited conditions. The very fact, however, that there is a *pound force* and a *pound mass* in the English system leads to confusion.

A pushing force

MAGNETIC FORCE

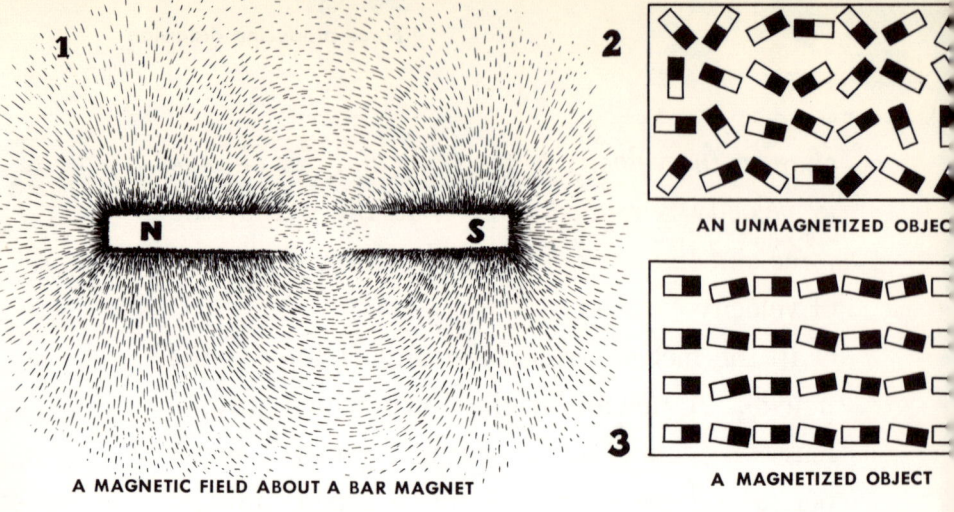

A MAGNETIC FIELD ABOUT A BAR MAGNET

AN UNMAGNETIZED OBJECT

A MAGNETIZED OBJECT

A MAGNET is an object which exerts a measurable force of attraction, many times greater than the normal attraction between two bodies, for iron, steel, and a few other substances. Lodestone, an iron ore, is a natural magnet. Artificial magnets are made from iron, steel, and mixtures of nickel, iron, and other metals.

If iron filings are sprinkled on a magnet, most of them adhere to its ends or poles. When a straight magnet, such as a compass needle, is free to rotate it will come to rest with one end pointing north. Near this end is its *north pole*. Near the other end is its *south pole*. Unlike poles (north and south) of magnets attract and like poles repel one another.

The space through which a magnet is effective is its magnetic field. If iron filings are sprinkled on a paper which has been laid over a bar magnet, the filings align themselves in paths which indicate lines of force of the magnetic field (Figure 1). These lines run through space from the north to the south pole and continue through the magnet.

The exact nature of magnetism is unknown. We do know that if a magnet is broken, each piece acts as a magnet. Even small groups of molecules (domains) of a magnetic substance must act as magnets, each with a north and a south pole. The domains of an unmagnetized object are haphazardly arranged (Figure 2). If the object is stroked with a magnet, the domains turn so that all of their north poles point in the same direction (Figure 3). The object then behaves as a magnet.

A body charged with static electricity possesses no special magnetic

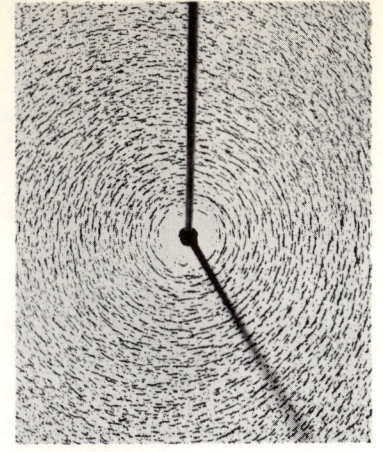

MAGNETIC FIELD AROUND A WIRE

hundred pounds of scrap iron. Others, such as those in door bells and telephone receivers, are very small.

properties, but moving electricity creates a magnetic field about it. The lines of force form concentric circles around a straight wire (Figure 4). If the wire is wound into a coil, the lines merge into a powerful magnetic field similar to that of a bar magnet. Such a coil is known as a solenoid. The solenoid is the basic element of the electromagnet. Some electromagnets are very large, such as this one which is lifting several

GRAVITATION

GRAVITATION IS THE MUTUAL FORCE, or pull, any two objects exert upon one another. Every particle of matter in the universe attracts every other particle with a force that increases as the mass of the particles becomes larger and decreases in proportion to the square of the distance between the centers of the particles.

The gravitational force between all but the largest bodies is small. For example, the force exerted between two giant ocean liners docked side by side would be less than 1 pound. But the attraction between the earth and the sun probably exceeds 1 billion trillion tons. The attraction between all of the planets, moons, and stars in the universe is fantastically great and is the force which holds the universe together.

The attraction between the earth and bodies on or near to its surface is known as *gravity*. It is gravity that is responsible for the weight of objects (see page 82). The force of gravity keeps our feet firmly on the ground, causes rain and snow to fall to earth, water to run downhill, and is of great importance in the occurrence of tides, ocean currents, and wind.

Although it is not uniform all over the earth (see page 83), gravity is generally stated in terms of the acceleration it imparts to a freely falling body. This is equal to about 32 feet per second per second. In a vacuum, all bodies fall at the same rate, such as the large ball and small ball shown in the photograph, but in the air friction may slow the descent of a body. For example, a baseball and a feather would strike the ground at the same instant in a vacuum, but in the air, the ball would drop rapidly while the feather drifts down more slowly.

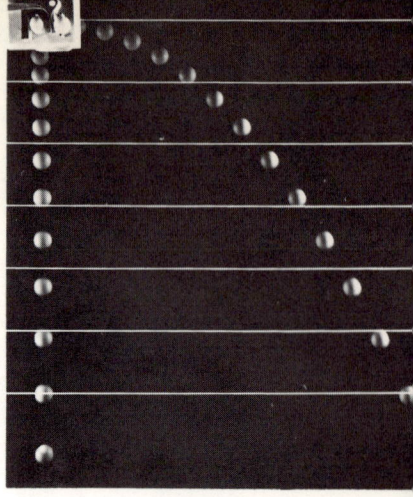

A ball dropped and a ball shot drop at the same rate

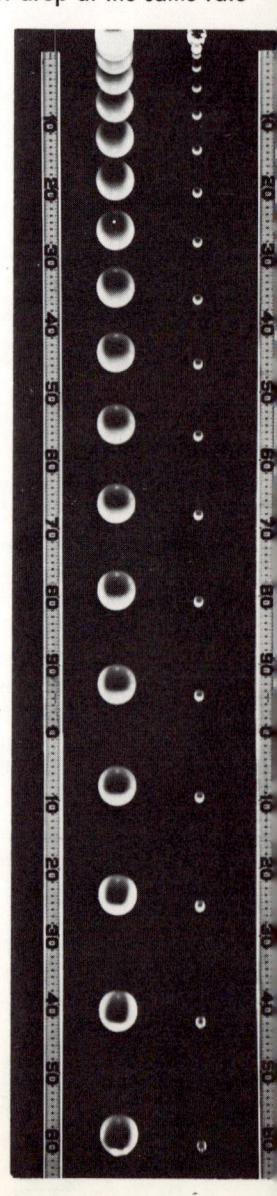

Large and small balls drop at the same rate

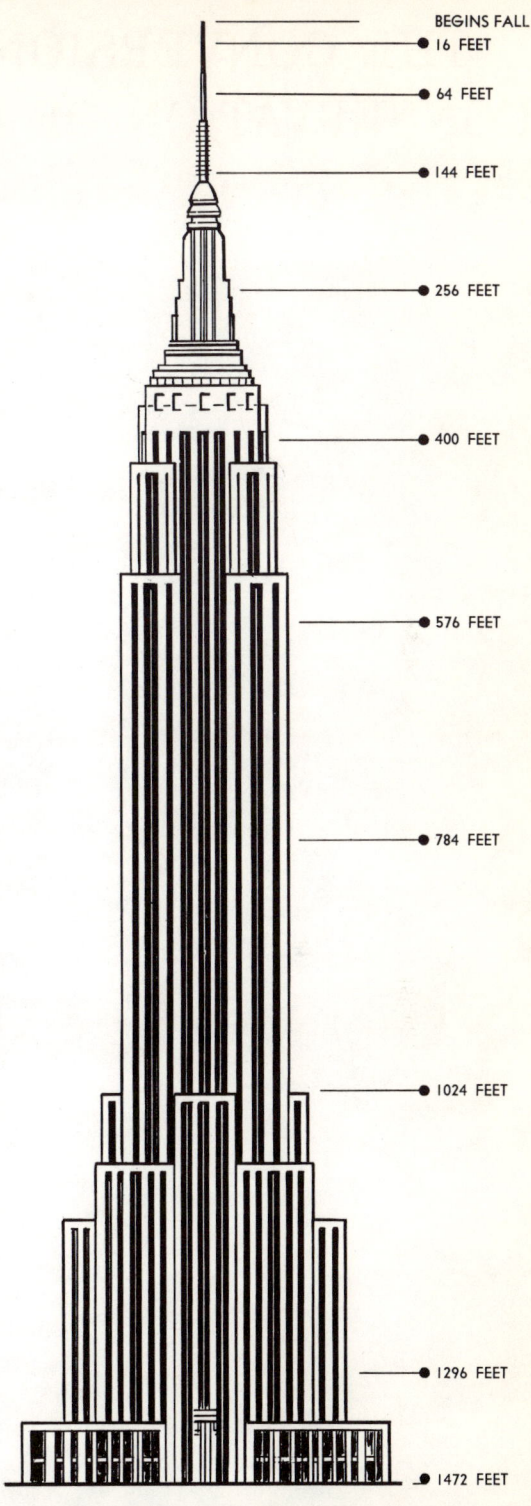

A BASEBALL WOULD REQUIRE NEARLY TEN SECONDS TO FALL FROM THE TV ANTENNA ON THE EMPIRE STATE BUILDING TO THE SIDEWALK

BEGINS FALL
● 16 FEET
● 64 FEET
● 144 FEET
● 256 FEET
● 400 FEET
● 576 FEET
● 784 FEET
● 1024 FEET
● 1296 FEET
● 1472 FEET

BEGINS FALL — VELOCITY = 0 FT./SEC.
16 FEET — END OF 1 SECOND, VELOCITY = 32 FT./SEC.
64 FEET — END OF 2 SECONDS, VELOCITY = 64 FT./SEC.
144 FEET — END OF 3 SECONDS, VELOCITY = 96 FT./SEC.
256 FEET — END OF 4 SECONDS, VELOCITY = 128 FT./SEC.
400 FEET — END OF 5 SECONDS, VELOCITY = 160 FT./SEC.
576 FEET — END OF 6 SECONDS, VELOCITY = 192 FT./SEC.
784 FEET — END OF 7 SECONDS, VELOCITY = 224 FT./SEC.
1024 FEET — END OF 8 SECONDS, VELOCITY = 256 FT./SEC.
1296 FEET — END OF 9 SECONDS, VELOCITY = 288 FT./SEC.
1472 FEET — END OF 9.55 SECONDS, STRIKES SIDEWALK WITH VELOCITY = 305.6 FT./SEC.

The diagram shows the acceleration of a ball by gravity when the ball is dropped from the Empire State Building in New York City. Although you might expect the ball to drop 32 feet during the first second, notice that it actually drops only about 16 feet. This is because the ball had a velocity of 0 at the start of its drop. If it accelerates uniformly to a speed of 32 feet per second at the end of one second, its average speed during the first second is the average of its beginning (initial) speed of 0 and its end (terminal) speed of 32 feet per second, or 16 feet per second. As you can see, it would take about 10 seconds for the ball to reach the ground.

A question that fascinates many people is this: If a bullet is fired horizontally from a gun and a second bullet is dropped from the same height, which bullet will strike the ground first? The answer is, they will strike the ground at the same instant! The reason for this is that the downward pull of gravity is independent of the horizontal motion of the body. If a bullet were fired at an angle upward at the same time a second bullet was dropped, would they fall at the same instant? Would the bullet that was fired upward travel as far from the gun as a bullet that was fired horizontally?

THE CONVERSION AND CONSERVATION OF ENERGY

AN IMPORTANT SERIES of energy transformations takes place in a hydroelectric plant, such as this one at Hungry Horse Dam, Montana. Water stored in the reservoir behind the tall dam has tremendous potential energy. When it drops nearly 600 feet through a long tubular flume to the base of the dam, the water's potential energy is changed to kinetic energy.

At the bottom of this flume the rushing water pushes against the paddles or blades of a huge turbine wheel (see page 160) and causes the wheel to rotate. The energy of running water is thereby converted to rotational energy. As the turbine wheel spins, the shaft to which it is attached turns. Then, in a room high above the turbine, the other end of the turning shaft drives a generator which converts mechanical to electrical energy. The electricity produced by four of these turbine-powered generators travels over wires to homes and factories in the region surrounding this dam.

This series of energy transformations illustrates a universal principle: *energy can be converted from one form to another*. Other examples are: the burning of coal, which converts potential chemical energy to kinetic heat and light energy; the work of an electric motor, which changes kinetic electric energy to kinetic mechanical energy; and the conversion of kinetic light energy to potential chemical energy by the activity of green plants. In a flashlight, chemical energy of the battery is changed to electrical energy and then, in the bulb, to light and heat energy.

A second principle, which is inseparably associated with conversion of energy, is that of conservation of energy. Basically, this principle states: *while energy can be changed from one form to another, the total amount of energy in a closed system remains unchanged.* (A closed system is one that can neither lose energy to or obtain energy from the outside.) For example, the work done by a machine, plus the frictional loss within the machine, always equals the effort put into the machine.

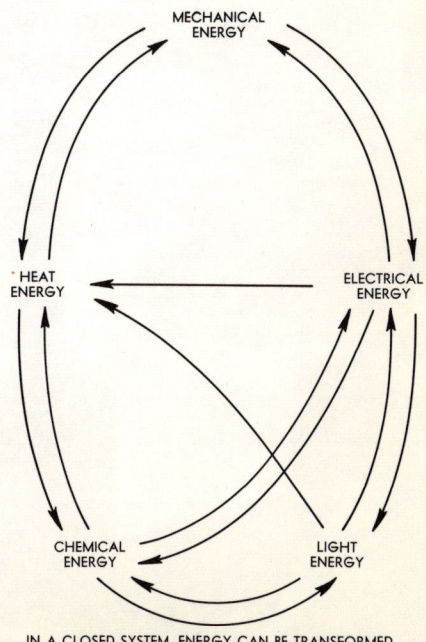

IN A CLOSED SYSTEM, ENERGY CAN BE TRANSFORMED FROM ONE STATE TO ANOTHER, BUT THE TOTAL AMOUNT OF ENERGY DOES NOT INCREASE OR DECREASE

CHAPTER III

HOW WE MEASURE

We make use of measurements every day. At the grocery, your mother may buy a *quart* of milk, a *pound* of meat, and several *fluid ounces* of sauce. Father figures the distance to work in *miles,* the time his trip takes in *minutes,* and the speed of his car in *miles per hour*.

The complex system of exchange, the standard of living, and the advanced state of science in our civilization would be impossible without adequate measurements. The manufacture of thousands of identical items by mass production permits the rapid construction of television sets, automobiles, washers, and thousands of other machines at prices most of us can afford. But mass production requires that a given part will fit interchangeably into any of hundreds of identical machines, rather than into just one machine for which it was specially made. This "interchangeability" is the basis of mass production and depends on precise measurement by units that are the same at one place as at another.

In scientific research, measurements are used to describe conditions of experiments or qualities of things being studied. Science could not progress if scientists in one country used a kind of measurement that was different from the kind used by scientists in other countries.

Man had to choose basic units of measurement. These units are arbitrary — there are no natural ones, although natural objects — tiny shells, parts of the body — or natural phenomena — length of day, phases of the moon — have been used in the past for measurements.

This chapter describes the ways we measure a number of characteristics of matter. As you read, you will find it helpful to look at the tables in the appendix (page 220) where many units of measurement are compared. These comparisons will be of value to you in many ways in the future. Keep them available for reference.

LINEAR MEASURES AND STANDARDS OF MEASUREMENTS

Whether he measures the diameter of an atom, the distance from one city to another, the depth of the ocean, or the thickness of a board, man needs a way to express distance. Because these measurements are made along a straight line, they are called *linear measurements*.

Parts of the body are convenient units for linear measurements. For centuries a system of measures was used which included: the *digit*, the width of the index finger; the *foot*, the length of a human foot; and the *inch*, the breadth of the thumb.

People differ in stature — so measurements varied from one person to another. The need for *standards* of measurement — samples recognized as the perfect example of each unit — soon became apparent. Perhaps the foot of a tribal chief was the first standard. Later, wooden, stone, or metal standards were made, but even these varied from tribe to tribe.

In the 15th century, the British government established new standards for units of length, volume, and weight to be used throughout the widespread British Kingdom. This *English system* later was adopted by other countries. But English units are not related systematically. For example, 12 inches equal 1 foot, and 1 mile contains 63,360 inches or 5,280 feet. It is not easy to convert measurements from one unit to another.

In 1791, the Paris Academy of Science developed a new system of measures, the *metric system*. The basic linear unit, the *meter*, originally was defined as one ten-millionth of the distance from the North Pole to the equator. Other units, including those of volume and mass, are based upon the meter and are related decimally. That is, they increase or decrease by multiples of 10 and are converted by moving the decimal point.

The systematic relation of metric units was recognized to be of value to science and these units now are used by scientists throughout the world. But acceptance of the metric system by non-scientists has been slow. The metric system was made legal in the United States by an Act of Congress in 1866, but its use was not required and has not yet become common.

From 1889 to 1960, a bar made of an alloy of platinum and iridium, a metal that is unaffected by most chemicals and does not change shape with age, was used as the standard for the meter length. This bar is kept at the International Bureau of Weights and Measures, near Paris, France. Copies, known as *prototypes,* are kept by various nations of the world. Prototype meter number 27 and prototype kilogram number 20, the United States standards of length and mass which are kept at the National Bureau of Standards near Gaithersburg, Maryland, are shown below on the left.

The new international metric standard of length, adopted in 1960, is the wavelength of the orange-red light emitted by krypton (isotope 86) when immersed in a low-temperature bath of liquid nitrogen. The second photograph shows a scientist adjusting a krypton lamp. The meter now is defined as 1,650,763.73 wavelengths of krypton-86 light, but this change in standards does not affect the actual length of the meter unit. It merely assures a more stable standard — one that is believed to be unchangeable — and one that can be reproduced with great accuracy in any well-equipped laboratory.

Even though several nations, including the United States, still use the English system, English units now are defined in terms of the international metric standard. The "inch" is equal to 41,929.399 wavelengths of krypton-86 light, or to 2.54 centimeters.

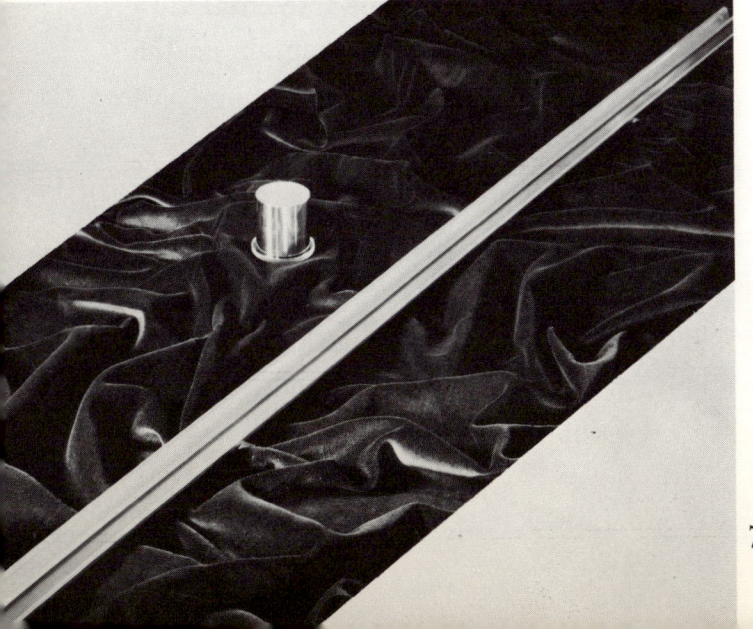

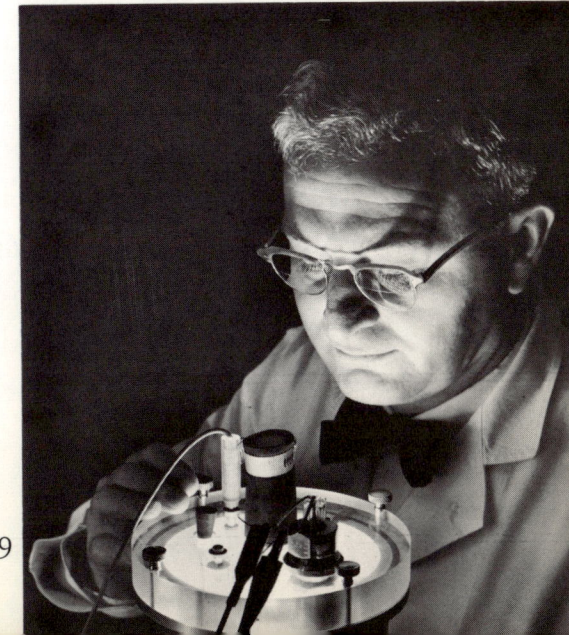

AREA AND VOLUME

AREA IS A MEASURE of the amount of space on a surface. While linear measurements consider only a line, or one dimension (length), areal measurements consider two: length and width. Width is a second linear measurement made at a right angle to that of length.

Area is obtained by multiplying the length of a surface by its width (length × width = area). For example, the square in the diagram on the facing page is 2 inches wide and 2 inches long. Its area, therefore, is 4 square inches (2 × 2 = 4).

Volume, the space occupied by a substance or enclosed by a container, is a 3-dimensional value obtained by multiplying length times width, times *thickness*. Thicknesses is a measurement made perpendicular to the surface which was measured by length and width. The block in the diagram is 2 inches wide, 2 inches long, and 2 inches thick. Its volume, thus, is 8 cubic inches (2 × 2 × 2 = 8). Count the smaller blocks shown by

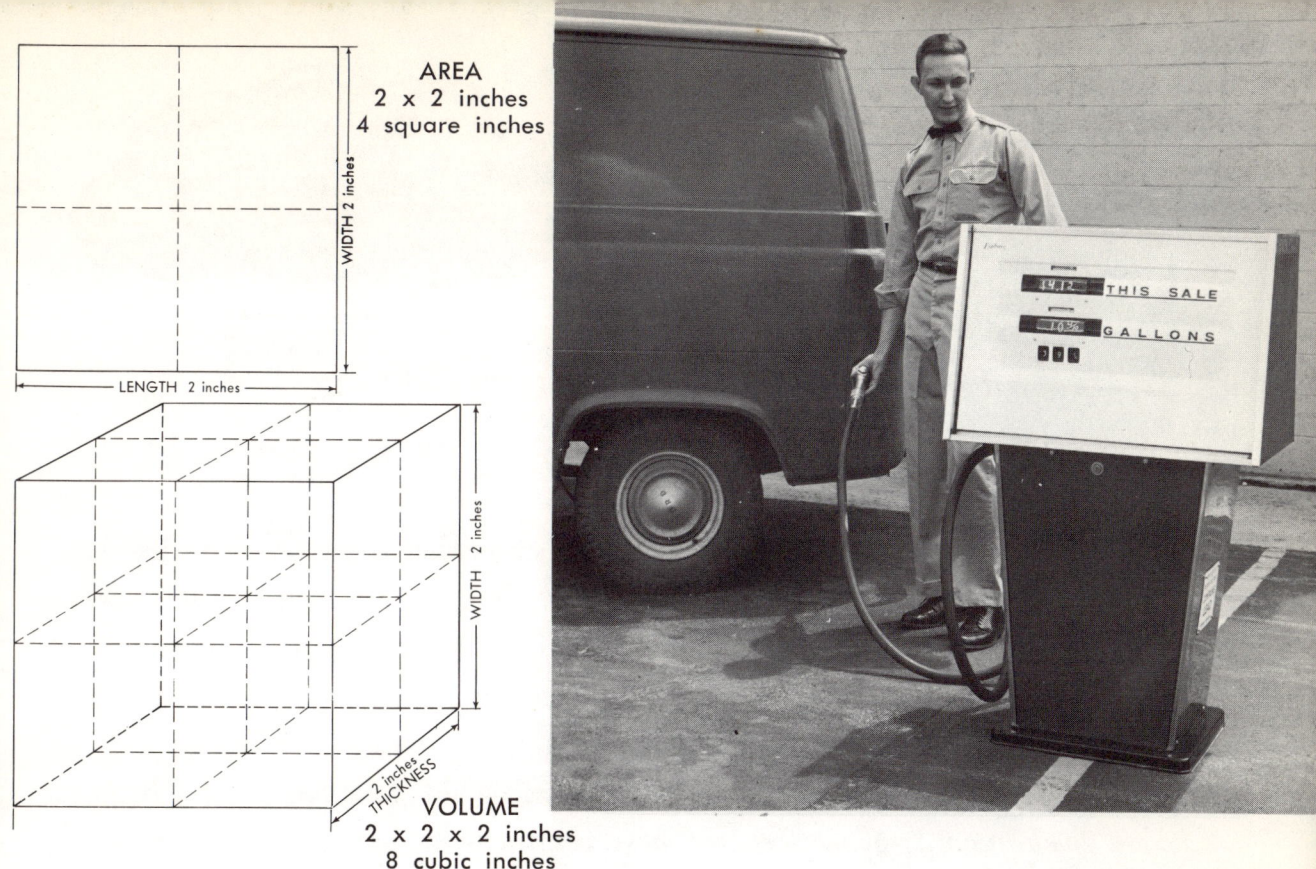

dotted lines inside this 8 cubic inch block.

All measurements must be expressed in the same unit before they can be multiplied to obtain area or volume. Length in inches must be multiplied by width and thickness in inches. Because a linear unit, such as an inch, is multiplied by itself once (squared) to obtain a unit of area, or by itself twice (cubed) to obtain a unit of volume, area and volume cannot be expressed by linear units. We use squares or cubes of those units — for example, *square* inches and *cubic* feet. There are also several special units of area and volume. These are listed in the appendix (page 220).

Measurements of area and volume are of great importance in science and commerce. In real estate transactions, the price of a parcel of land is determined largely by its size (area). A farmer must know the area of his fields to calculate the amount of seed and fertilizer needed for his crops.

Solids usually are measured by weight (you buy sugar and flour by the pound), but liquids and gases are measured more easily by volume. At the filling station, therefore, you do not buy gasoline by the pound, but by the gallon. Milk is sold by the quart and cooking gas by the cubic foot.

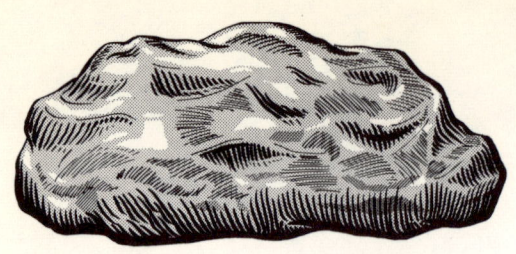
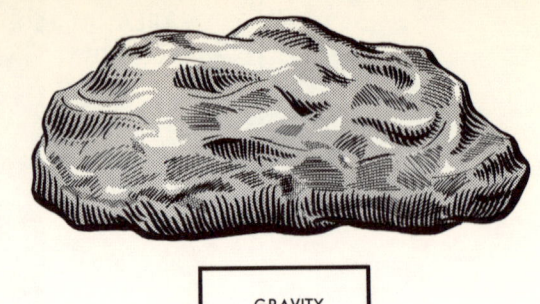

MASS AND WEIGHT

THE FIRST LAW OF MOTION (page 40) states that every object resists a force which tends to change its velocity. Thus, an object at rest will not move until a force is applied to it which is strong enough to overcome its resistance to movement, or inertia. The amount of inertia depends on the quantity of matter present in the body. *Mass is a measure of inertia* and, thus, also of quantity of matter. In contrast, *weight is the force with which a given quantity of matter, or a mass, is attracted toward the center of the earth by a standard gravity.* The international gravity standard is approximately equal to the acceleration of gravity at sea level half way between the equator and the north or south pole.

Mass and weight are measured in different units. In the metric system, mass is measured in such units as the *gram* and *kilogram*. Weight is measured in units of force, such as the *dyne* and *newton* (see page 69). Units of mass and force in the English system bear identical names — such as *ounce*, *pound*, and *ton*. Where standard gravity exists, weight and mass are similar in value: a 1 pound mass weighs 1 pound.

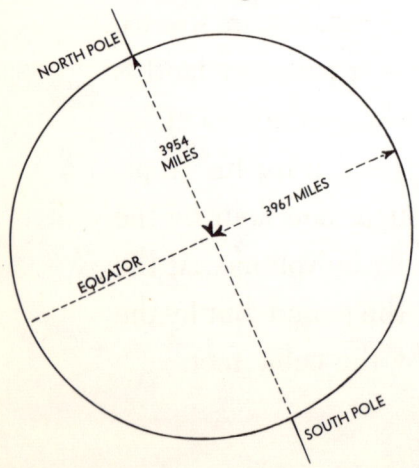

As long as no matter is added or taken away, the mass of an object remains the same, regardless of where it is located in space. However, the force with which an object is attracted toward the earth — its weight — decreases as its distance from the earth's center increases. This decrease is rapid because the force of gravity lessens in proportion to the square of the distance from the center of the earth (see page 72).

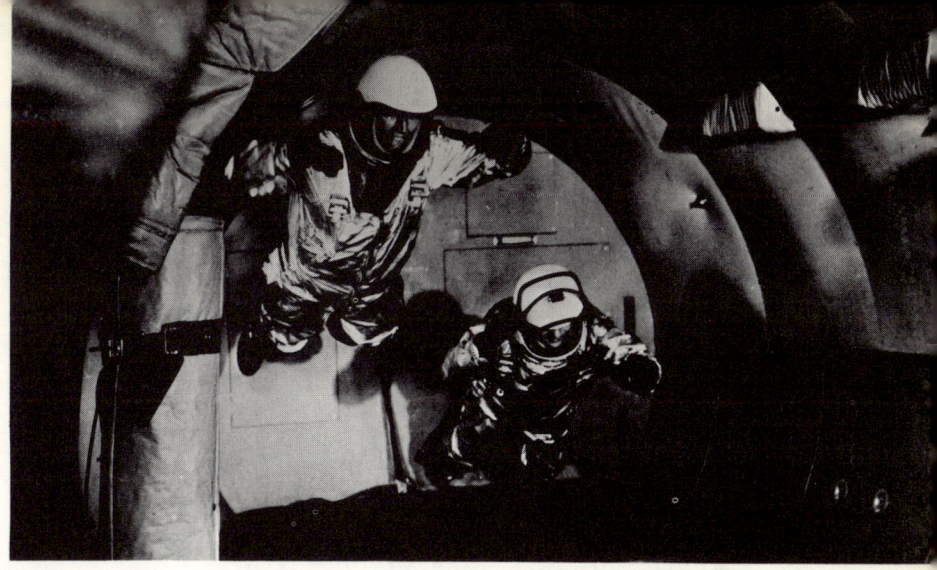

Variations of weight with altitude on the earth are small, because the distance from sea level to the highest mountain peak (about 5.5 miles) is slight compared to the distance from sea level to the earth's center (about 4,000 miles). Even at sea level, though, weight varies because our earth bulges at the equator and is flattened at the poles. Thus, an object which weighs 1,000 pounds with standard gravity would weigh only 999.3 pounds at the equator, because it would be farther from the earth's center. At the north pole, it would weigh about 1,000.3 pounds. Why?

Our new ability to probe into space with rockets has brought a new problem — how will our bodies function when we are weightless, as the men are in the photograph above. If you weigh 100 pounds at sea level, you would weigh only 25 pounds in a space capsule 4,000 miles high (2 times as far from the earth's center; ¼ as much gravity); 11 pounds at 8,000 miles; and only 1 pound at 36,000 miles. Weightlessness also occurs for short periods during dives when an airplane accelerates at a rate equal to that of gravity. And an astronaut in low altitude orbital flight also experiences weightlessness when the centrifugal force of his orbiting capsule — a force which acts opposite to gravity — equals gravity (see page 44).

Objects on the surface of the earth also are subjected to centrifugal force because the earth rotates. But this force is slight, so that the weight of any object is reduced only a little — about 0.3% at the equator — from what it would be if the earth were not rotating.

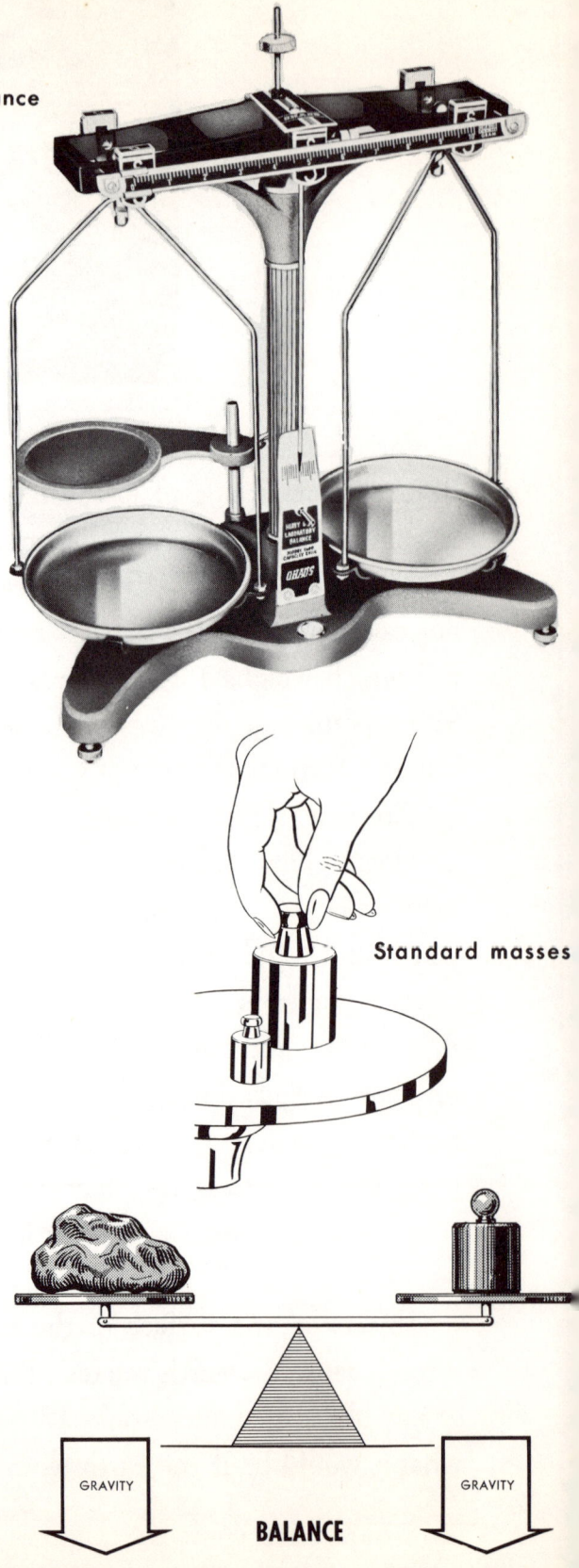

Beam balance

Standard masses

BALANCE

GRAVITY GRAVITY

Two kinds of machines commonly are used to measure mass or weight: the *beam balance* and *spring scale*. A beam balance, such as the one shown in this photograph, is a first-class lever (see page 104) with arms of equal length. An object placed on the platform at the end of one arm will balance an object of equal mass at the end of the other arm. Standard masses of different sizes, usually in the form of small brass cylinders, are placed on one platform until a combination is found which will balance an unknown object. Then, the total mass of the standards is equal to the mass of the unknown object. If the mass is determined in pounds, we generally say that its weight also is that many pounds, even though the value of gravity at the place of measurement may not be standard.

In a spring scale, the stretching of a steel spring or some other elastic material is used to determine the mass or weight of an unknown object. Such a scale first must be

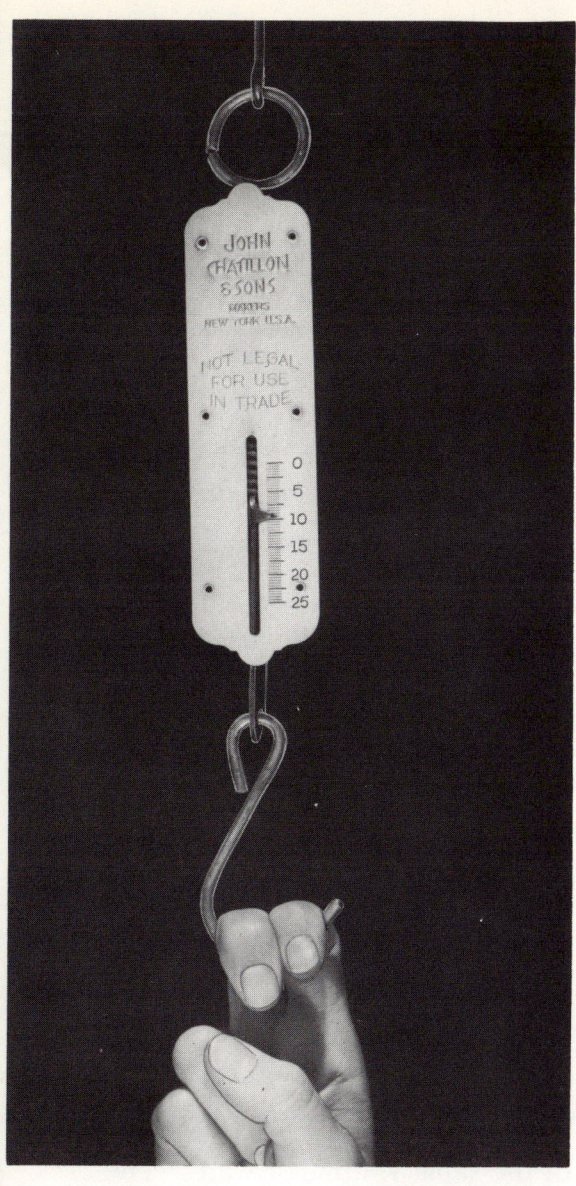

Spring scale

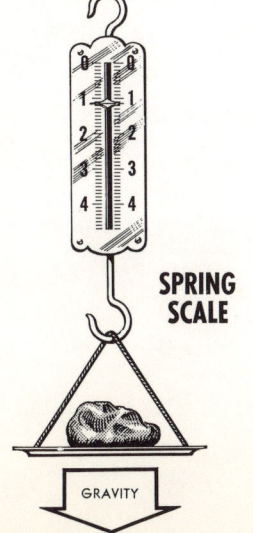

SPRING SCALE

GRAVITY

calibrated by measuring the extension of the spring caused by a standard mass. Then, an unknown object which stretches the spring to the same extent is considered to equal the standard mass. Because a given mass would weigh more in one place (at the sea shore) than at another (on a mountain top) because of changes in gravity, the mass could stretch the spring more at one place than another. Thus, a spring scale can be used to determine mass or weight accurately only at the place where it was calibrated.

An object has mass, but no weight in outer space. Thus, we cannot use a balance or spring to measure mass because there would be no force to pull the mass downward. However, masses could be compared by a method similar to the one used in the experiment illustrated on page 43. If an equal force is applied to two different objects, the object which has the greater mass will accelerate more rapidly. By measuring the acceleration of each object, we could determine the relative size of their masses.

DENSITY AND SPECIFIC GRAVITY

ALL MATTER HAS MASS. But from experience we know that some pieces of matter are heavier than others. A lump of iron, for instance, may feel much heavier than a similar lump of aluminum. But a large piece of aluminum may weigh as much as, or more than a smaller piece of iron. So, to compare the weights of different objects (especially if they differ greatly in size) their weights must be given in terms of portions of equal size.

Density is an expression of the masses of various substances expressed in identical units of volume. The density of this large chunk of plastic foam is obviously much less than the density of the meringue pie it is balancing.

To determine the density of a substance, its mass is divided by its volume. For example, the density of iron is 490 pounds per cubic foot in English measures, or 7,900 kilograms per cubic meter in metric units. The density of aluminum is 164 pounds per cubic foot, or 2,650 kilograms per cubic meter, and the density of water is 62.5 pounds per cubic foot or 1000 kilograms per cubic meter.

Specific gravity is a handy measure of the relative densities of various substances. It is obtained by dividing the density of a substance by the density of water. Thus, the specific gravity of a substance indicates how many times heavier the substance is than the same volume of water. The specific gravity of gold, for example, is 19.3. Thus, we know that any volume of gold will weigh 19.3 times as much as an equal volume of water.

DENSITY AND SPECIFIC GRAVITY OF SOME COMMON SUBSTANCES

	Pounds/ Cubic Foot	Kilograms/ Cubic Meter	Specific Gravity		Pounds/ Cubic Foot	Kilograms/ Cubic Meter	Specific Gravity
Pine wood ..	30	500	0.5	Aluminum .	164	2,700	2.7
Ice	57	900	0.9	Iron	493	7,900	7.9
Water	62.5	1,000	1.0	Gold	1,206	19,300	19.3

TIME

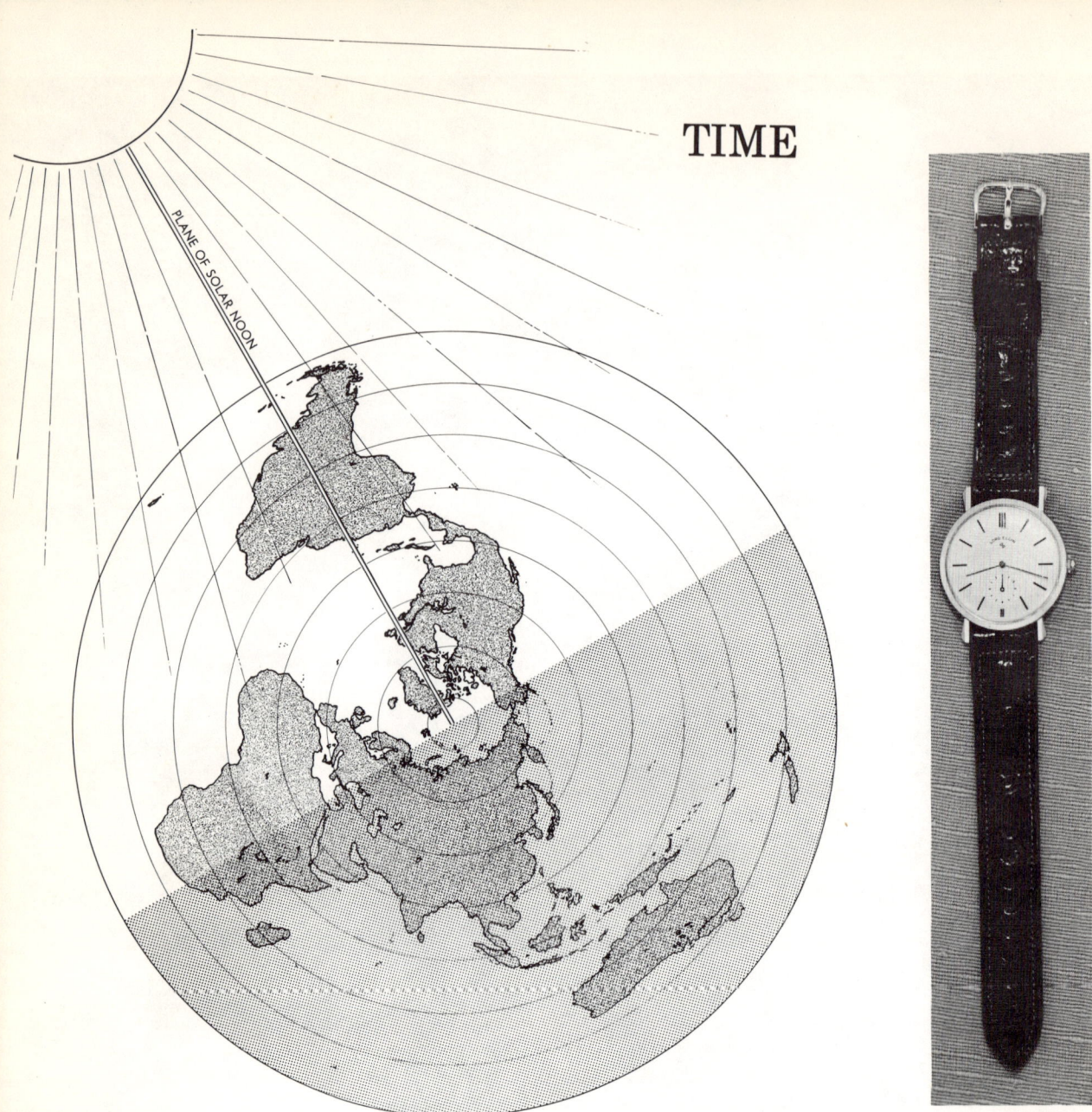

Although we normally are not aware of it, the earth is constantly revolving. Because the earth turns toward the east, we see the sun apparently rise in the eastern sky, pass overhead during the day, and then set in the west. After a period of darkness, caused by our side of the earth being turned away from the sun, we see the sun rise again. Primitive man doubtless used the periods of night (sleep) and the periods of daylight (activity) to reckon time. For longer periods, he may have referred to the phases of the moon.

Our modern methods of reckoning time still are based on the time it takes the earth to rotate. Both the English and metric systems employ the same units to measure time. These units begin with the *mean solar day*, the average period between two successive *solar noons*. A solar noon is the precise instant when the sun appears to pass through the meridian, an imaginary, vertical plane which extends from a given place to the north and south geographical poles of the earth. You can find the solar noon of your area by standing a broom stick or pipe perfectly vertical in your yard and determining the moment when it either casts no shadow or when its shadow is cast toward the true north. A compass needle points to magnetic north, so you will have to ask your teacher or librarian to help you find what correction must be made to obtain true north from a compass reading.

The mean solar day is divided into 86,400 equal parts, called *seconds*. The *minute* is a unit equal to 60 seconds and an *hour* is a larger unit equal to 60 minutes or 360 seconds. A solar day contains 24 hours.

Seven solar days make one *week* and approximately 365¼ solar days form a *year*. In our calendars, we make up for this extra ¼ day by having three of every four years with 365 days and one of every four years with 366 days. This extra day is added to the month of February in the years we call "leap year."

All measurements of time are based on exacting observations of the positions of the sun. However, the most popular time-keeping devices are clocks. They are made in an amazing array of sizes and shapes. But all clocks are based on the same principle: If the circumstances are exactly the same, a given object requires precisely the same time to move through a specified distance in one case as in another. Thus, the hands of a clock, in one hour, move through exactly the same distance as they did in the hour before and as they will in each hour afterward. Of course, this principle is shown best by the apparent movement through the sky of the sun, upon which our measurements of time are based.

SPEED, VELOCITY, AND ACCELERATION

Speed and velocity are often used interchangeably to describe the rate at which something moves. Scientists, however, use these terms to express two different but closely related concepts.

Speed is the rate of motion of a body, stated as the distance traveled in a given time. Average speed is calculated by dividing the distance traveled by the time required to travel that distance. A runner may be clocked at 10.9 seconds in the 100-yard dash, an average speed of 9.2 yards per second. What is the average speed of an automobile that travels 120 miles in 3 hours?

Scientists employ Mach numbers (pronounced mock) to measure high speeds. A Mach number is the ratio of an object's speed to the speed of sound, Mach 1. Mach .8 is less than the speed of sound (subsonic). Mach 3 is three times as fast as the speed of sound (supersonic). Because the speed of sound varies with the temperature, Mach 1 may be equal to 700 m.p.h. at sea level on a cold day and over 800 m.p.h. on a hot day. In the cold air at high altitudes, Mach 1 may be equivalent to a speed of only 660 m.p.h. Because sound requires some substance, such as the atmosphere, to transmit it, there can be no sound in space. Mach numbers, therefore, are meaningless for a space probe, such as Pioneer V, launched from Cape Canaveral on March 11, 1960, and now in orbit around the sun. This probe reaches a maximum speed of 78,000 miles per hour.

The *velocity* of a body is its speed in a given direction. The velocity of an express train on a straight stretch of track, for example, might be 96 m.p.h. toward the northwest. A change in velocity occurs when there is a change in speed or direction. The rate of change of velocity is termed *acceleration*, and it may be positive (increased) or negative (decreased). For example, if the speed of an automobile on a straight road is increased from 35 m.p.h. to 55 m.p.h. in two minutes, the velocity is increased 20 miles per hour. The acceleration during this change of velocity is 10 miles per hour per minute. On the other hand, an automobile on a curve could increase its speed, but because it also would change direction, its velocity with regard to its original direction of travel would decrease.

FOUR POUND BOOK IS RAISED TWO FEET ABOVE TABLE

WORK AND POWER

BOX 10 LBS.
BOY 90 LBS.
STAIRS 10 FT. HIGH

IN SCIENCE, work is defined as a transfer of energy which involves movement of the point to which a force is applied.

Work is measured by the product of the force exerted upon an object and the distance through which the force moves (work = force x distance). The quantity of work can be expressed by any unit of force multiplied by any unit of distance. Measurements in the English system commonly are given in *foot-pounds*. For example, a laborer does 1,500 foot-pounds of work when he carries a 30-pound stone up a 50-foot-high hill (30 lbs. x 50 ft.). How many foot-pounds of work would you do to raise this 4 pound book 2 feet above the table? How many foot-pounds of work will this 90 pound boy do by carrying a 10 pound box to the top of a 10 foot stair?

A unit of work in the metric system is the *erg,* which is the work done when a force of one dyne (see page 69) is exerted through a distance of one centimeter. An erg is approximately equal to the work done when a mosquito is lifted three-eighths of an inch. The *joule,* which is equal to 10 million ergs, is a more convenient unit for most purposes. It is also equal to 0.738 foot-pounds.

Power is the rate at which work is done. It is determined by dividing the quantity of work by the period of time during which the work was done (average power = work ÷ time). *Horsepower* is a common unit used to measure the power of various engines. It is equal to 550 foot-pounds per second, or 746 watts. The watt, which equals one joule per second, and the kilowatt (1,000 watts) are common metric units used to measure the power of electric motors, generators, and lights.

TEMPERATURE, TOTAL HEAT AND SPECIFIC HEAT

Air Force sergeant takes a free air temperature at Ice Island.

NEARLY EVERY SUBSTANCE expands when it is heated and contracts to its original size when it is cooled to the starting temperature. On a cold, winter day the Empire State Building in New York City is 1,472 feet tall. But it stretches upward an extra foot when warmed by the midsummer sun. This stretch is an example of thermal expansion, the phenomenon which underlies the operation of the thermometer, an instrument used to measure heat intensity.

Thermometers contain a liquid especially chosen for its expansion properties. Alcohol is used in less-expensive instruments and in those to be used in cold regions, such as in this Weather Bureau instrument shelter in the Arctic. Mercury is used in medium and high-temperature ranges.

Doctor takes a human temperature

94

There are two temperature scales in common use. On one scale, the *Celsius* scale* of the metric system (formerly called the centigrade scale), a value of 0.01° C is assigned to the triple-point of water (the temperature at which ice, liquid water, and water vapor are in equilibrium) and 100° C to the steam point (the temperature of equilibrium between liquid water and its vapor under a pressure of one atmosphere). On the *Fahrenheit* scale, an English measure, the temperature of the triple-point is equal to 32° F and that of the steam point is 212° F, with 180 equal units between. The units can be extended above and below the standard temperatures as far as required. Each centigrade degree is equal to 1.8 Fahrenheit degrees. The scales are compared in the diagram. In this book, temperatures are given on the Celsius scale, the scale used by scientists all over the world. Fahrenheit temperatures are given in parentheses.

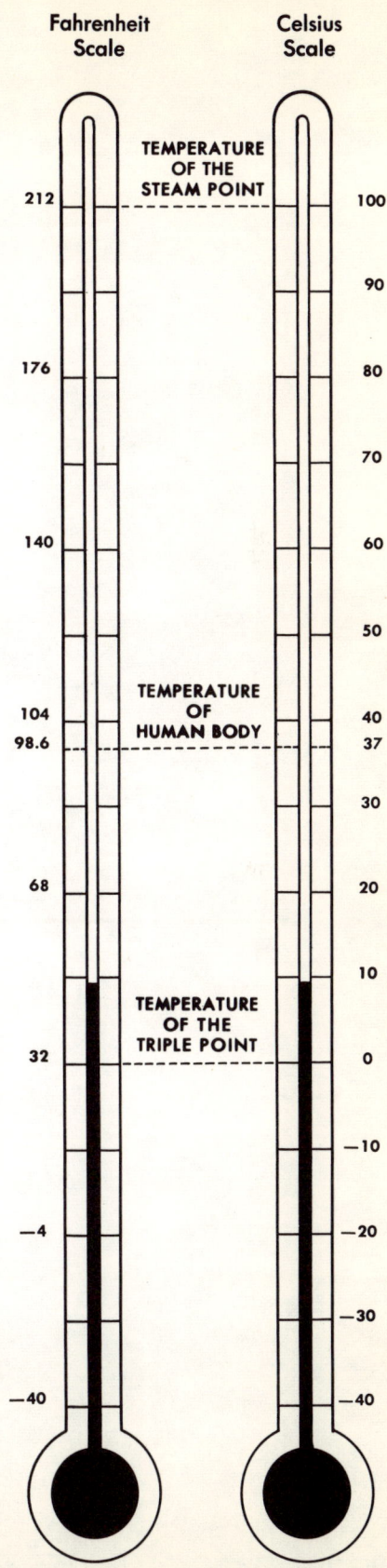

---

*Anders Celsius, a Swedish astronomer, invented a thermometer in 1742 whose scale had 100 degrees between the ice point and steam point.

Thermometers measure only the intensity of heat. This relative measure gives no indication of the quantity of heat in any body or the differences in total heat possessed by different bodies. Thus, water in a tea kettle may be at the same temperature as water spouting skyward from Old Faithful Geyser in Yellowstone National Park. But the quantity of heat present in the kettle is a small fraction of that in the thousands of gallons of water issuing from the geyser. Temperature measurements are the basis of another series of units which are used to determine quantitatively the amount of heat in a body.

In the metric system the basic unit of heat quantity is the *calorie,* the heat required to raise the temperature of one gram of water one degree Celsius. It is equivalent to 4.18 joules of mechanical energy.

The British thermal unit (B.t.u.), the heat required to raise the temperature of one pound of water one Fahrenheit degree, is the basic heat measure of the English system. One B.t.u. is equal to 252 calories or to 778 foot-pounds of mechanical energy. The British thermal unit is customarily used to measure the heat produced by various fuels, such as coal, oil, gas, and gasoline.

The temperature of one substance may rise much more rapidly than that of another substance when both are subjected to the same heat. For example, to raise the temperature of one gram of water one degree Celsius requires 1.0 calorie. But only one-fifth as much heat is needed to raise the temperature of a similar mass of aluminum one degree (0.22 calorie), and just one-thirtieth as much for lead (0.03 calorie). The ratio of the quantity of heat required to raise a given mass of a substance through a given degree of temperature to the quantity required to raise an equal mass of water through the same range is the *specific heat* of the substance. The specific heat of water is 1, aluminum is 0.22, and lead is 0.03.

Specific heats of various substances are accurately determined in this ice calorimeter at the National Bureau of Standards. The material is first heated to a known temperature in the small cylinder to the left of the operator's head. Then the material is dropped down into the calorimeter where the heat it releases while cooling is measured by observing the temperature to which it raises a known mass of water.

ELECTRICITY

Periodically the "light man" reads the dials of a glass-enclosed electric meter in your home to determine the amount of electrical energy used. Later, his company will send a bill for this energy. The charge is based on the number of kilowatt hours used. In order to understand how much energy a kilowatt hour represents, we must first learn about several units that are more basic.

The number of electrons that pass through a conductor in a given time determines the size of the current. The *ampere* is the unit used to measure electric current. One ampere is equivalent to a flow of about 6.3 billion electrons per second through a conductor.

Every substance resists, more or less, the passage of an electric current. The practical unit of measurement of resistance is the *ohm*. By agreement, it is the resistance offered by a column of mercury 106.3 centimeters (42.2 in.) long, 1 square millimeter (.0016 sq. in.) in cross-sectional area, at 0° C (32° F).

Electrons are driven through a conductor by a pressure known as an *electromotive force* (e.m.f.) which is measured in a unit known as the *volt*. One volt equals the e.m.f. that will cause a current of one ampere to flow through a conductor having a resistance of one ohm. Ordinarily, there is an e.m.f. of 110-120 volts in the wires of homes. Lightning involves e.m.f.'s of several million volts.

The *watt* is a unit used to measure the power or rate of consumption of electrical energy. It is the potential rate of work of a current of one ampere maintained by an e.m.f. of one volt (watts = volts x amperes). A 60-watt bulb uses exactly twice as much current as a 30-watt bulb.

Commercially, electrical energy is measured in kilowatt-hours (kw.hr.). One kw.hr. is equivalent to 1,000 watts of power delivered for one hour. This amount of electrical energy will operate a large television set for more than five hours, a 100-watt bulb for ten hours, or an electric toaster for about one hour.

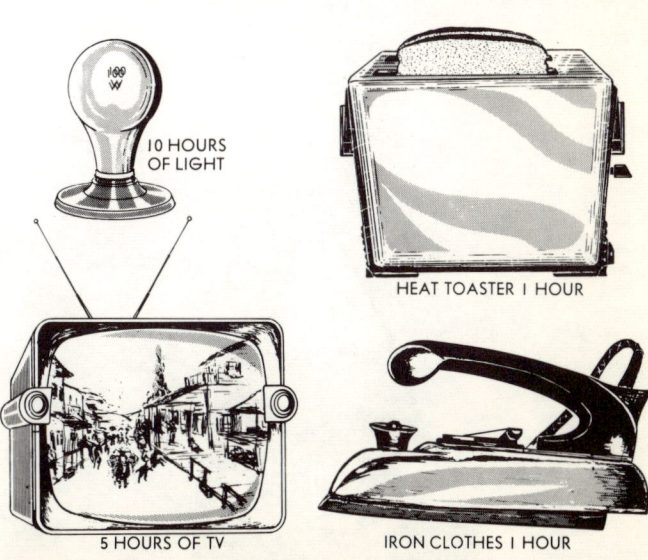

WHAT ONE KILOWATT-HOUR OF ELECTRICAL ENERGY WILL DO

CHAPTER IV

THE PHYSICS OF SIMPLE MACHINES

EARLIEST MAN had only his body with which to push, pull, lift, fling, pound, or crush objects. Then, perhaps man found that a sharp stone would cut the skin from an animal more easily than he could tear it with his hands. However his first invention came about, man learned that simple machines could ease his labors and extend his abilities to do work.

A simple machine is merely an object which is able to modify a force which is exerted upon it (known as the *effort*) to do work on some other object (known as the *resistance*). The machine may *multiply a force,* so that a small effort can move a large resistance. It may merely *change the direction of a force.* Or, it may *increase the velocity of a force.*

The relation between the sizes of the effort and the resistance is known as the *mechanical advantage* (M. A.) of the machine. Thus, if an effort of 3 pounds will lift a 6 pound object, the mechanical advantage of the machine is 2 (M. A. $= \frac{\text{resistance}}{\text{effort}} = \frac{6}{3} = 2$). At first, it may seem that a machine can create force, but this is not true. *The work done on a machine is always equal to the work done by the machine.* (Friction losses are ignored when principles are discussed. The work done on a machine actually equals the work done by the machine plus these friction losses.) Work (see page 93) is measured in terms of the size of a force and the distance through which it moves. Thus, if the mechanical advantage of a machine is greater than 1, the effort must move farther than the resistance. If the mechanical advantage is 3, the effort will move three times as far as the resistance. If the mechanical advantage is less than 1, the resistance travels farther than the effort and the machine will increase the speed of a force, but reduce its size.

This chapter will do more than acquaint you with the principle of a lever, or a screw, or a wheel. An understanding of simple machines is basic to the understanding of all machines, for even an airplane, a printing press, or a giant crane is a combination of simple machines.

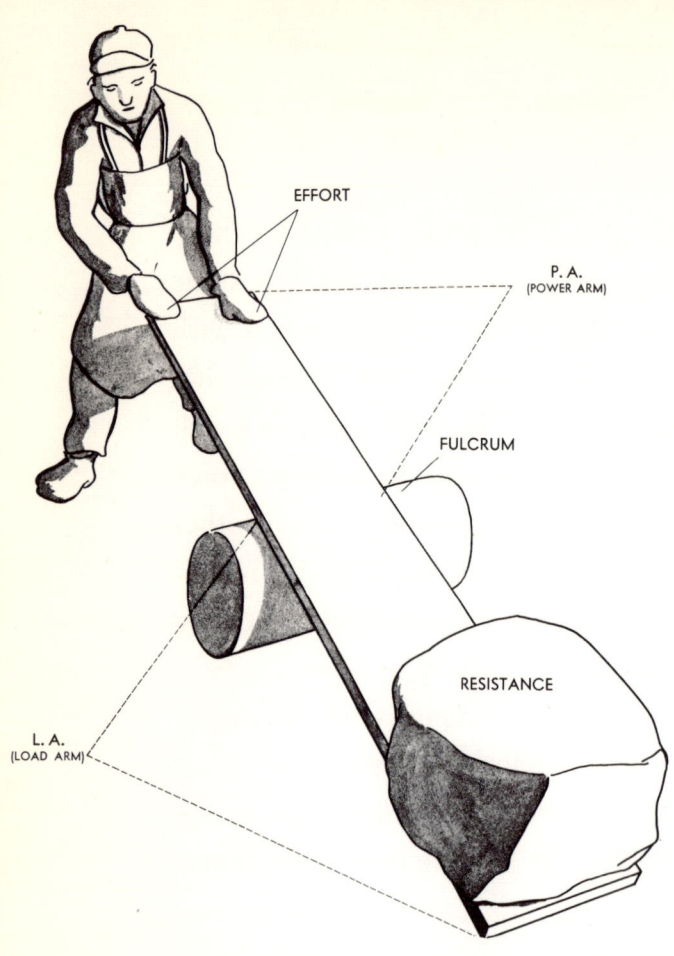

THE LEVER

You use many levers each day. Scissors, pliers, bottle openers — even parts of your own body — are levers. Although we use them so often, few of us know what a lever is or how it operates. A lever is just a rigid object, usually a bar, rod, or pole, which can be turned about a point which is called its *fulcrum*.

Two forces act upon a lever. One force, called the *effort* or *power*, is applied to the lever to oppose a second force, the *resistance* or *load*. The portion of the lever between the fulcrum and the effort is called the *power arm*. The portion between the fulcrum and the resistance is the *load arm*. The mechanical advantage of a lever depends on the lengths of its two arms and can be obtained by dividing the length of the power arm by the length of the load arm (M. A. $= \frac{\text{power arm length}}{\text{load arm length}}$).

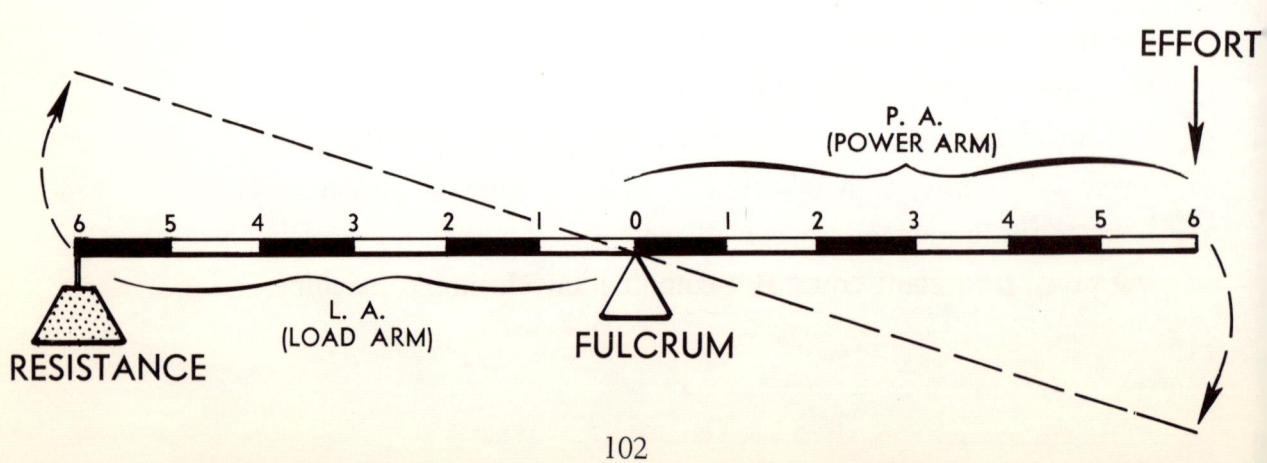

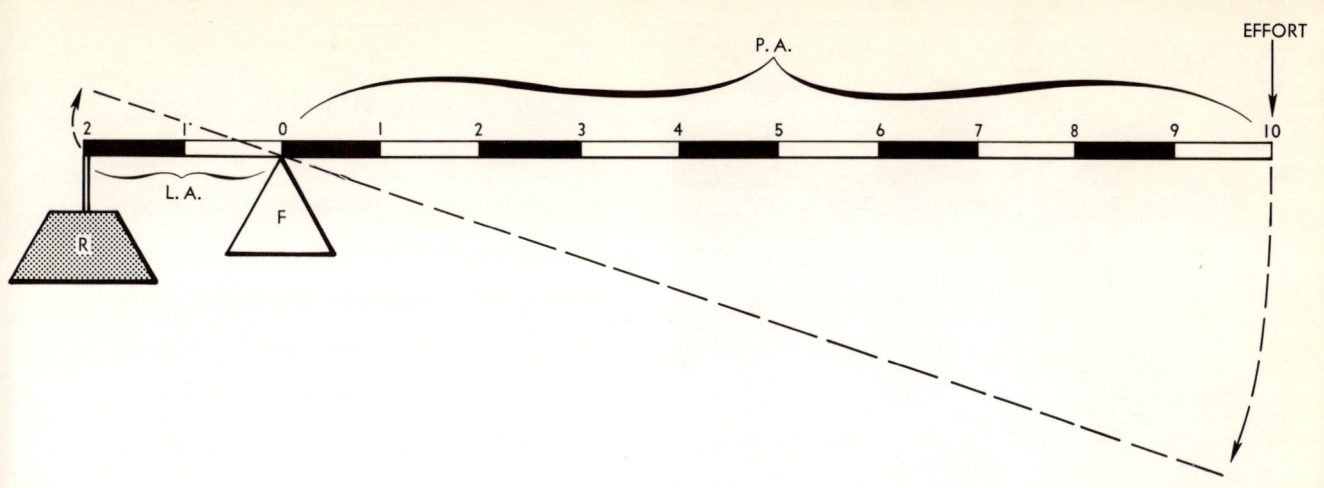

If the arms of a lever are of equal length, the effort will balance a resistance of the same size. The only use for such a lever is to change the direction of a force or to compare the sizes of two forces (see page 84).

If the power arm is longer, the mechanical advantage of the lever is greater than 1, because the effort will move farther than the resistance. Such a lever will multiply force, with a loss of speed. If the load arm is longer, the mechanical advantage of the lever is less than 1, because the resistance will move farther than the effort. In this case, the lever multiplies speed at the expense of force. A large, slow-moving force applied near to the fulcrum can cause a smaller resistance farther removed from the fulcrum to move more rapidly. This principle is used in the catapult.

By varying the location of the fulcrum of a lever in relation to the effort and the resistance, we can use a lever for different purposes. These variations give rise to three classes of levers:

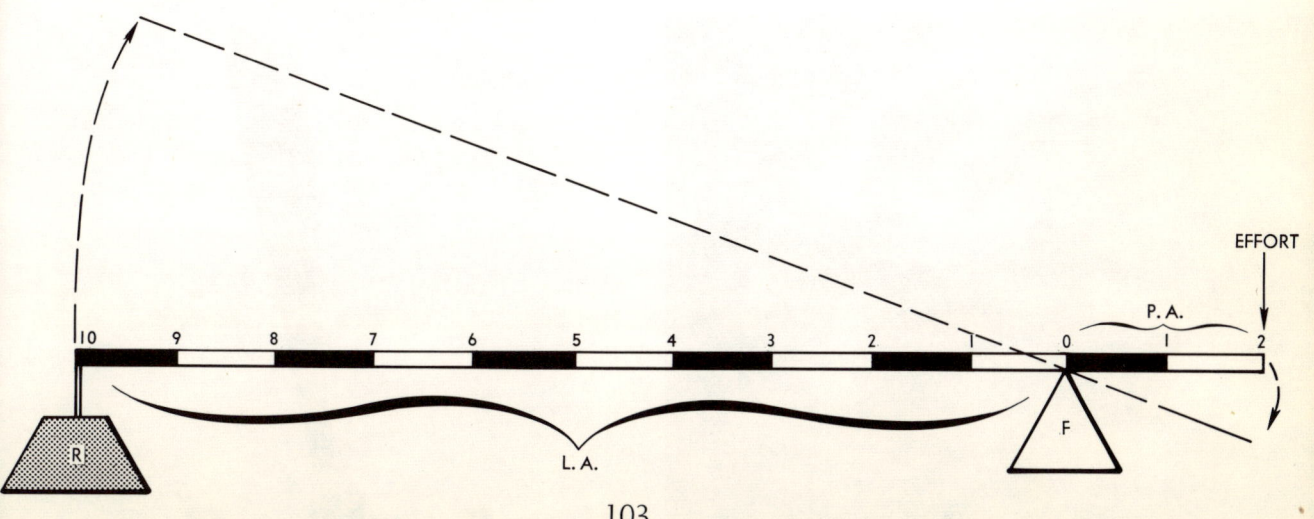

Class I levers. When the fulcrum is located between the effort and the resistance, the lever is a first-class lever. If the power arm is longer than the load arm, a lever of this class can be used to increase force. If the reverse is true, and the power arm is the shorter, the lever will increase the speed. The direction of the applied force is always reversed, so that the load moves up when the applied force moves down. A seesaw is a lever of the first class. Other examples are scissors, balances, and crowbars.

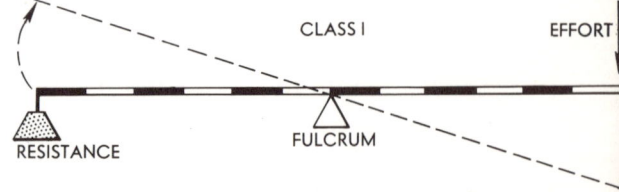

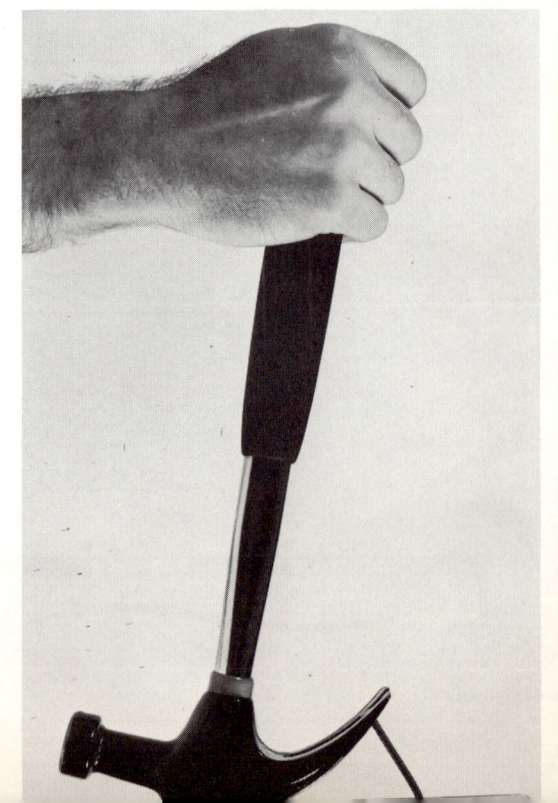

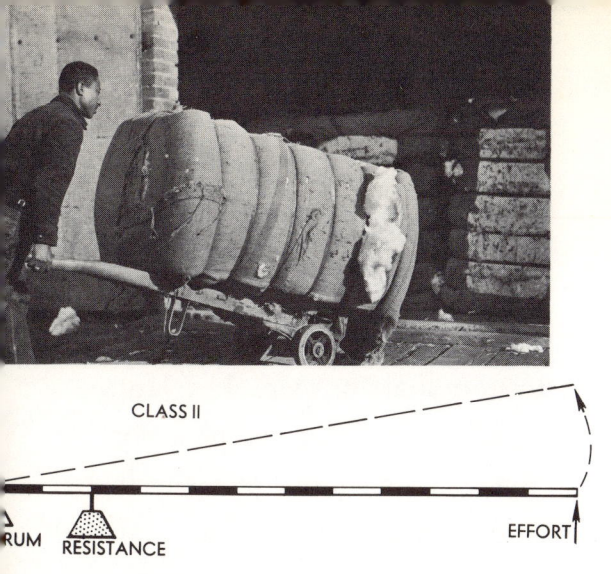

Class II levers. When the resistance is situated between the fulcrum and the effort, the lever is a second-class lever. Because the effort is always located farther from the fulcrum than is the resistance, a lever of the second class always multiplies force at the expense of speed. The nearer the resistance is to the fulcrum, the greater this gain will be. The effort and the resistance move in the same direction, so a class II lever does not alter the direction of the applied force. Wheelbarrows and two-wheeled carts are second-class levers. Nutcrackers, bottle openers, rowboat oars, and doors also are levers of this class.

Class III levers. When the effort is between the fulcrum and the resistance, the lever is a third-class lever. There is always a gain in speed and a consequent loss of force with a third-class lever, because the effort is nearer to the fulcrum than is the resistance. Baseball bats, golf clubs, shovels, the human jaw and forearm, canoe paddles, mouse traps, and some types of grass shears are all third-class levers.

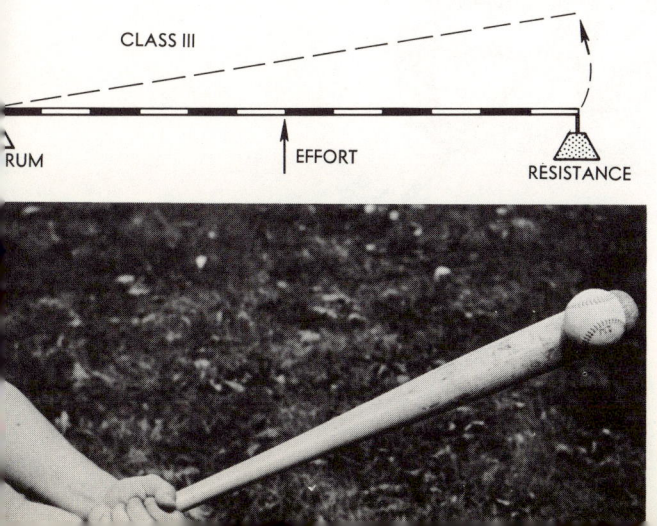

THE WHEEL AND AXLE

THE DEVICE we call the wheel and axle consists of a large wheel with a smaller wheel attached at its center so that they rotate together. Most often, the smaller wheel is elongated to form a shaft or *axle*. The large wheel itself may be modified by removing all of its body except a portion along one radius. In this case, we call the device a *crank*. On a bicycle, the pedals are attached to the ends of two cranks which are fixed to a modified axle — a toothed wheel which moves the chain to drive the bicycle.

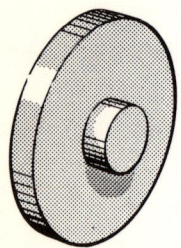  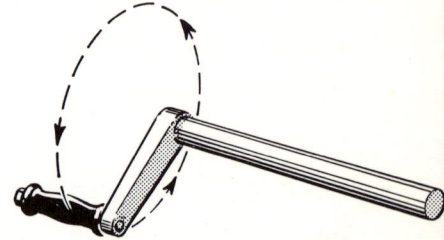

VARIATIONS OF THE WHEEL AND AXLE

In use, a rope or cable is often attached to and wound around the rim of the wheel. Another rope is fixed to, and wound in the opposite direction around the axle. Because the wheel and axle are securely fastened together, each time the wheel is turned the axle also turns. Thus, when a force is applied to the wheel's rope the load which is secured to the axle's rope is raised.

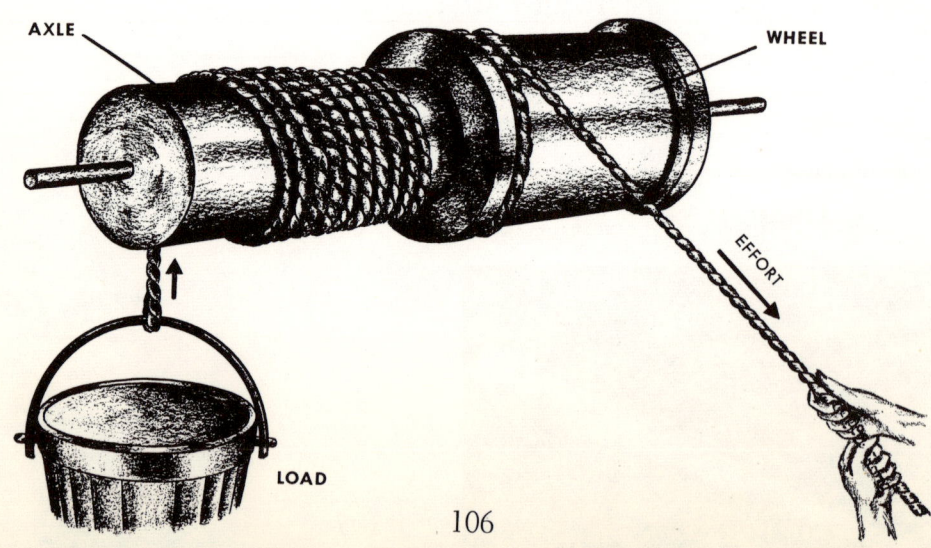

If we picture the radius of the wheel and that of the axle as being continuous, we notice that the principle of the wheel and axle is the same as the principle of the class I lever. The radius of the wheel is one arm of the lever and the radius of the axle is the other arm of the lever. The common center of the wheel and axle then is the fulcrum. The mechanical advantage of a wheel and axle, therefore, depends on the length of the radius of the wheel, the length of the radius of the axle, and the point to which the effort is applied.

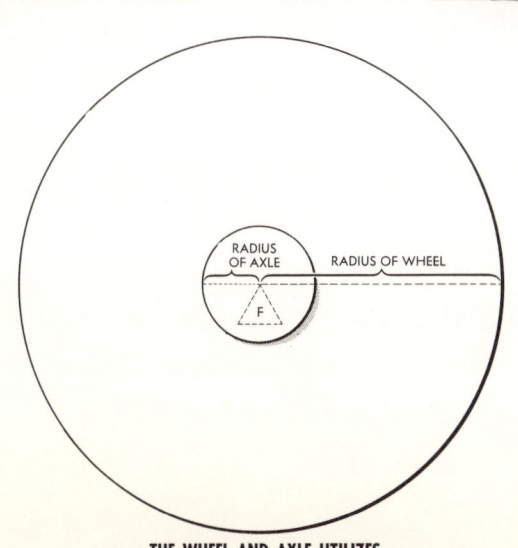

THE WHEEL AND AXLE UTILIZES
THE PRINCIPLE OF A CLASS ONE LEVER

107

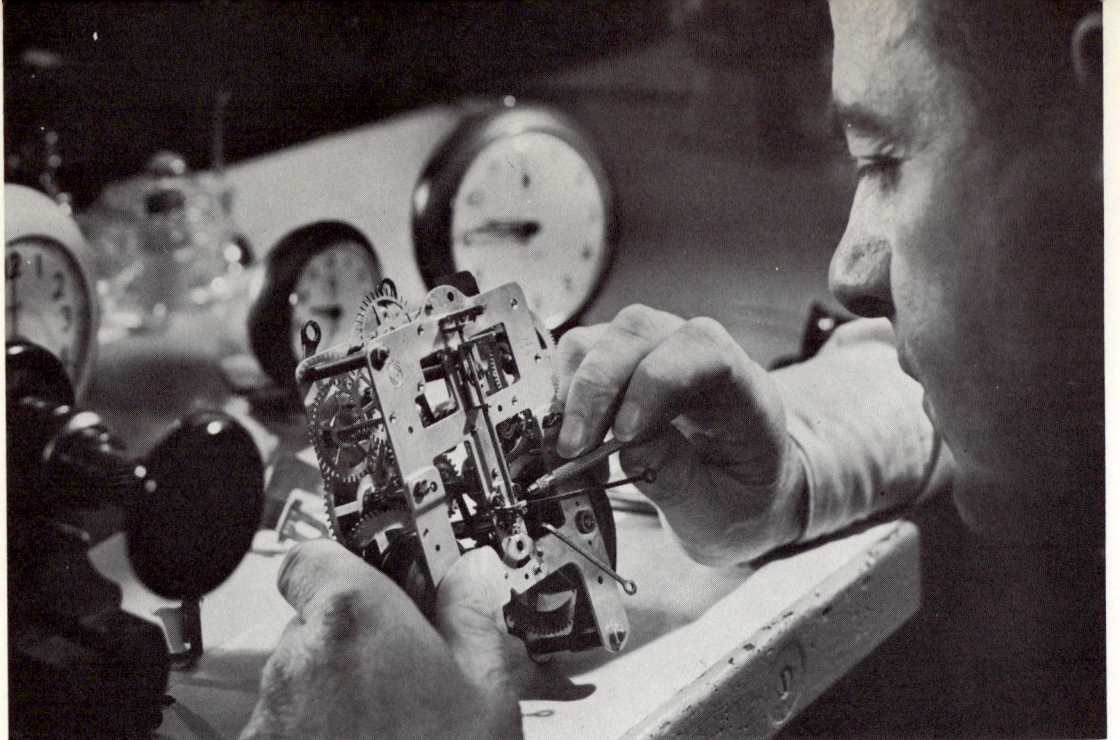

The wheel and axle can be used for a number of purposes: to change the size of a force, to change its speed, to change the direction of its motion, or to transmit a force from one place to another or from one object to another.

A few common wheel and axle devices are: doorknobs, egg beaters, clothes wringers, screw drivers, clockworks, hand drills, and telephone dials. In some of these, the wheel (perhaps the axle, too) is toothed to form a gear. Gears which fit together or mesh have teeth of the same size. The relative speed of meshing gears and their mechanical advantage, therefore, depends upon the ratio between the number of teeth on the gears. For example, a gear with five teeth will revolve twice as rapidly as one with ten teeth that is meshed with it and the system will double the effort applied to the smaller gear.

When the effort is applied to the wheel, the power arm is longer than the load arm. The mechanical advantage of the machine, therefore, is greater than 1 and the machine multiplies force at the sacrifice of speed. On the other hand, if the effort is applied to the axle (as it is in an automobile), the shorter arm of the imaginary lever is the power arm. The mechanical advantage of the machine, then, is less than 1 and it is used to increase speed at the expense of force.

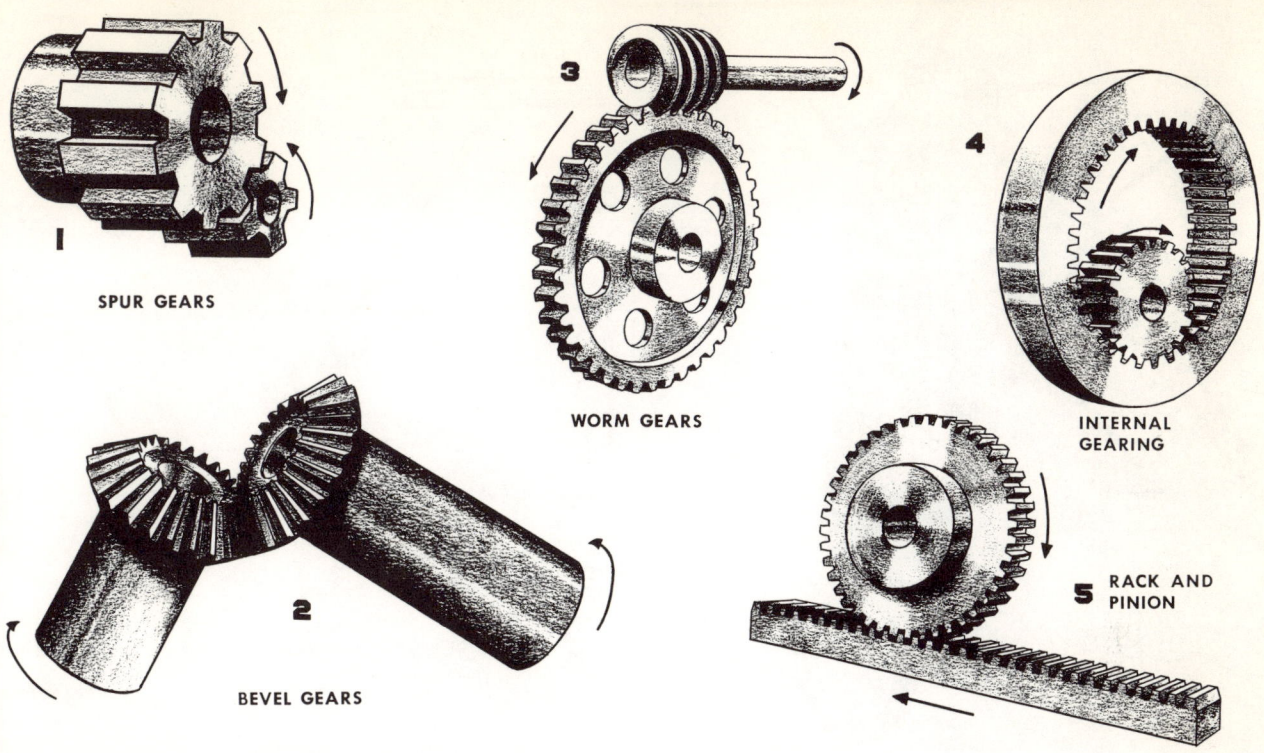

1 SPUR GEARS
2 BEVEL GEARS
3 WORM GEARS
4 INTERNAL GEARING
5 RACK AND PINION

There are several basic types of gears. The most common kind is the *spur gear*. The surfaces of its teeth are parallel to the axle. The teeth of a *bevel gear* are at an angle to the axle. Bevel gears are used to change the axis of the force.

A *worm gear* consists of a short, revolving screw (the worm) whose threads mesh with the teeth of a spur gear (worm wheel). Such gearing is used to transmit a force where two axles cross at right angles, but in different planes. By use of the screw (see page 116), the mechanical advantage of the gear is made very large. Such a gear is used in the steering system of an automobile.

Internal gearing allows the power gear and the load gear to rotate in the same direction. The smaller gear is a normal spur gear and the larger one is a hollow rim that is toothed on its inner side.

If the hollow gear of an internal gear were split and flattened, the device would be a *rack and pinion*. This combination converts the rotary motion of a spur gear, or pinion, to a flat or plane motion in a movable toothed bar, the rack. A printer's proof press uses a rack and pinion. In this case, the pinion moves and the rack is stationary.

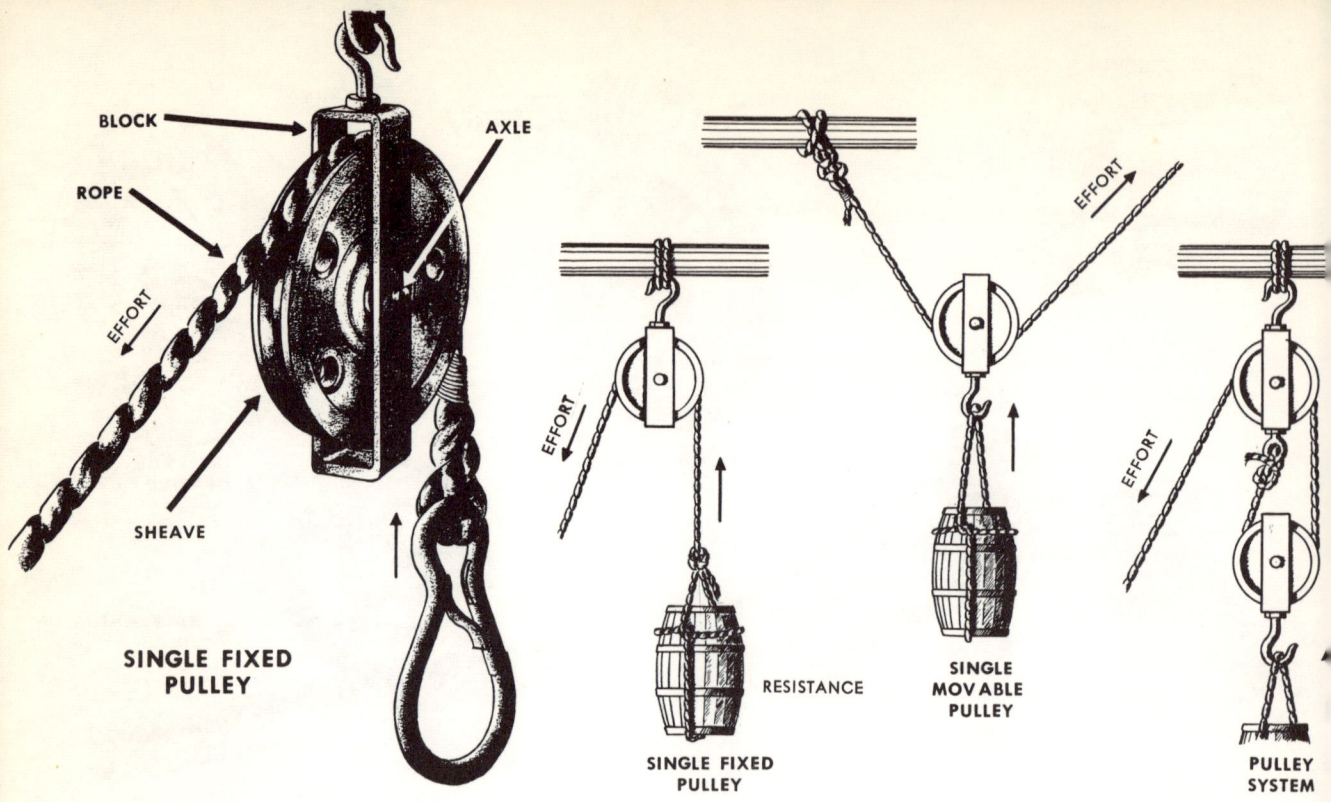

A WHEEL, an axle, and a frame are the components of a simple machine known as the *pulley*. The wheel and axle of the pulley are not rigidly joined together as in the wheel and axle machine. Instead, the wheel is free to spin on the axle. The axle and the wheel are mounted in a rigid frame called a block. A rope or flexible chain is fitted into the grooved rim of the wheel, or sheave, to prepare the pulley for use.

If the pulley is hung from a stationary object, it is said to be fixed. An effort applied to one end of the rope in a single, fixed pulley will balance a resistance of equal size hung on the other end of the rope, and both the effort and resistance will move the same distance. The mechanical advantage of such a machine, therefore, is 1. It can multiply neither force nor speed, so it is only a convenience which allows a downward pull to move a resistance upward.

If the load is hung directly on the pulley and one end of the rope is attached to a fixed object, the pulley is *movable*. A force applied to the free end of the rope will balance a load twice as large, but the resistance will move through only half the distance covered by the free end of the rope. The mechanical advantage of a single movable pulley is, therefore, 2.

THE PULLEY

The mechanical advantage of a pulley system can be made large by combining fixed and movable pulleys. The theoretical mechanical advantage of a system with one continuous rope is equal to the number of rope segments which support the resistance. In the diagram, the mechanical advantage of the pulley system is 2, because two strands of rope support the resistance.

Two factors limit the number of pulleys which can be used in a system. First, the work done by a machine cannot exceed the work done on it. Therefore, if the mechanical advantage of a pulley system is 2, the applied force must move twice as far as the load; when it is 4, four times as far, and so on. For very large values, the applied force would have to move so far to lift the load that the use of the pulley would not be worthwhile. Second, there is a considerable loss of energy in each pulley due to friction (see page 60). A point would be reached at which more work would need to be done to offset friction in the pulleys than to lift the load.

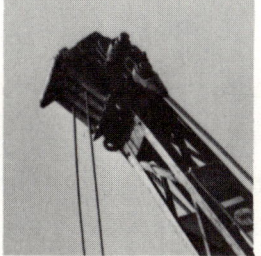

THE INCLINED PLANE, WEDGE, AND SCREW

An INCLINED PLANE is a simple machine used to raise heavy objects with less effort than is needed to lift them straight up. It is stationary and has no moving parts — it is merely a straight, sloping surface. Hillsides, stairways, mountain roads, ramps, and chutes are all inclined planes.

A horizontal plane, such as the floor of your home, supports the entire weight of an object placed upon it. A vertical plane, such as a wall, supports none of the weight of an object placed against it. Inclined planes are intermediate between these extremes. They support part of the object's weight.

To cause an object to move up an inclined plane, you must exert a force slightly greater than the unsupported weight of the object (F_r in the diagram). A gently sloping inclined plane will support a greater portion of the weight of an object than will a steeper plane. Because the slope of an inclined plane of a given height varies with the length of the plane, the mechanical advantage of the plane (if friction is ignored) is equal to the length of the plane divided by its height. The plane in the diagram is 12 feet long and 4 feet high. The mechanical advantage of this plane is 3 (M. A. = $\frac{length}{height}$ = $\frac{12}{4}$ = 3). The longer the plane is in relation to its height, the more gentle its slope will be and the greater will be its mechanical advantage. Although a smaller effort is needed to raise an object on a gentle plane, the object must be moved through a longer distance. Therefore, the total amount of work done to raise an object to a given height will be the same (if friction is ignored) regardless of whether 1) a long,

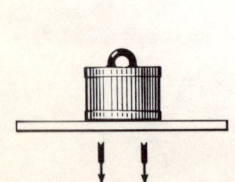
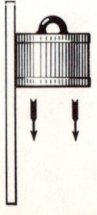
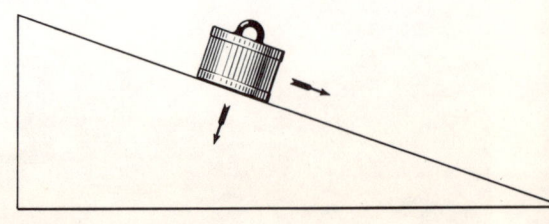

gently-inclined plane is used with a small force; 2) a short, steeply-inclined plane is used with a larger force; or 3) a force equal to the weight of the object is used to lift the object straight upward.

Every sloping street or road is an inclined plane. Highway engineers express the slope or grade of a road as the ratio of the height of the plane to the length of its base. A rise of four feet in a horizontal distance of 100 feet is equal to a 4 percent grade. Neglecting friction, a horizontal force equal in magnitude to 4 percent of the weight of an object will cause the object to move up this slope. Engineers attempt to keep the grades of roads as gentle as possible. Some highways have grades of as much as 12 percent; railroad grades rarely exceed 2 percent.

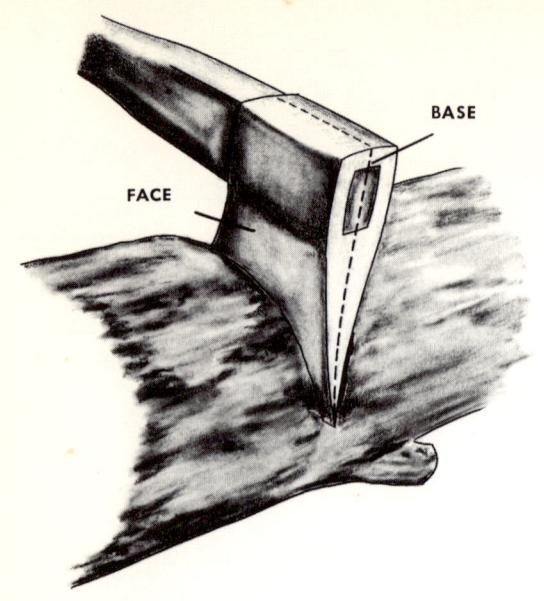

lization. The ancient inhabitants of the earth found that odd-shaped stones were useful for hunting wild animals, cutting meat, scraping animal skins, hoeing the ground, and digging. The wedge still is prominent in many cutting tools. Simple wedges, formed by a single inclined

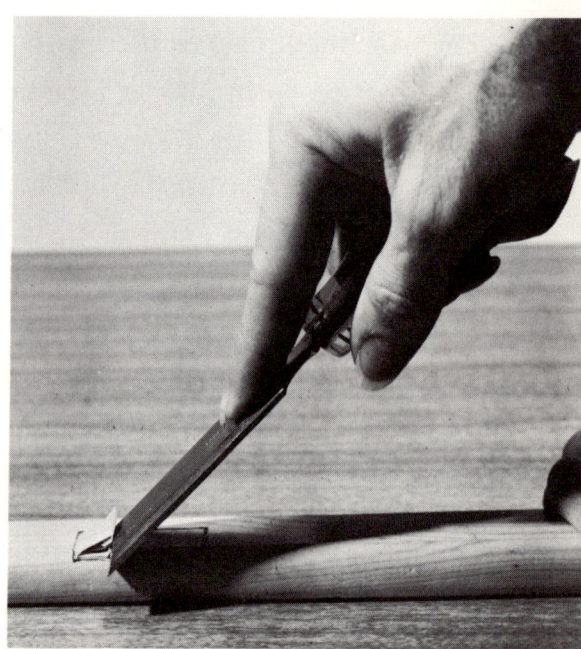

The *wedge* is a modified inclined plane. Instead of pushing a load up a wedge, we push the wedge under the load. The wedge, of course, must be made of a substance which is harder than the object on which it is used.

Man learned the value of the wedge long before the dawn of civi-

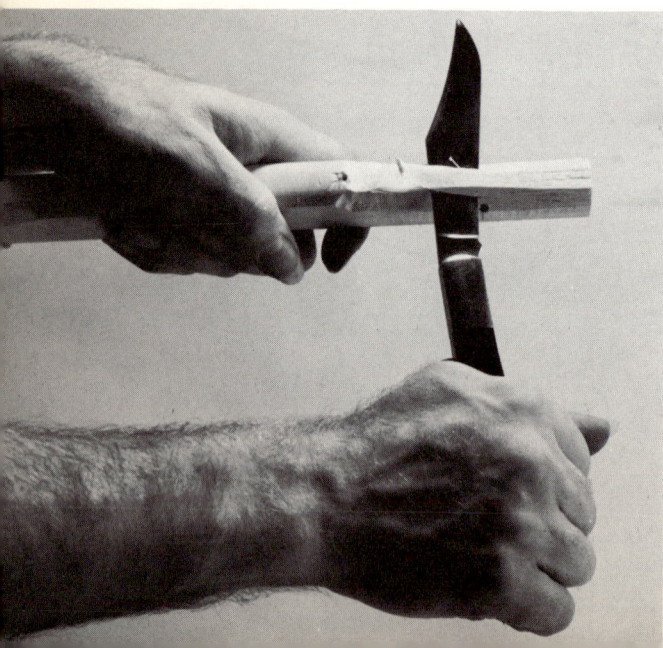

plane, are used in chisels, wood planes, picks, plows, draw blades, hoes, saw teeth, and your own front teeth. Tools which feature compound wedges, formed by two or more inclined planes joined base to base, are nails, bullets, axes, knives, pins, and arrowheads.

Because of the enormous effort necessary to overcome the friction encountered in using a wedge, there is no simple expression for its mechanical advantage. However, the principle of the inclined plane also applies to the wedge. To make the mechanical advantage of the wedge as large as possible, the angle of the blade of the wedge (the intersection of its faces) should be as small as possible. In any case, the force or effort will move through a greater distance than will the resistance. If a wedge 3 inches wide and 15 inches long is used to split a log, the wedge must move 15 inches to spread the wood only 3 inches. The effort, therefore, travels 5 times as far as the resistance is moved. The wedge multiplies force at the expense of speed.

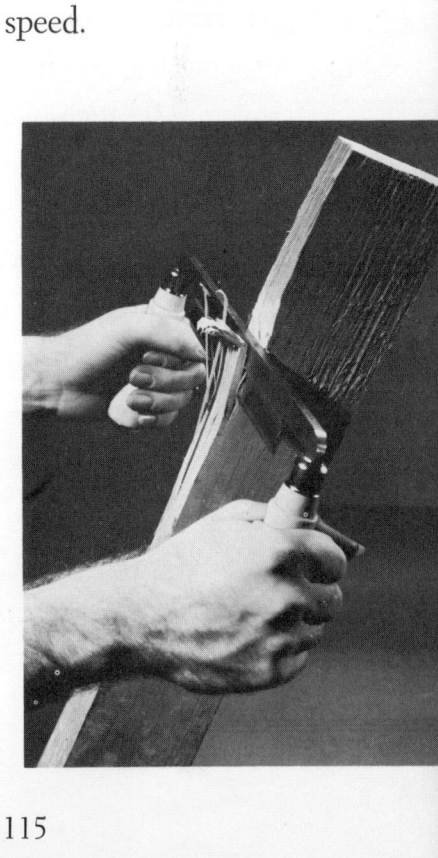

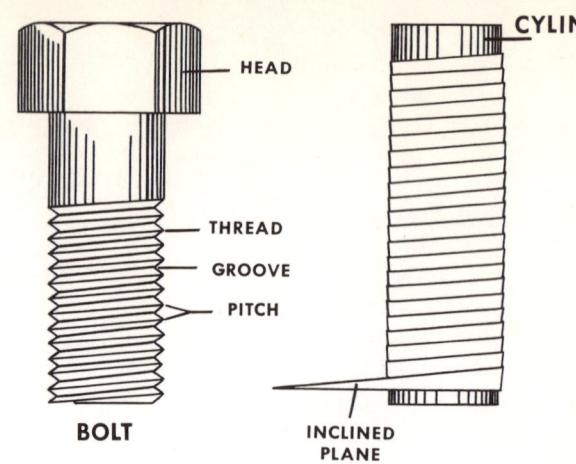

The *screw* also is a modified inclined plane. In the screw the plane is coiled tightly around a rigid cylinder or rod, so that it forms a spiral or helical ridge, called the *thread*. The successive turns of the thread are separated by a spiral *groove* whose width is uniform throughout the length of the screw. The width of this groove, measured parallel to the long axis of the screw and between the crests of two successive turns of the thread, is called the *pitch* of the screw.

Enormous multiplication of force is possible with the screw, particularly when a wheel and axle, screw driver, or crank is used to turn the screw. The theoretical mechanical advantage of such a combination is equal to the distance through which the effort travels in one rotation, divided by the pitch of the screw. If a 7-inch long crank were used to turn a screw, the effort would travel in a circle of 44 inches circumference. The theoretical mechanical advantage of the machine, if the pitch of the screw were 0.04 inch, would be 1,100. Friction usually reduces the actual mechanical advantage to a small fraction of this.

The principle of the screw is used in the brace and bit and in many other common devices, including vises, faucets, swivel chairs, food grinders, jar lids, some types of automobile jacks, bench clamps, and, of course, in wood screws and nuts and bolts.

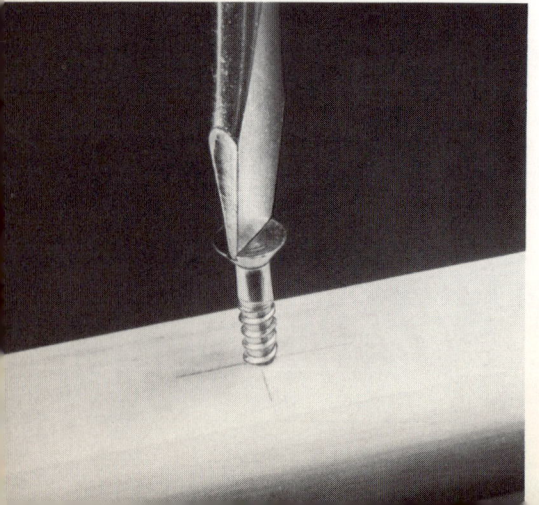

CHAPTER V

A WORLD OF LIFE

Our bodies are composed of billions of atoms arranged in systems which function in accordance with the laws of chemistry and physics.

ALTHOUGH WE ALL EXPERIENCE it from the moment we are born, our understanding of the process called "life" is incomplete. Perhaps the most accurate definition we can give now is that life is a typical condition of living things. A "living thing" is an object which can absorb substances from its surroundings and use them to make more of its own matter. For example, you are a living thing. From food and drink, your body makes new bone, flesh, muscle, and blood so that it grows and repairs itself.

The bodies of all living things — plants, animals, people — are made chiefly of four elements: carbon, nitrogen, oxygen, and hydrogen. An amoeba, one of the simplest animals, is made of 5 billion or more atoms of these elements combined into many kinds of complex molecules. Each microscopic cell of your body is nearly as complex as an amoeba and is composed of about as many atoms. Yet there are more cells in your body than there are atoms in any single cell. Thus, you are a Gulliver in the Lilliput-land of the atom.

The scientists who study the chemistry and physics of life are known as *biochemists* and *biophysicists* (*bio-* is a Greek prefix meaning "life"). Their work has taught us a great deal about the structure and operation of living things, but even though we know almost exactly how many atoms combine to make some of the simplest forms of life, we do not know what gives a collection of molecules the unique quality we call "life."

In this chapter, we will discuss some of the substances of which living things are composed, the chemical environment or surroundings of life, and certain chemicals which make life possible on earth. This is but a sample of our vast knowledge of the chemistry and physics of life. But more significant than what we know is what we *do not know* about living things.

AIR AND AIR PRESSURE

We live at the bottom of a deep sea of gases which we call the *atmosphere*. The atmosphere is not formed by a compound, nor by an element. It is a mixture of gases we call *air* and is composed principally of nitrogen and oxygen. About 99% of the volume of dry air at sea level is formed by these two elements: 78.03% nitrogen, 20.99% oxygen. Carbon dioxide, a gaseous compound released as a waste product by all plants and animals and used by green plants to manufacture food, composes about 0.04% of the air. Hydrogen, the lightest element, forms about 0.01% of the volume of the atmosphere and rare gases make up most of the remainder: argon, 0.93% and neon, helium, krypton, xenon, and radon combined, 0.0015%.

Two other components of the atmosphere — water vapor and dust — are present in amounts which vary widely from place to place. Over every square mile of the eastern United States, there may be 100,000 tons of water vapor present in the air. Air over tropical regions may contain three or four times this much water vapor, but air over a desert region may contain only a fraction as much. The billions of tons of water in the atmosphere is but one phase in the cycle through which water travels on the earth. (See pages 136, 137.)

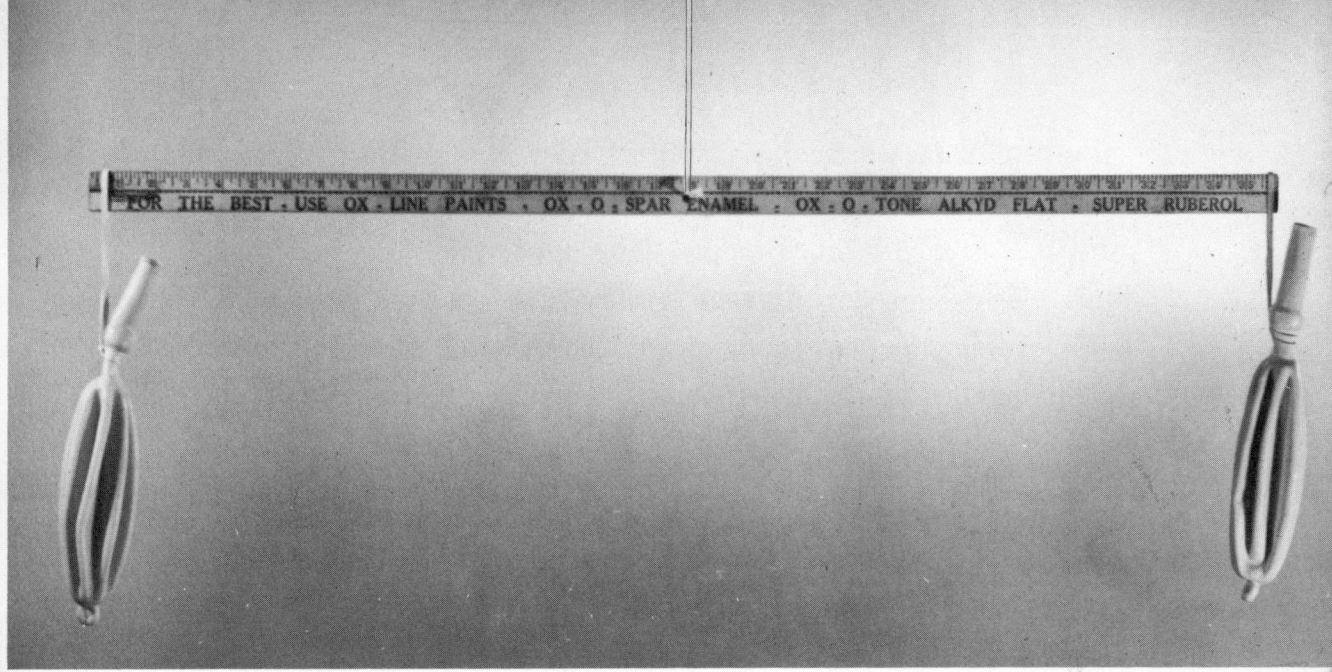

Air is matter and, like all matter, air has mass. Near the earth, all mass has weight because of its attraction by gravity. Therefore, we know that air must have weight, although we normally are not aware of it. The simple experiment pictured here demonstrates that air has weight. In this experiment, a yardstick is used as a balance. An empty balloon is hung on each end of the yardstick, which is suspended from the ceiling by a string. After the empty balloons are balanced, one is filled with air. Which balloon now weighs the most? What gave it this extra weight? (Do not forget that the air in a balloon is compressed and thus has a greater density than air outside the balloon.)

By careful measurements, scientists know that at sea level the column of air that rests on a square foot of the earth's surface and extends upward at least 1,900 miles weighs about 2,117 pounds — more than a ton. Thus, every plant, animal, rock, building, or other surface on the earth at sea level is under a pressure of 14.7 pounds per square inch due to the weight of air pressing down on it. A simple experiment will show the great pressure to which each of us is exposed. If you boil water in a gallon can, the air in the can will be forced out by water vapor. Now, place a lid on the can and allow it to cool. As the water vapor cools, it condenses and returns to the liquid phase. The volume of water in gas form is 1,650 times as large as its volume in liquid form. Thus, as the vapor condenses to a liquid, the pressure inside the can is reduced and a partial vacuum is formed. The force pushing outward on the sides of the can may be only 1 or 2 pounds per square inch, but the air pressure pushing in on the sides is 14.7 pounds per square inch. What happens to the can? Our bodies are adapted to normal air pressure. Our bodies press outward against our skin with the same pressure that air presses inward against it. What do you think might happen to an astronaut without special equipment if he stepped from a space ship into the vacuum between the stars (where there is no air pressure)?

The tremendous force exerted on a body by air pressure was dramatically demonstrated by Otto von Guericke, a German, in 1654. He fashioned a metal ball of two tightly-fitting halves. By pumping the air from within this ball, he formed a partial vacuum in the ball. The more dense air outside the ball then pressed the two halves of the ball together. Von Guericke hitched eight horses to each half of the ball and tried to pull them apart. The horses could not separate them!

Air pressure decreases with altitude above sea level. Because of the tremendous weight pressing down on it, the air near the ground is highly compressed and most dense. As we rise higher above sea level, the air column above us is shorter and is formed by less dense air. At the summit of Mt. Everest in the Himalaya Mountains (29,141 feet above sea level), the air pressure is only about 5 pounds per square inch. Because it is less dense, a given volume of air at high altitudes contains fewer molecules of oxygen and other gases. Our bodies require a large amount of oxygen. As we climb a mountain or fly upward in an airplane, we find it more difficult to breathe and we tire more easily because of oxygen shortages. How has this difficulty been overcome in airplanes? How do astronauts obtain oxygen during space flights?

The atmosphere is also important to life on earth because it forms a protective covering for the earth which filters the sun's rays and prevents the living things on the earth's surface from being burned to a crisp in only a few minutes. At night, the blanket of air prevents too rapid escape of heat from the earth into space and keeps us from being frozen at temperatures far below zero.

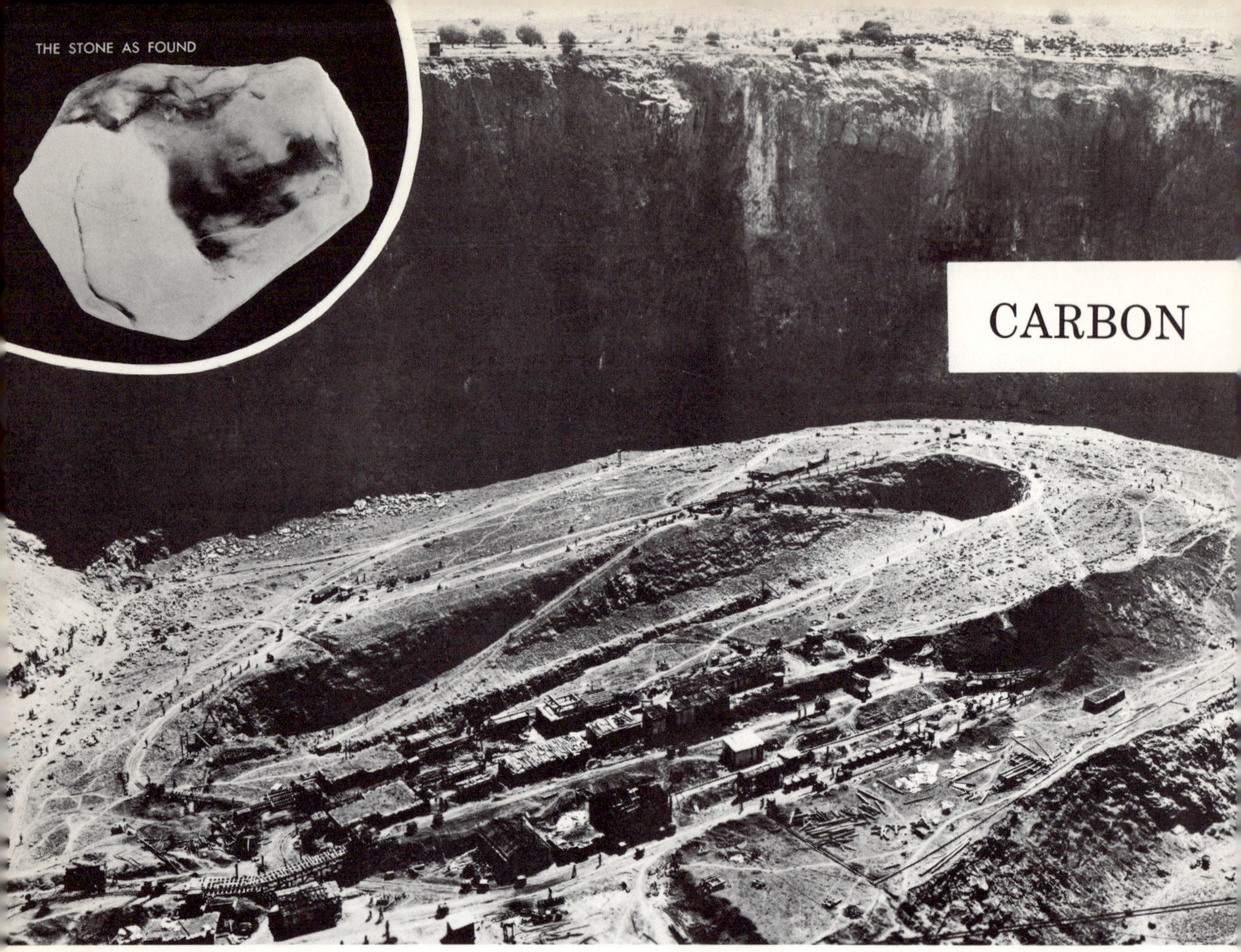

CARBON

Diamond mine in South Africa

Cut Diamonds

CARBON is the most amazing element. Although it forms but 0.03 percent of the crust of the earth, carbon is a constituent of more than 300,000 different substances—ten times the number of all other compounds.

Carbon is able to form such a tremendous variety of compounds because its atoms combine readily with many other kinds of atoms. Each carbon atom has four valence bonds with which it can combine with other atoms. These may be the atoms of other elements. But carbon atoms have the unusual ability to link with other carbon atoms to form rings and long chains.

Pure carbon appears in two crystalline forms and an amorphous, or structureless, condition. One of carbon's crystalline forms is uniform in structure in all directions. In this form, carbon is colorless, transparent, insoluble in all common solvents, a non-conductor of electricity, and it is the hardest of all natural substances. We call it a diamond.

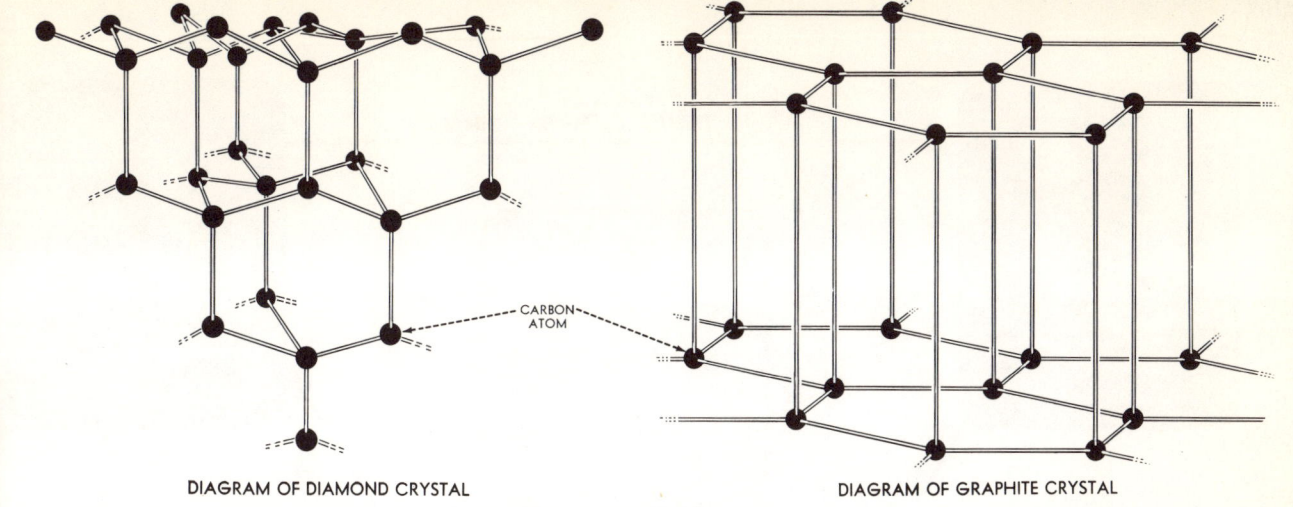

DIAGRAM OF DIAMOND CRYSTAL

DIAGRAM OF GRAPHITE CRYSTAL

Its other crystalline form is known as graphite. In this form, carbon is black, opaque, very soft, greasy to the touch, a conductor of electricity, and is insoluble in the common solvents. The "lead" in your pencil is a mixture of graphite and clay.

Charcoal, peat, coke, lamp black, and the various grades of coal are more or less pure forms of amorphous carbon. These substances differ from the crystalline forms of carbon in that their atoms do not appear to have an organized arrangement.

Carbon is our most useful element because of the many forms in which it occurs. In combination with hydrogen as coal, coke, charcoal, and petroleum, it is the most important source of energy to power our machines and to heat our buildings. Even more important, carbon forms a considerable portion of all plants and animals. In fact, about 18 percent of you is carbon. Because carbon compounds were once believed to be produced only by living organisms, they are called organic compounds. The chemistry of carbon compounds still is known as organic chemistry.

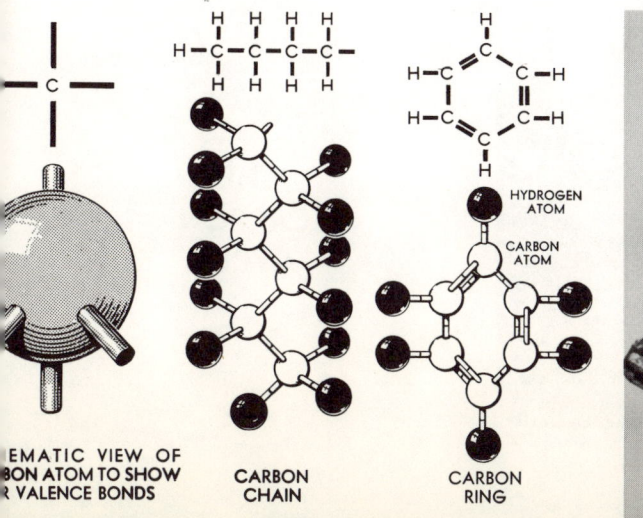

SCHEMATIC VIEW OF CARBON ATOM TO SHOW FOUR VALENCE BONDS

CARBON CHAIN

CARBON RING

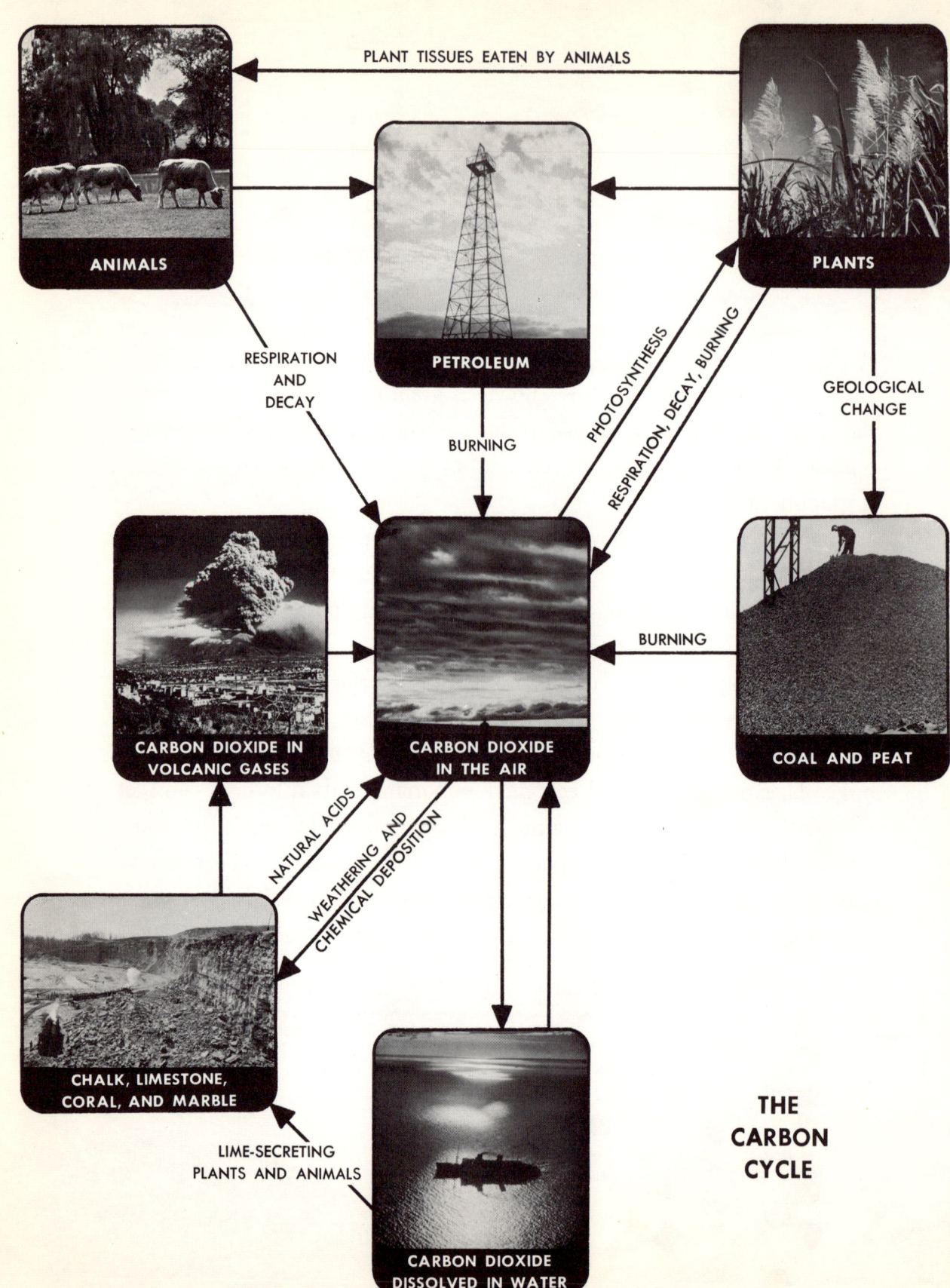

THE CARBON CYCLE

CARBON is the most basic constituent of living matter and of many other natural substances. But the supply of carbon is very limited. In nature, therefore, carbon atoms must be circulated in a manner similar to the way in which we circulate money. Just as a single dollar bill may be used by many people, a single carbon atom may be a part of a lump of coal at one time, part of a molecule of carbon dioxide gas at another time, and at still another time, a part of your own body. This circulation of carbon atoms is called the carbon cycle.

Carbon dioxide is a colorless, odorless gas that comprises about one-thirtieth of the volume of the air. Just as a bank is the main agency for the circulation of money, carbon dioxide in the atmosphere is the main agency for the circulation of carbon.

Green plants continually withdraw carbon dioxide from the atmospheric bank. By combining it with hydrogen, plants manufacture simple sugars. If these sugars are used to supply energy to the plant, carbon dioxide is a by-product of this energy-producing reaction. Or the sugars may be converted into new plant tissue. Thus the carbon is stored in the tissues of a plant and is returned to the atmosphere when the plant burns or decays.

Of course, the plant may be eaten by an animal. In this case, the tissue may be oxidized (see page 129) to supply energy to the animal. The animal exhales carbon dioxide as a by-product. Animals (including people) depend upon plants to supply all the carbon needed to build their bodies. Carbon in animal tissue is circulated when one animal is eaten by another, or when an animal dies and its tissues decay. Decay is another form of oxidation which releases carbon dioxide.

The complete carbon cycle is even more complicated. It includes carbon in the form of limestone and coral, peat and coal, volcanic gases, and petroleum. Regardless of the form in which an atom of carbon may be found, it will eventually be returned to the atmospheric bank. Once returned to the bank, it is ready to begin its circulation once again.

OXYGEN

THE MOST ABUNDANT THING in the world comprises 50 percent of the weight of the earth's hard crust, 25 percent of the atmosphere, 80 percent of the oceans, and 65 percent of you. We call it oxygen.

At normal temperatures, pure oxygen is a tasteless, odorless, colorless gas. But when it is cooled below its boiling point, $-182.5°$ C ($-360.5°$ F), oxygen is a pale blue, strongly magnetic liquid. It turns to a brittle solid at $-227.0°$ C ($-440.6°$ F).

Oxygen is so active chemically that it combines with every other stable element except the inert rare gases. Pure oxygen, therefore, occurs principally in the atmosphere. Oxygen is withdrawn continuously from the atmosphere by many chemical reactions, but it is replenished during the daylight hours by the activities of green plants. The remaining natural supply of oxygen, with the exception of the small amount dissolved in fresh waters and the oceans, is chemically united with other elements in the form of various compounds.

Nearly all living things require a continuous supply of free oxygen for respiration, the process which enables you to derive energy from your food. To allow your body to carry on its life functions, you breathe in enough air each day to fill 13,000 milk bottles. About 500 quarts of oxygen are subtracted from this air as it passes through your lungs, used in oxidation processes, and later released through your lungs as carbon dioxide. When men go where oxygen is scarce (such as deep below the earth in mines, or high above it in airplanes and space capsules) they must carry a supply of the gas with them.

A chemical reaction in which oxygen combines with another substance is termed an *oxidation reaction*. Rapid oxidation reactions release noticeable heat and light. They are usually described as *combustion*, or *burning*. This roaring fire in the pine forests of southern New Jersey is an example of rapid oxidation. When trees burn, oxygen combines with compounds of carbon, hydrogen, and oxygen present in the leaves and wood. The products of this reaction are primarily carbon dioxide and water.

Slow oxidation reactions are less spectacular than rapid ones. They produce no light, but release an amount of heat equal to that of rapid reactions. The heat is released over such a long period of time that it is often not noticeable. The rusting of iron, drying of oil paints, and decay of plant and animal remains are slow oxidation reactions.

Reduction is the reverse of oxidation. In a reduction reaction, oxygen is removed from, rather than added to a substance. Reduction is brought about by mixing a substance with a chemical which has a stronger attraction for oxygen, known as a *reducing agent*. During the reaction, oxygen is transferred from the substance to this reducing agent. Therefore, every reduction reaction is accompanied by an oxidation reaction. Reduction reactions are especially important in refining ores to obtain pure metals (see page 188).

The term oxidation is now applied to any chemical reaction in which a substance loses electrons and thereby increases its valence (see page 18). The term reduction is applied to a reaction in which a substance gains electrons and decreases its valence.

HYDROGEN

Its atom is the simplest possible—one electron whirling around a single proton. By virtue of this simple construction, hydrogen has the smallest mass of all substances; consequently, it is the lightest thing in the world. It weighs only one-fourteenth as much as the air you breathe.

Because it is so light, hydrogen has long been used in balloons and other lighter-than-air craft. It was once thought that giant dirigibles—as long as 10 football fields, and weighing more than 20 elephants—would serve as luxury liners of the air. But, hydrogen and oxygen form a highly explosive mixture. On May 6, 1937 the giant German dirigible, *Hindenburg,* burst into flames and crashed at Lakehurst, New Jersey. This accident, pictured here, marked the end of an era.

Hydrogen is still used for weather balloons. Helium, a heavier but non-inflammable rare gas, has supplanted hydrogen in large, lighter-than-air passenger craft. But the short supply of helium and the development of larger and speedier airplanes have made helium-filled aircraft a rarity.

Astronomers believe that free hydrogen comprises a significant portion of the sun and other stars, and it probably exists throughout space between celestial bodies. In fact, hydrogen seems to be the most abundant thing in the universe, and about 90% of all the atoms are thought to be hydrogen atoms.

In the atmosphere at sea level, hydrogen occurs in a free, gaseous state in infinitely small amounts. In a combined form it is found in all plant and animal tissue, and in petroleum and natural gas. It makes up 11 percent of water by weight, and is a vital component of all acids and bases (page 132).

Hydrogen is relatively inactive at ordinary temperatures. A mixture of hydrogen and oxygen, however, combines with a violent explosion when ignited, producing ordinary water (H_2O). Because it combines so readily with oxygen, hydrogen is used as a reducing agent in many industrial refining processes.

After release, this hydrogen-filled weather balloon will be used to calculate the direction and velocity of the air up to 30,000 feet.

ACIDS AND BASES

AN ACID is formed if the molecules of a hydrogen compound break up into negatively and positively-charged particles (ions) when the compound is dissolved in water. Acids share several characteristics: 1) they contain hydrogen ions; 2) they taste sour (the sour taste of a ripe lemon is due to its citric acid); 3) they conduct electricity; 4) they turn blue litmus paper red; 5) when magnesium, aluminum, manganese, zinc, chromium, iron, nickel, tin, or lead is placed in an acid solution, the metal replaces the hydrogen in the acid and bubbles of hydrogen gas are released. We often say in regard to this last reaction that acids corrode metals.

Most people believe that an acid is a liquid that will make holes in their clothing, cause agonizing pain if accidentally dropped on their skin, and cause almost instantaneous death if swallowed. Sulfuric acid (H_2SO_4), hydrochloric acid (HCl), and nitric acid (HNO_3), the acids most often used in the chemical laboratory and in industry, live up to these dire standards. But boric acid (H_2BO_3) is used as a soothing eye wash. Vinegar, a weak solution of acetic acid (CH_3COOH), is used in cooking. Carbonic acid (H_2CO_3) produces the soda water from which soft drinks are made. Ascorbic acid ($C_6H_8O_{16}$), better known as Vitamin C, is an important part of our daily diet.

Bases or *hydroxides* are another important class of chemicals. They are formed by compounds whose molecules break up into negatively-charged hydroxyl ions, composed of oxygen and hydrogen (OH$^-$), and some positive ion. Bases have several characteristics in common: 1) They have a bitter taste; 2) they feel slippery or soapy; 3) like acids, they conduct electricity; 4) they have a *caustic action,* that is they will dissolve skin, wool, and hair; 5) they turn red litmus paper blue. Two bases which are used frequently around the home are ammonia, which is the same as the ammonium hydroxide (NH$_4$OH) in the laboratory bottle pictured here, and lye, which is used to clean the drains of sinks.

When an acid and a base are mixed, they neutralize one another by a double replacement reaction (see page 26). One product of this reaction is a compound formed by the negative ion of the acid and the positive ion of the base. It is known as a *salt.* The second product is always water (H$_2$O), formed by the combination of the positive hydrogen ion of the acid (H$^+$) and the negative hydroxyl ion (OH$^-$) of the base. The solution which results from the reaction may look similar to the original base and acid, but it will not change the color of litmus paper. One of the most common reactions of this type occurs when a farmer or homeowner puts lime on an acid soil. The lime combines with water in the soil to form a base which then reacts with the soil acids.

WATER

Water is the most common chemical compound and the most abundant liquid on earth. Lakes, ponds, rivers, and oceans of water occupy about three-fourths of the surface of our planet; masses of ice and extensive snow fields cover large portions of the polar and high mountain regions; vast quantities of water are found in the air and soil; and a large part of the body of every plant and animal is formed by water.

Under ordinary circumstances, water is a clear, colorless liquid. In deep layers, as in oceans and lakes, water may appear to be bluish-green. When cooled to 0° C (32° F), water changes into a colorless solid called *ice*. When heated to 100° C (212° F) at sea level air pressure, it boils and changes into a vapor. Water vapor, or steam, is invisible. What we commonly call "steam" — the white clouds which rise from a boiling coffee pot or tea kettle — really is composed of tiny droplets of liquid water suspended in invisible water vapor.

A very unusual property of water is that it reaches its greatest density when it is near, but still above its freezing point. The specific gravity of water at 4° C (39° F) is 1.0, whereas at its freezing point (0° C) it has a specific gravity of only 0.9 in its solid form as ice. This reduction of specific gravity is due to the expansion of water when it freezes. You know that a bottle of water or a water pipe will burst when it freezes. This is because a quantity of water will occupy 1.1 times as much space in the form of ice as it will in the form of a liquid.

In nature, the expansion of water as it freezes is of great importance. For example, as the moisture in a rock freezes and expands, it may cause small grains or even large pieces to break off. Over thousands of years, repeated freezing and thawing wears down rock surfaces and plays an important part in forming soil. An even more important aspect of this unusual behavior of water is its relation to the plants and animals which live in streams, ponds, and lakes. In the winter, as the water cools, it becomes most dense at 4° C and sinks to the bottom. Warmer, less dense water rises and replaces it until it, too, is cooled. Finally, when the water is the same temperature throughout, the water layer at the top is cooled further and changes into ice. Even though it is a solid, the ice floats, because it is less dense than liquid water (see pages 86, 150). This is of great importance to water life, because if the ice sank to the bottom, the pond or stream would freeze solid and there would be no liquid water beneath the ice in which living things could survive the winter. The layer of ice also is an excellent insulator, especially when snow falls on it. This insulation protects the deeper water from further cooling and thus prevents it from freezing.

The earth's supply of water is in continuous circulation — through lakes, ponds, streams, oceans, through the air, the soil and underlying rocks, and living plants and animals. Some natural chemical processes decompose water molecules, and remove them from circulation (for example, photosynthesis, see page 144). Other natural processes, such as respiration and the burning of organic matter, produce new water molecules.

The circulation of water in nature is called the *water cycle*. The principal steps in the earth's water cycle are shown on pages 136-137. Because it is a cycle, or circular flow, it has no beginning or end. But we can begin with water vapor as it evaporates from the soil, from vegetation, or from a water surface. This gaseous form of water is lighter than air and therefore rises in the atmosphere. It is carried by winds across oceans and continents. As air containing moisture rises over mountains, or is forced upward by colder air, the water vapor cools and condenses into fine droplets which form a mist or cloud. These droplets may fuse and fall as rain, snow, sleet, or hail. All are forms of *precipitation*.

Part of the precipitation evaporates back into the air before it reaches the earth. Part of it wets the surfaces of vegetation and rocks and later evaporates. Another portion runs over the surface of the ground and into streams or lakes. Still another portion seeps into the soil.

Some of the water which enters the soil reappears in springs or rivers. Some flows underground to the oceans, which contain more than 85% of all the earth's water. And some evaporates directly from the soil or is absorbed by vegetation and then evaporated from the plants. Evaporation from the inner portions of plants is known as *transpiration*.

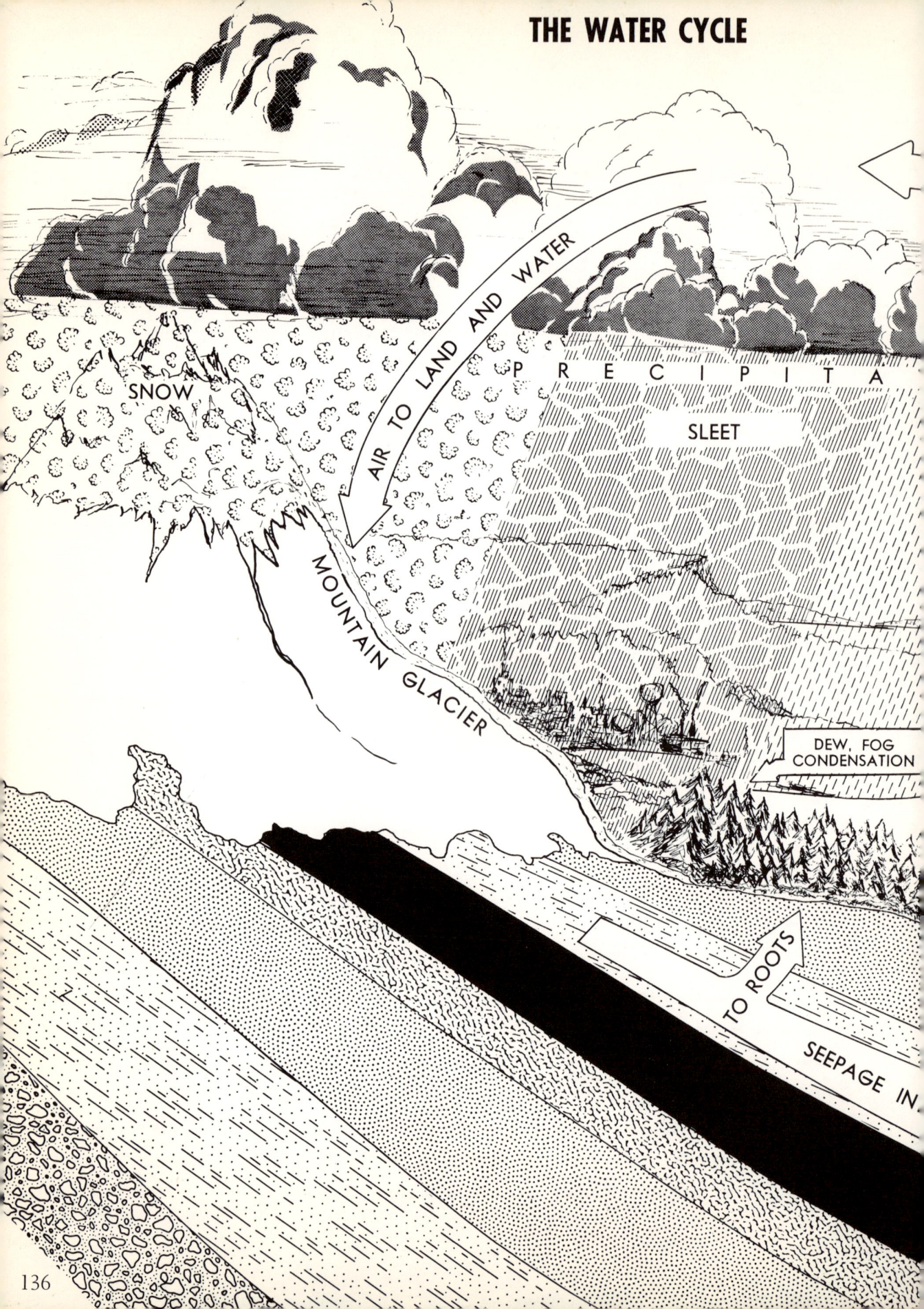

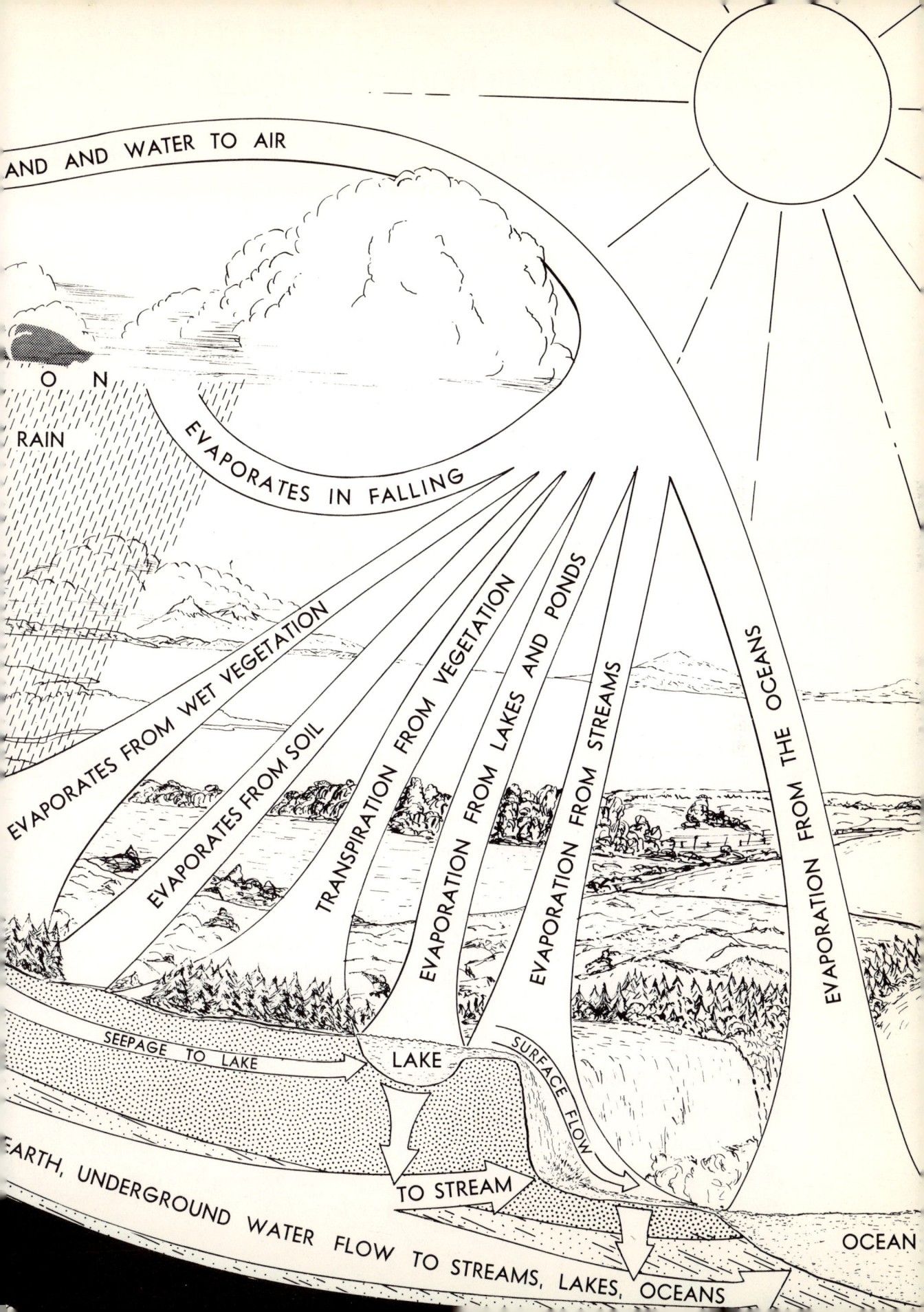

THE NITROGEN CYCLE

N COMPRISES more than three-fourths of the air. N extends high above the earth and rests upon every acre with a weight of 300 million pounds. You are completely surrounded by N; and N is present in every cell and in every drop of blood in your body.

N, of course, is the chemical symbol for the element nitrogen. Pure nitrogen is an odorless, colorless gas which neither burns nor supports combustion. It liquefies at $-196°$ C ($-321°$ F) and freezes to a white solid at $-210°$ C ($-346°$ F). Although nitrogen is relatively inert, it occurs in a pure state, under natural conditions, only in the atmosphere.

Nitrogen is essential to all living things. Its atoms join with those of carbon, hydrogen, and oxygen and at times with those of sulfur and phosphorus, to form complex protein molecules. Proteins are the basic components of protoplasm, the substance contained in all living cells. Some familiar proteins are the white of an egg, the venom of a poisonous snake, and gamma globulin, a blood derivative now widely used to protect people from polio and other diseases.

Even though every plant and animal requires a continuous supply of nitrogen, only a few simple plants (mostly bacteria) can use uncombined nitrogen. These bacteria live in the soil, or in swellings or tubercles on the roots of certain green plants. They can combine nitrogen into simple compounds, in which form the nitrogen can be absorbed by green plants. Animals obtain their nitrogen by eating plant tissues.

When an animal or plant dies, other kinds of bacteria break down the complex protein molecules in its remains, leaving the nitrogen combined with hydrogen in simple ammonia molecules. Some ammonium compounds can be used immediately by higher plants. Others are oxidized later by soil bacteria into the form of nitrates which can be used by all higher plants.

Each year, throughout the world, many millions of tons of nitrogen are removed from the atmosphere. But the atmospheric supply is not diminished, because a like amount is returned to the air by burning and decay of plant and animal remains. This entire process by which nitrogen is circulated in nature is called the *nitrogen cycle*.

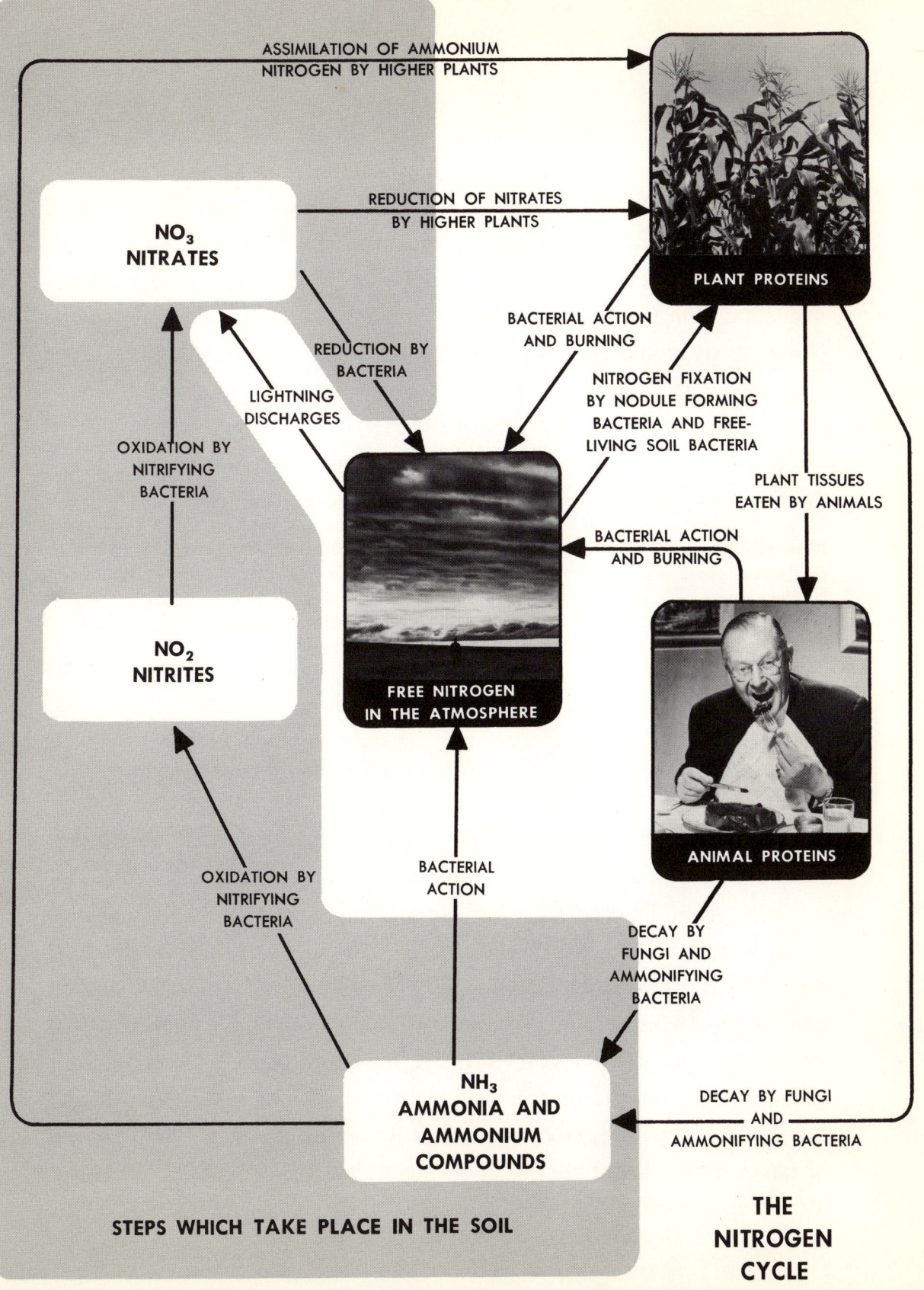

WHAT MAKES A MAN?

ENOUGH IRON to make a nail; enough potassium to make a shotgun shell; enough magnesium for a dose of magnesia; enough sugar to sweeten a gallon of lemonade; enough sulfur to give your dog a flea bath; and enough phosphorus to make 2,200 match heads — these are a few of the 20 elements found in the body of a man. Sold as raw materials, the components of your body would be worth a little more than a dollar. This table lists these elements:

COMPOSITION OF THE HUMAN BODY

Element	Percentage	Place of Occurrence in Body
Oxygen	65.00%	water, carbohydrates, proteins, fats
Carbon	18.00	carbohydrates, proteins, fats
Hydrogen	10.00	water, carbohydrates, proteins, fats, stomach acids
Nitrogen	3.00	proteins
Calcium	2.00	bones, teeth, blood
Phosphorus	1.00	bones, teeth, muscles, nerves, brain
Potassium	0.35	soft tissues, milky secretions
Sulfur	0.25	proteins
Sodium	0.15	common salt
Chlorine	0.15	common salt, stomach acids
Magnesium	0.05	bones, soft tissues, body fluids
Iron	0.004	red blood cells, muscles, liver, kidneys, spleen
Manganese	0.003	?

Fluorine, silicon, iodine, copper, cobalt, zinc, bromine, aluminum, selenium, and boron are present as traces.

Their places of occurrence largely are unknown.

An average person in a lifetime of 70 years will eat a total of about 40 tons of food, from which his body will obtain raw materials for growth and energy for its various processes and for movement.* This food will be: 33,600 pounds of vegetables, fruits, nuts, and berries; 13,300 pounds of grain in the form of bread and cereals; 11,900 pounds of meat, fish, and poultry; 9,100 pounds of potatoes; 7,700 pounds of sugar; 4,500 pounds of fats and oils; 1,400 pounds of tea, chocolate, and coffee; 25,200 eggs; 17,500 quarts of milk.

*Norman J. Berrill, "How Long Can the Earth Keep U Eating?" *MacLean's Magazine,* 68:16-20, June 11, 195

This photograph shows some of the meat that each of us probably will eat during a lifetime. The girl indicates the size of this collection.

In addition to water, salts, and vitamins (none of which furnish energy), foodstuffs are composed of several chemical classes of foods. *Carbohydrates*, which comprise about 70 percent of our diet, are our chief source of energy. In their molecules, carbon is combined with hydrogen and oxygen which are present in the same ratio as they occur in water (H_2O). *Fats* are a more concentrated, but less abundant source of energy. They comprise slightly less than 30 percent of our diet. Fats are also composed only of carbon, hydrogen, and oxygen, but hydrogen and oxygen do not occur in the same ratio as in water. *Proteins* are compounds of carbon, hydrogen, oxygen, and nitrogen, and sometimes sulfur and phosphorus. Proteins furnish the body with materials for growth and repair.

THE CHEMISTRY OF A PLANT

IN THE mid-1600's, scientists believed that plants were made of five "elements," earth, air, fire, water, and nitre. To develop better farming methods, scientists wished to find which of these "elements" was most important. An experiment, by Johan Baptisa Van Helmot, a Belgian, has become a classic. Van Helmot planted a willow cutting which weighed 5 pounds in a tub containing 200 pounds of soil. The plant was watered frequently, but no other substance was allowed to enter the tub. After 5 years, when the willow tree was removed it was found to weigh 169 pounds and 3 ounces, but the soil had lost only 2 ounces. Van Helmot concluded that water was the only "element" needed for plant growth.

Another scientist, John Woodward, later found that sediments present in water resulted in greater plant growth. This indicated that the 2 ounces of soil lost in Van

Helmot's experiment were significant to the growth of the willow tree.

Today, we know that Van Helmot's willow increased in weight partly as a result of the construction of new tissues from foods manufactured from water and a gas, carbon dioxide, by the process of photosynthesis (page 144). However, we also know that plant tissues contain much water —a cucumber is about 96% water and a corn plant is 80% water. The remaining portion of the plant, its *dry weight,* is composed on a number of other substances.

Any element present in the soil is likely to be taken up by plant roots. At least 60 elements have been found in plant tissues, and it is likely that every stable element occurs in plants on soils in which the elements occur. However, we know of only 15 elements which are necessary for the growth and reproduction of plants. These elements can be divided into two groups: 1) the *major elements,* which are needed in relatively large amounts, and 2) the *minor elements,* which are needed in very small amounts. Oxygen, carbon, hydrogen, nitrogen, sulfur, phosphorus, calcium, potassium, and magnesium are major elements. Iron, manganese, zinc, copper, boron, and molybdenum are minor elements.

A ton of corn contains about 890 pounds of oxygen, 870 pounds of carbon, 125 pounds of hydrogen, 30 pounds of nitrogen and smaller amounts of the other necessary elements which would weigh, combined, less than a pound. Molybdenum alone would weigh a fraction of an ounce. Even though the minor elements are used in small amounts, they are as important to plant growth as the major elements. There are several areas on the earth where one or more minor elements are absent. These areas are nearly as barren of plants as a desert. However, they can be farmed if the missing elements are introduced in quantities as small as an ounce an acre.

The elements needed for plant growth are obtained from the air, from the soil, and from water. Water is made up of hydrogen and oxygen. Carbon dioxide, a compound of carbon and oxygen, is present in the air and is the main source of the plant's carbon. Thus, the three elements which make up more than 90% of the dry weight of the plant are supplied by water and air. The remaining 12 elements needed by the plant are absorbed from the soil.

PHOTOSYNTHESIS

WE COULD NOT LIVE if there were no green plants, for they are the source of all food. Green plants, such as this sugar cane, can manufacture food from inorganic raw materials. Animals do not possess this ability, and therefore must either feed upon plants or upon other animals which have eaten plants. You may eat plant material in the form of bread, cereal, fruits, and vegetables. Or, when you eat meat, you may eat plant food which has been transformed into the tissues of cattle, sheep, or hogs.

Chlorophyll is the green coloring matter in plants. Its molecules are complex organic networks of more than 100 atoms. In some way, these molecules can absorb the energy of sunlight and use it to drive the entire food-making process. This process is called *photosynthesis* (*photo* = light, *synthesis* = to make). It is the earth's most widespread single chemical process and produces more material than any other single process (about 240 billion tons of sugar per year).

Through this process of photosynthesis, green plants are able to combine two inorganic raw materials — water and carbon dioxide — into an organic compound, sugar. By careful measurement, scientists have found that 112 kilocalories of light energy are needed to make one molecule of simple sugar. We can outline the photosynthetic process by the formula:

$$\text{water} + \text{carbon dioxide} + \text{light energy} = \text{sugar} + \text{oxygen}$$
$$H_2O \qquad CO_2 \qquad 112\,Kcal \qquad (CH_2O) \qquad O_2$$

Actually, there are several steps, most of which are not yet fully understood, in the photosynthetic process. The first reaction, and the only one for which light is necessary, decomposes water (H_2O) into hydrogen (H_2) and oxygen (O). The oxygen is immediately released to the air. The two hydrogen atoms which are set free are transferred to a carbon dioxide molecule (CO_2). When the hydrogen combines with the carbon dioxide, they form a

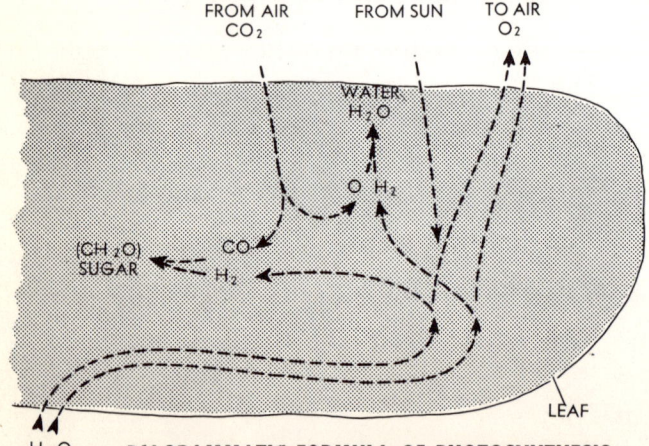

DIAGRAMMATIC FORMULA OF PHOTOSYNTHESIS

basic sugar unit (CH_2O) and release an oxygen atom. However, this oxygen atom from the carbon dioxide does not pass into the air. With two hydrogen atoms, freed by the decomposition of another water molecule, it combines to form a new water molecule.

The basic sugar units produced by photosynthesis subsequently are used to build more complex molecules of the various food substances: carbohydrates, fats, and proteins. Each unit contains a small store of sun energy which has been converted to chemical energy. Later, when the foods which are composed of these units are oxidized in our bodies, the sun energy is released for our use.

VITAMINS

STOP-AND-GO LIGHTS regulate the flow of traffic on our highways. Thermostats regulate the temperature of our homes and offices. In a similar way, vitamins seem to regulate many of the processes within our bodies.

Vitamins, or the compounds which unite to form them, are complex carbon compounds produced chiefly by plants. The final step in their synthesis, however, may occur within our bodies. Because many vitamins are stored by animals, we obtain them from meats, dairy products, and other animal foods.

Vitamins are needed only in very small quantities — they compose only about one ten-thousandth of the weight of the food we eat. Although vitamins furnish the body with neither energy nor building materials, without vitamins the body is unable to utilize properly the foods it receives. Various "deficiency" diseases, such as scurvy, beriberi or pellagra may result from a lack of certain vitamins. A well-balanced diet is the best protection against these diseases.

Before their chemical composition was discovered, vitamins were identified by letters. Even today most vitamins are known by the letter names. Among the vitamins in your diet are:

Vitamin A ($C_{20}H_{30}O$). Promotes growth, good vision, healthy condition of nose, mouth, and internal organ linings. Obtained by eating liver, dairy products, and certain vegetables.

Vitamin B_1 or Thiamine ($C_{12}H_{18}ON_4SC_{12}$). Promotes appetite, vital to growth and reproduction; regulates utilization of carbohydrates by body; prevents beriberi, a crippling disease. Supplied by milk, green vegetables, egg yolks, meats, and yeast.

Vitamin D ($C_{27}H_{43}OH$). Regulates the body's use of calcium and phosphorus; promotes the growth of strong teeth and bones; prevents rickets. Supplied by dairy products and fish. Also synthesized in the body from simpler compounds in the skin under the influence of sunlight.

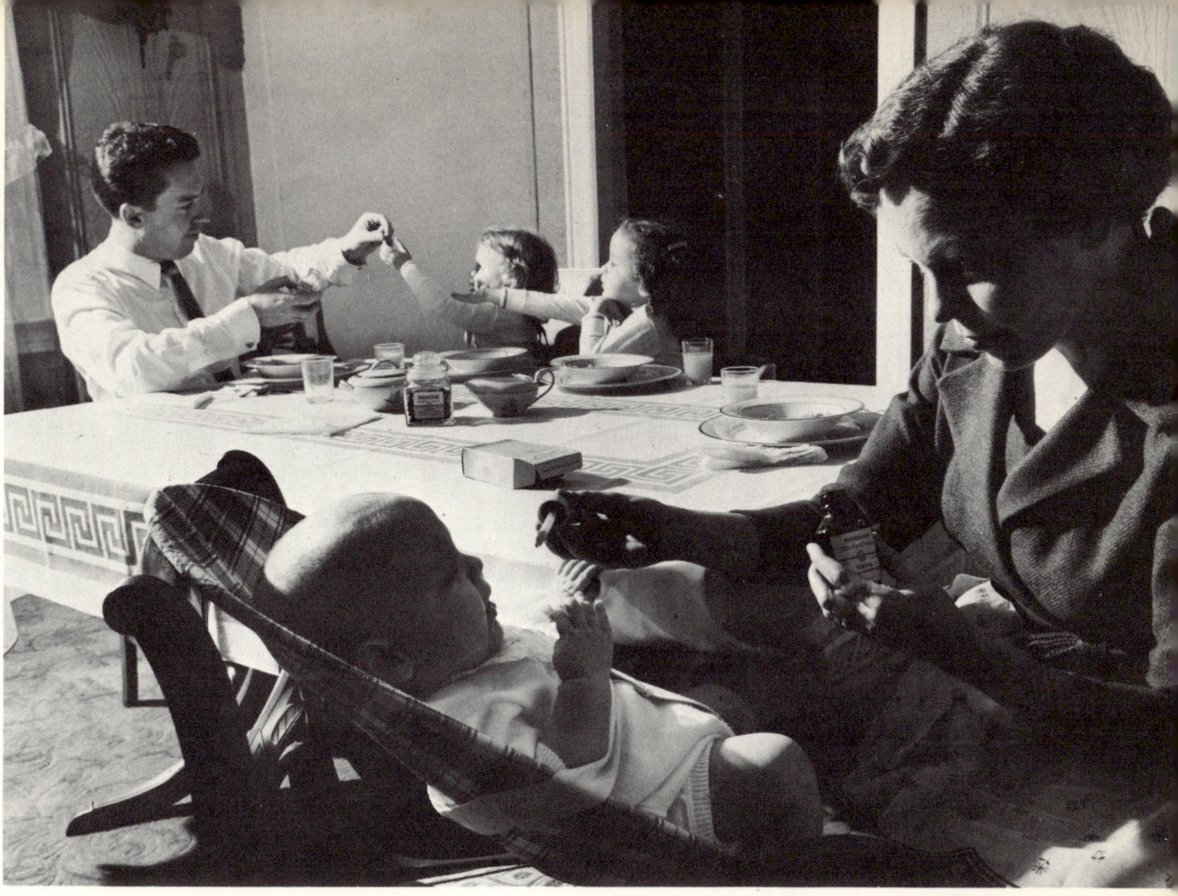

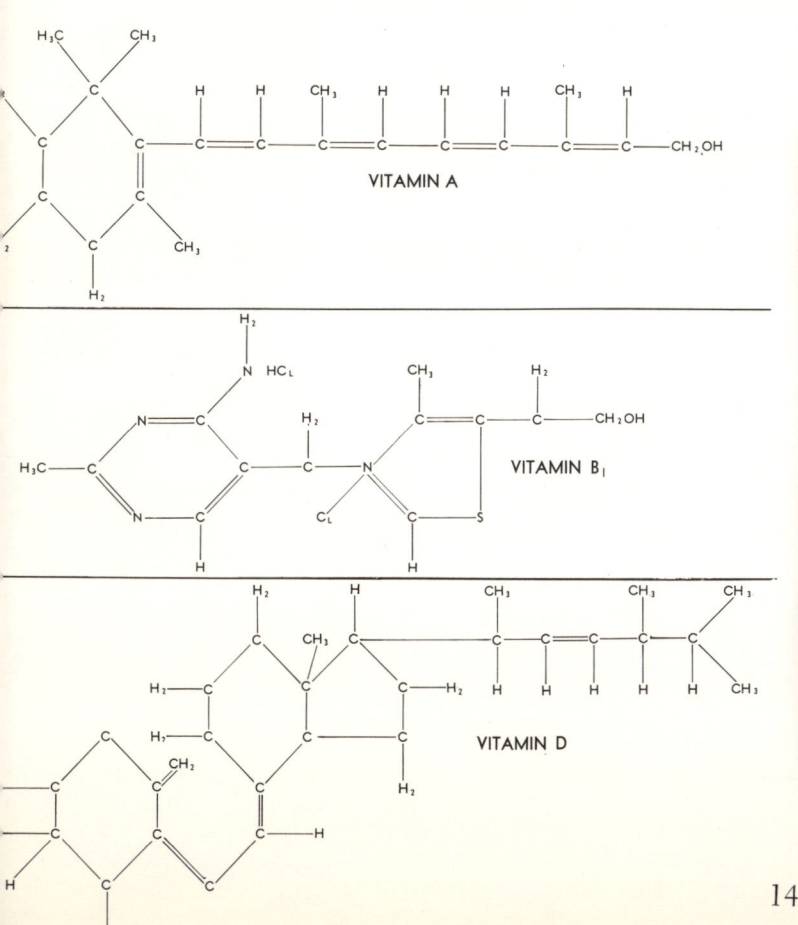

All the family takes supplemental vitamins

VITAMIN A

VITAMIN B$_1$

VITAMIN D

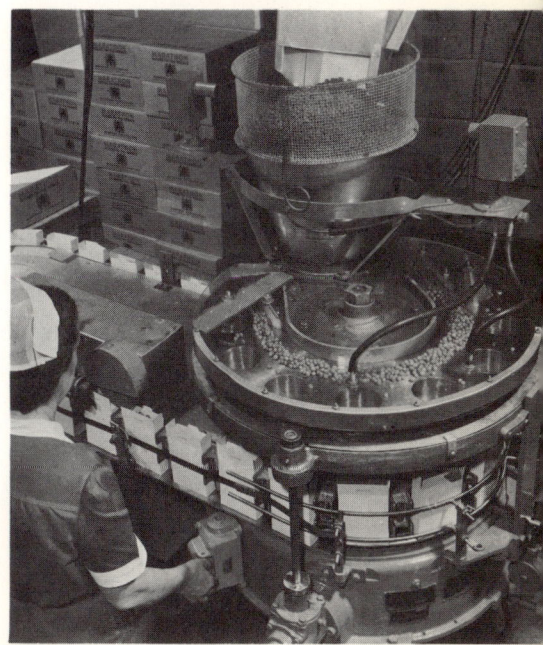

Processing peas for freezing

CHAPTER VI

PHYSICS IN EVERYDAY LIFE

EVERY MODERN HOUSEHOLD is filled with appliances, tools, and complex machines which make practical use of the basic principles of matter and energy. Our highways, airlines, railroads, and factories are filled with machines which employ these basic principles.

We are now able to control sources of energy which were beyond imagination only a few years ago. Man devised workable theories about the nature of energy and the ways by which it could be transformed, then designed and built the engines and machines to use this energy to do work. On the opposite page, you can see one energy-converting device that is useful in allowing man to travel further during a given period of time and to transport materials more rapidly than ever before. This, of course, is a jet airplane.

In this chapter are shown some of the greatest inventions that our civilization has produced. Many of these inventions would have been considered impossible only a generation or two ago. Many of them may be replaced by new inventions within our generation or the next.

BOATS
BALLOONS
AND SUBMARINES

ARCHIMEDES, a mathematician who lived 22 centuries ago, discovered the secret of things that float. *The buoyant force exerted by a fluid on any object is equal to the weight of fluid that the object displaces.* If the buoyant force is greater than the weight of the object, the object will float. Even if an object sinks, its apparent weight will be reduced by an amount equal to the weight of the fluid it displaces. This is why a rock seems to weigh less in water than it does in the air.

When the specific gravity of an object is less than the specific gravity of the fluid in which it is immersed, the object will displace a volume of fluid with a weight greater than its own. The object, therefore, will float.

The specific gravity of iron is 7.9, so solid iron will not float in water (specific gravity = 1). But if a piece of iron is flattened and shaped into a hollow vessel which will displace a weight of water greater than its own, the iron will float. This principle is employed by huge ocean liners, such as the *S.S. United States* shown here in New York harbor.

The Mayflower and its sister ship, the Columbia, are the only operational blimps in the Western Hemisphere.

Steel-framed airships, as this Goodyear blimp, and heavy plastic or fabric and rubber balloons that float in the air operate on the same principle. Because they are filled with helium or some other gas that has a specific gravity which is less than that of air, the gas-filled bags displace a volume of air with a greater weight than their own. Therefore, they float.

A submarine is able to sink or float by varying its specific gravity. Basically, a submarine is a hollow steel cylinder with compartments which can be filled with water or air as desired. When they are filled with air, the ship is light enough to float. When the compartments are water-filled, however, the over-all specific gravity of the ship is greater than that of water, and the submarine sinks.

THE STEAM ENGINE

When heated to its boiling point, water expands and forms steam. This simple fact led to the development of the steam engine, the first machine that enabled men to generate power where and when it was desired. It provided a portable power source to drive railroad trains and ocean-going vessels.

The heart of the steam engine is its boiler. Here water, the lifeblood of the engine, is heated by a fire until it boils. The steam generated in the boiler passes, under high pressure, to the steam chest. From this distributing point the steam is fed through a small opening, or port, into a cylinder.

Upon entering the cylinder, the steam expands and pushes against a snug-fitting but movable piston. As the piston is pushed toward the end of the cylinder, a valve in the steam chest slides over the port which had admitted steam to the cylinder, thereby closing it, and at the same time opens another port. This permits steam to enter in front of the piston. The piston then is forced back to its former position, whereupon the valve again reverses the steam ports and initiates the piston cycle anew. The movement of the piston forces out the spent steam of the last stroke through the exhaust.

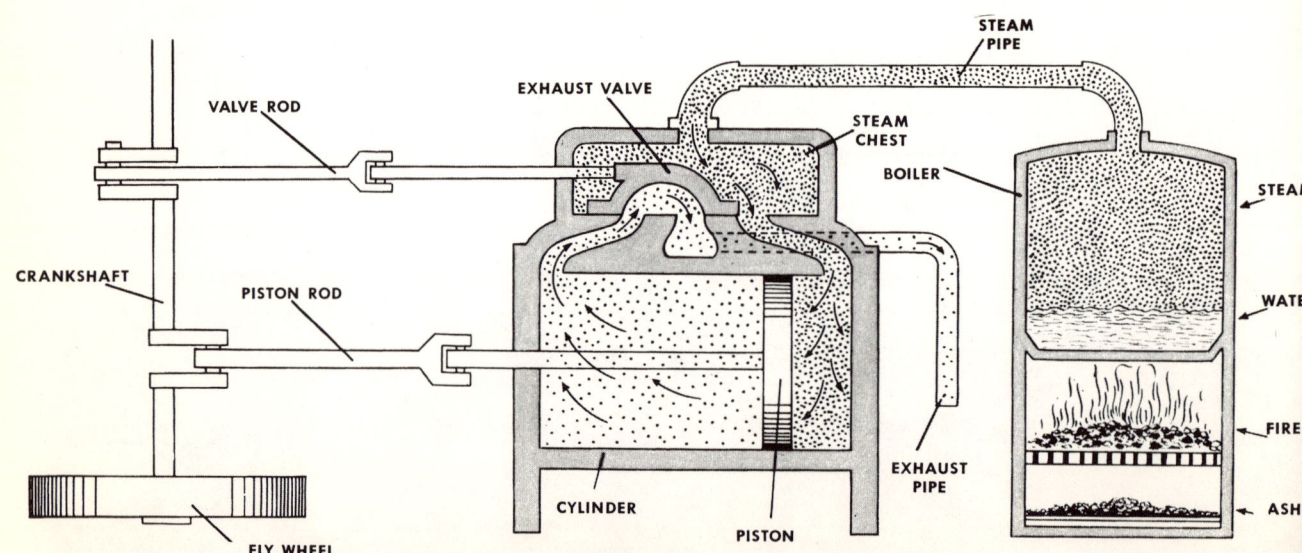

DIAGRAM OF STEAM ENGINE

The piston is attached to the crankshaft by a driving rod. As the piston is pushed back and forth by the steam, it turns the crankshaft. A heavy flywheel attached to the crankshaft gains sufficient momentum from this movement to enable it to give back some energy to the piston, moving it past the "blind spots" at each end of the cylinder. Machines that are to be powered by a steam engine may be attached directly to the crankshaft or may be driven by a belt fixed to the flywheel. In a railroad locomotive, the part of the flywheel actually is played by driving wheels that propel the locomotive.

273-CU IN. V-8 ENGINE ASSEMBLY — CUTAWAY

THE GAS ENGINE

The United States has more than 50 million portable chemical factories. These factories are gas engines in which oxygen is combined with a fuel, usually gasoline, and ignited to produce carbon dioxide and water. But we are primarily interested in another product — power.

A gas engine is like a steam engine in that an expanding gas pushing against a piston is the source of power. It differs from a steam engine in that its fire is intermittent and occurs within the cylinder. Gas engines, therefore, are called *internal combustion engines*. Gas engines drive most of the automobiles on our highways.

In most gas engines, there are four piston strokes for each fuel explosion: (1) *The intake stroke*. As the piston moves downward, a valve in the cylinder head momentarily opens to allow the fuel-air mixture to enter. (2) *The compression stroke*. The piston moves upward and compresses the

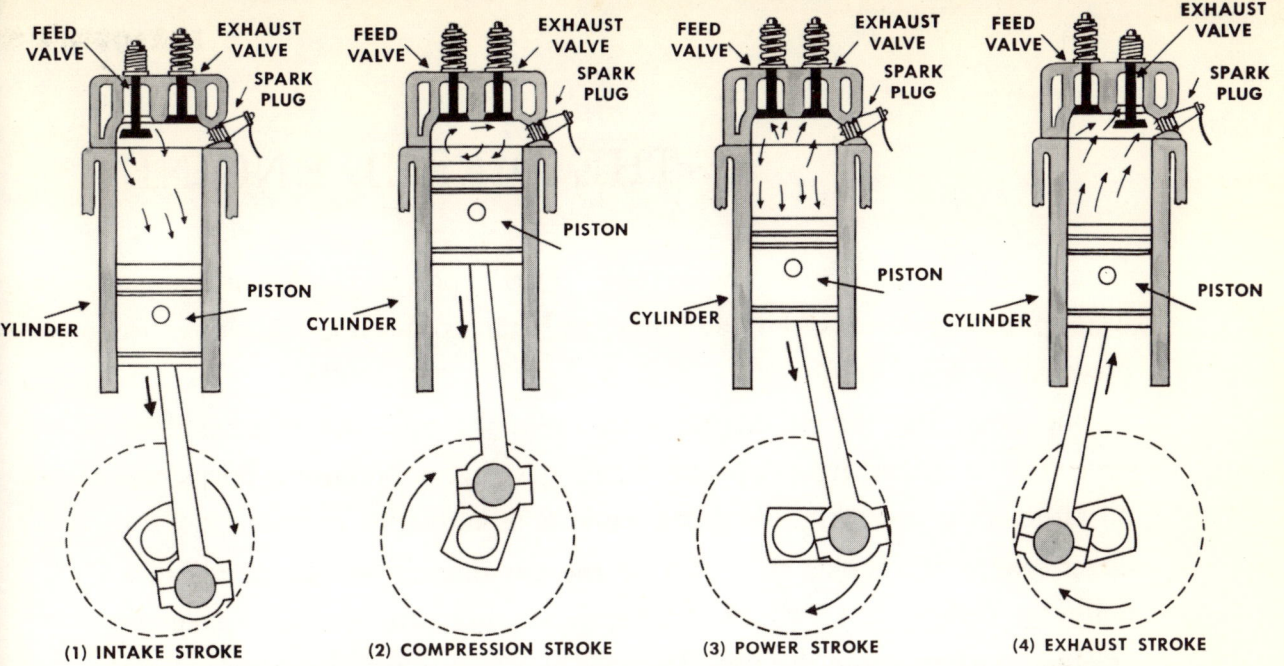

(1) INTAKE STROKE   (2) COMPRESSION STROKE   (3) POWER STROKE   (4) EXHAUST STROKE

mixture into the upper portion of the cylinder. (3) *The power stroke.* An electric spark, produced at the base of the spark plug, ignites the mixture. The heat of combustion causes the gaseous products, carbon dioxide and water vapor, to expand rapidly. The gases push the piston downward, turning the crankshaft to which it is attached. (4) *The exhaust stroke.* As the piston again rises, another valve in the cylinder head momentarily opens to allow the spent gases to escape through the exhaust pipe. The next stroke is a new intake stroke.

The flywheel, which is attached to the crankshaft, gains enough momentum during the power stroke to carry the piston through the other three strokes.

In a gas engine, the fuel and air are mixed in a device known as a *carburetor.* The fuel is injected into the carburetor as a fine spray and immediately vaporizes and mixes with the air. The resulting gaseous mixture is then fed into the cylinder. When the *accelerator,* or gas pedal, is pushed down, more fuel is mixed with the air in the carburetor. As this "richer" mixture enters the cylinder and explodes, it pushes against the piston with more force and supplies more power to the machine driven by the engine.

Most gas engines have several cylinders connected to the crankshaft. The crankshaft may be used to transfer power directly to some machine. A belt, gears, or other transfer system also can be used.

THE DIESEL ENGINE

Large trucks and buses, bulldozers, electric power plants, municipal water-pumping stations, railroad trains, and many other huge machines are powered by diesel engines.

The diesel, like the gas engine, is an internal combustion engine. However, it is less expensive to operate than a gas engine because it burns fuel oil rather than more highly-refined gasoline or kerosene. The design of the diesel engine is simpler than that of the gas engine because it requires neither a carburetor to mix its fuel with air, nor an electrical system to create a spark to ignite the fuel. In place of a carburetor, the diesel engine has a fuel pump and a nozzle which spray fuel into the cylinder. The power delivered by the engine is controlled by the quantity of fuel injected into the cylinder, rather than by the richness of a fuel-air mixture. No electric spark is needed to ignite the fuel because the compression of air in the cylinder raises the temperature of the air above the ignition temperature of the fuel. The principal disadvantages of the diesel engine are that it is comparatively large and heavy in relation to the power it develops.

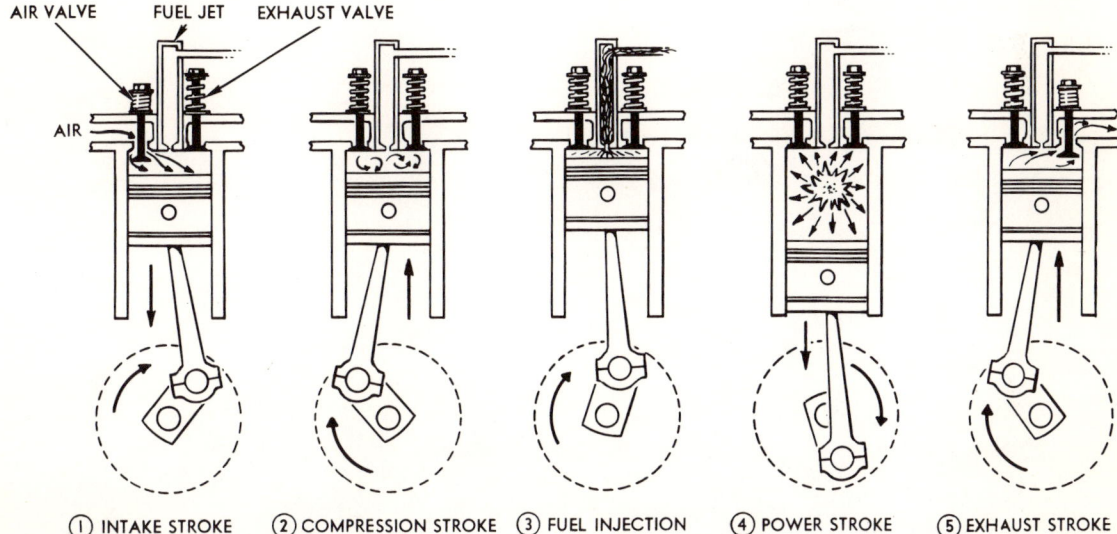

① INTAKE STROKE ② COMPRESSION STROKE ③ FUEL INJECTION ④ POWER STROKE ⑤ EXHAUST STROKE

The operation of a diesel engine is similar to that of a gas engine. As the piston surges downward, air is drawn into the cylinder (1). On the return stroke of the piston, the air is compressed to about one-sixteenth of its original volume (2). This great compression raises the temperature of the air to about 1,000° F. Fuel oil is sprayed into the cylinder just before the piston reaches the top of its stroke (3). The high temperature of the compressed air ignites the fuel and the rapidly expanding gases produced by the explosion drive the piston downward (4). The piston turns the crankshaft and, thus, supplies power to operate the machine to which it is connected. As the piston rises again, the spent gases are pushed out of the cylinder into the exhaust (5).

1
N
N
+ BRUSH
S
S
BRUSH
ARMATURE

N
2
ARMATURE
COMMUTATOR
N
S
STATIONARY MAGNET
STATIONARY MAGNET
S

4868

3
N
N
S
S

4
N
N
S
S

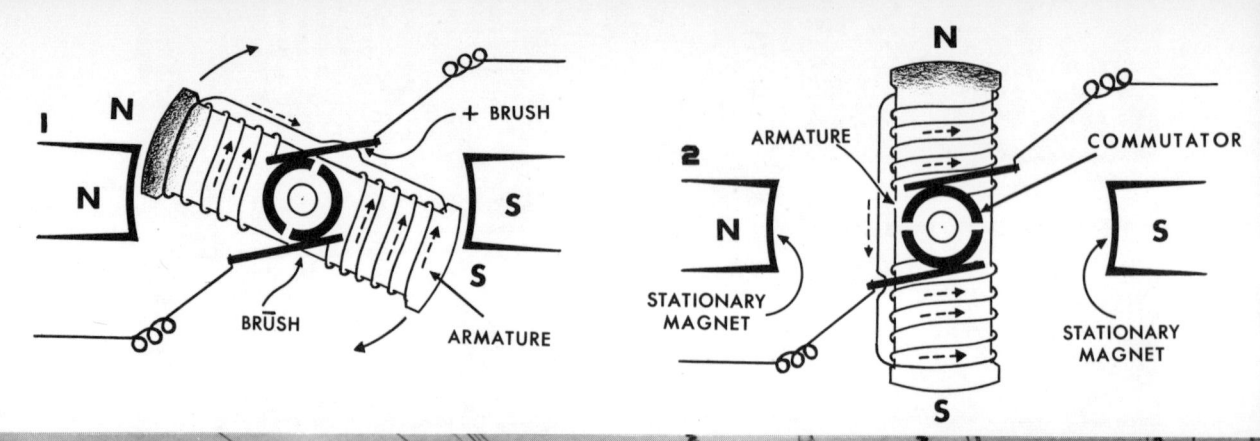

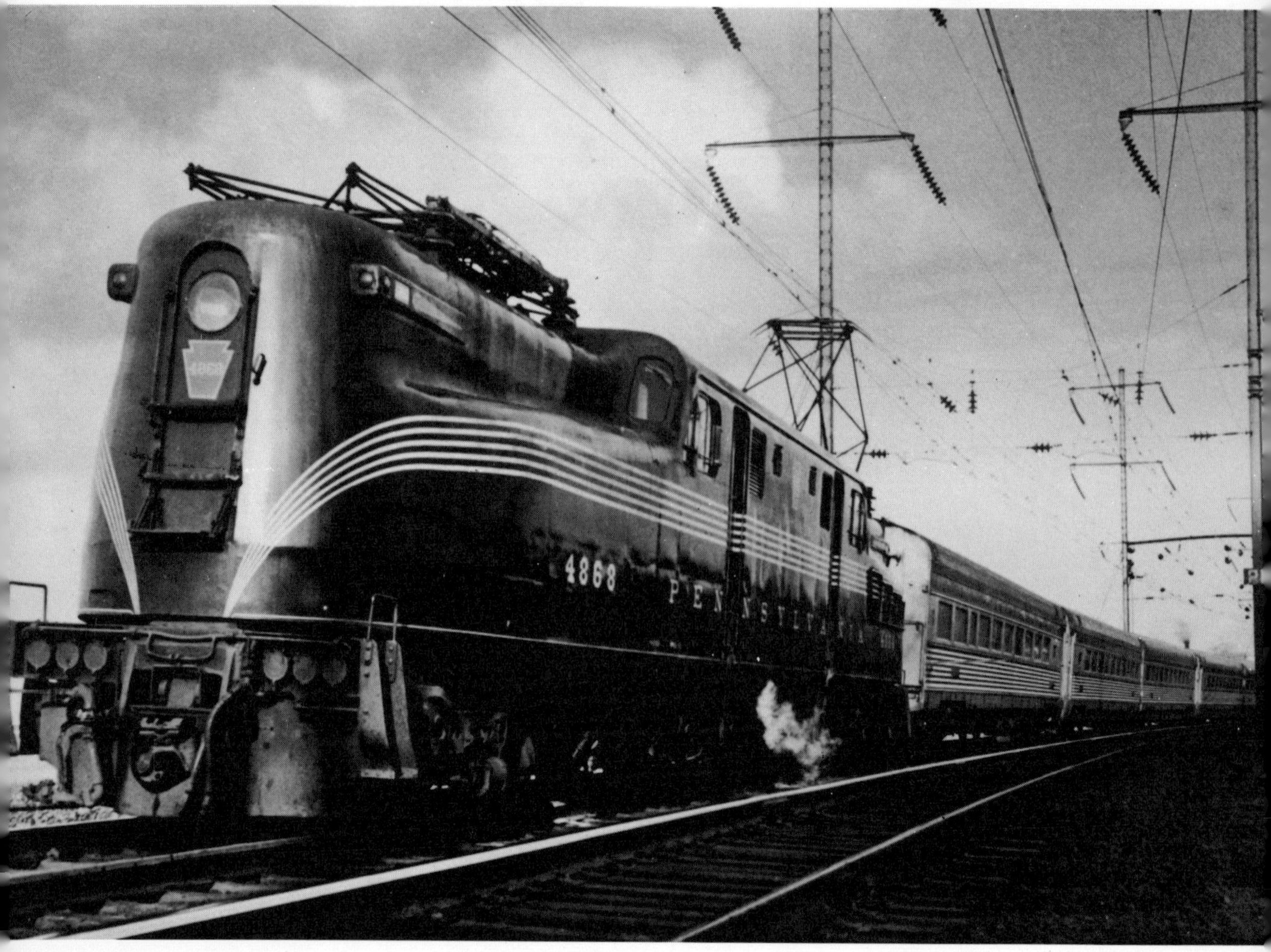

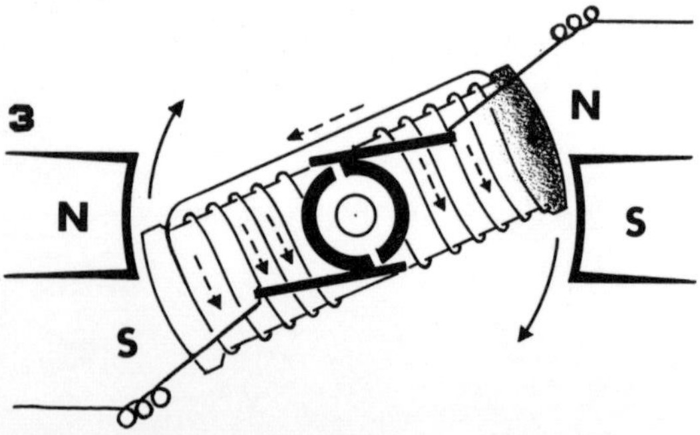

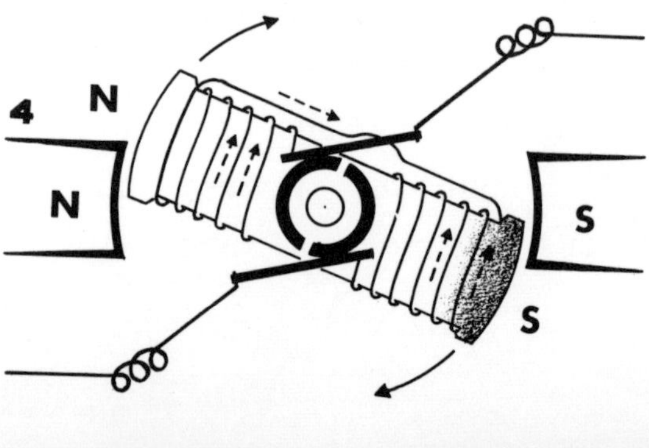

THE ELECTRIC MOTOR

GIANT LOCOMOTIVES, huge industrial machines, and tiny electric razors are but a few of the millions of devices powered by electric motors. Regardless of size, every electric motor is designed to do one thing, to convert electrical energy to mechanical energy.

A simple electric motor has three basic parts: a rotating electromagnet (*the armature*), a *stationary magnet,* and a pair of contact strips (*brushes*) which carry electricity to the armature.

When an electric current surges through wires of the armature, the armature becomes an electromagnet (see page 71). When the poles of the armature are opposite like poles of the stationary magnet, the poles repel one another and the armature is forced to turn (A). As it turns, the poles are attracted by the opposite poles of the stationary magnet (B). But, just as the opposite poles of the two magnets come together, the direction of flow of electricity through the armature is reversed (C). This reverses the armature poles and brings like poles of the magnets opposite again (D), to continue the rotation.

Reversal of current is accomplished by the use of a metal ring, *the commutator,* which is split into two sections. Each section is connected to one end of the armature coil. As the armature rotates, each commutator section is alternately in contact with the positive and then with the negative brush. Each end, therefore, is alternately the north and then the south pole of the armature.

The intermittent reversal of poles keeps the armature and its axle continuously rotating. The mechanical energy of the rotating armature is used to drive machines connected either directly or indirectly to the axle.

THE TURBINE

STEAM, GAS, AND DIESEL engines are reciprocating engines; that is, they depend on the alternate back-and-forth movement of a piston. At the end of each stroke the piston stops for a split-second before its motion is reversed. A large portion of the energy of the fuel is used alternately to oppose the piston's inertia of motion, and then its inertia of rest. In contrast, the motion of a turbine is rotary and continuous. No energy is wasted by alternately reversing direction.

Turbines are driven by the kinetic energy of a moving stream of fluid — usually steam, air, or water. The earliest and simplest turbines were water wheels and windmills. A modern water turbine is illustrated on page 74. Turbines driven by falling water or by jets of steam turn generators which furnish virtually all of the electricity used in the world. The moving fluid is directed against the blades of the turbine wheel or rotor and causes it to spin. But the velocity of the steam is so great that its energy cannot be efficiently absorbed by a single rotor, unless the rotor were to spin at a fantastic speed. Therefore, several rotors are attached to the turbine shaft, as shown in the photograph.

Steam from several nozzles strikes the curved blades of the rotor, thereby turning it. The steam then passes through the rotor to a set of stationary blades. These blades are curved so that the steam is directed against the next rotor at the proper angle. The number of rotors, usually about 26, varies according to the pressure of the steam used to drive the turbine.

Jet engines are modified gas turbines. They are similar in design to the stationary gas turbine. But stationary turbines differ in that all of the surplus kinetic energy of the hot gases is expanded against the rotors. The gases expand to normal atmospheric pressure before being allowed to escape from the engine.

THE JET ENGINE

Have you ever watched an escaped toy balloon dart swiftly about the room? If so, you have witnessed a demonstration of the fundamental law that *for every action there is an equal and opposite reaction* (see page 45). In this case, the backward escape of air from the balloon is the action, and the forward motion of the balloon is the reaction.

Jet engines, primarily used in airplanes, are based on this reaction principle. Air is drawn into the front of the engine, compressed, and mixed with fuel. A spark then ignites the mixture, producing superheated gases which escape at a high speed from the rear of the engine. This backward rush of gas, pushing against the combustion chamber of the engine, causes the plane to speed forward.

Bomarc ramjet interceptor missile streaks skyward.

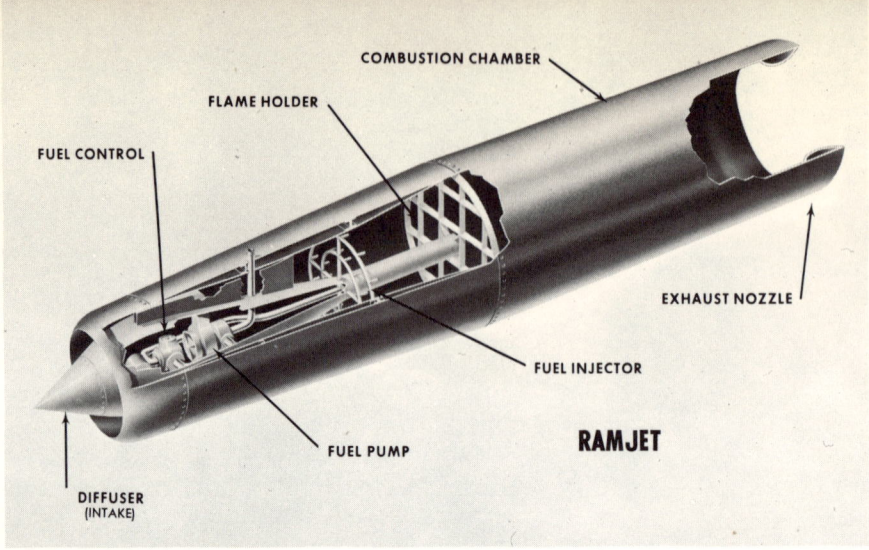

Although they are among our most advanced machines, jets are the most simple of all engines. The *ramjet*, the simplest jet, is little more than a hollow tube fitted with a fuel combustion chamber. Because it has no way to draw air into itself, air must be rammed into the ramjet. This is done by launching the ramjet plane from a "mother plane" at a high speed, or by using the ramjet to supply extra power for planes already in flight.

The *turbojet* (turbine-jet) needs no flying start. Blades in a compressor near its mouth draw in air and force it into the combustion chambers. Here, fuel is mixed wtih the air and ignited. As the hot, rapidly expanding gases escape from the combustion chambers, they are led into a small turbine. The rushing gases cause the turbine rotors and the shaft to which they are attached to spin. This shaft extends forward through the engine to the compressor and as the shaft turns, it moves the compressor blades which draw more air into the engine.

The *turboprop* engine is a slightly modified turbojet. The turbine not only supplies air to the engine, but also turns a regular propeller which gives added thrust to the plane.

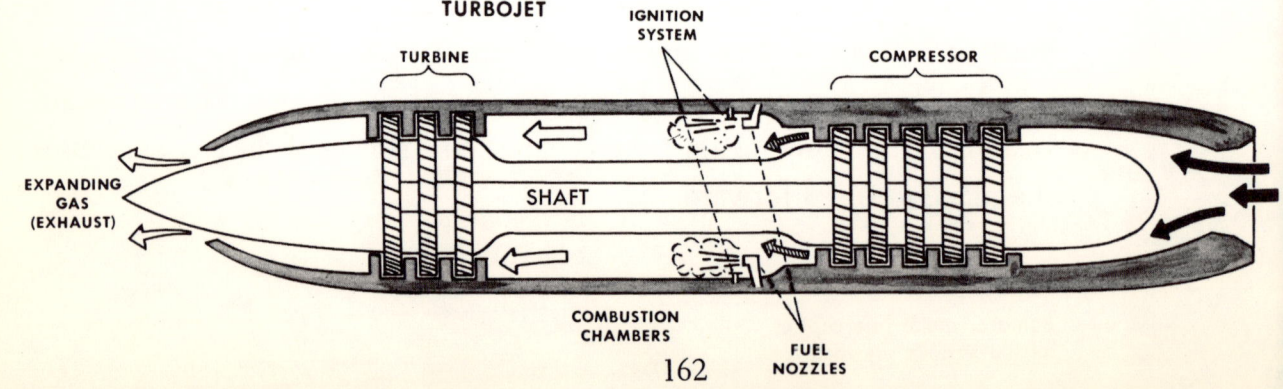

162

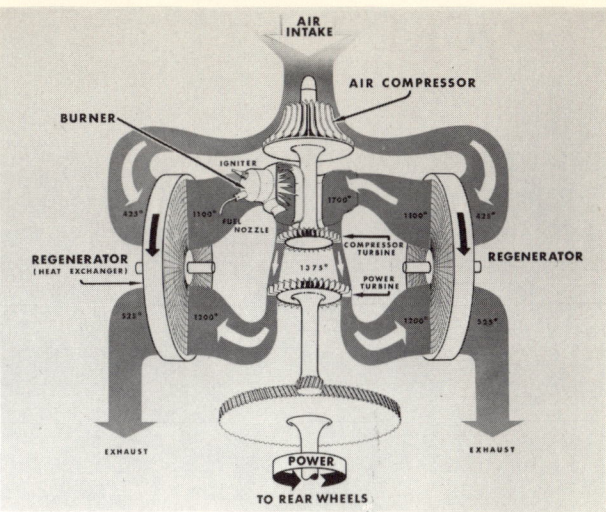

Photos of the Chrysler Turbine automobile. Air flow through a Gas Turbine engine.

A greater modification of the turbojet is being developed by the Chrysler Corporation for use in automobiles. In the Chrysler *Gas Turbine Engine,* the hot exhaust gases pass from the turbine which drives the compressor to a second turbine which drives the rear wheels of the automobile. The exhaust gases then are cooled and allowed to expand before they enter the air. Thus, no jet-push, or reaction, is produced. To be of practical value, an automotive gas turbine engine has to be made from readily available, low-cost materials by mass production techniques. It must be compact and light in weight. The gas issuing from its exhaust must be cool, the engine must have a low noise level, and it must operate economically. Many of these problems have been overcome and from 1963 to 1966 more than 200 people in various parts of the United States drove specially designed, hand built turbine cars as part of a test program. Results of this test will be used to develop plans to market a turbine powered, production-line car in the future.

The gas turbine engine has many advantages over gas engines. It has only one-fifth as many moving parts and requires much less maintenance. It is smoother, quieter, and more free of vibration. There are no pistons or valve gears, so there is less friction and oil use is negligible. The exhaust gases are cooler and cleaner than those of a gas engine. It has no radiator, so it needs no water or anti-freeze. It starts up immediately, even when the temperature is below freezing, and needs no warm-up period. And it will operate on a wide variety of fuels, including white gasoline, kerosene, diesel oil, aircraft turbine engine fuel, or a mixture of any of these.

ROCKETS

Movie hero James Bond (Sean Connery) adjusts rocket belt.

Rocket-propelled Flying Chair can carry men and supplies on earth or moon.

LIKE THE JET, the rocket engine works on the reaction principle. It differs from the jet in that it requires no outside supply of oxygen. Rocket engines, therefore, can operate in the near-vacuum which exists at high altitudes and in space. Rocket-powered missiles have attained speeds in excess of 22,000 miles per hour, and have carried payloads into orbit around the earth and the sun, and on missions to the moon, Mars, and Venus. In contrast, the small rockets shown above have been developed to lift a man over obstacles on the earth or moon at speeds up to 60 miles per hour.

Rockets are completely self-contained. In addition to a supply of fuel, they also carry a supply of oxygen. Their oxygen may be carried separately, or it may be in a combined form in one of the fuels. Because rockets need no air, their noses are solid and not open, as are those of jet engines.

There are two basic types of rockets, depending on the fuel they use:

Solid-fuel rockets are similar to those in use as fireworks for centuries. Many are used to assist airplanes during take-offs. Others are used as auxiliary power sources for airplanes and missiles in flight. They are also widely used to supplement artillery and as armament on fighter planes. The pencil-shaped Scout launch vehicle is a solid-fuel rocket used for upper atmosphere probes. Much larger solid-fuel rockets with tremendous thrusts are being developed for deep space shots.

Liquid-fuel rockets are of more recent development. They are more complex and more efficient than solid-fuel types. One type of liquid-fuel rocket uses nitric acid (HNO_3) and aniline ($C_6H_5NH_2$) as fuel. When these liquids are mixed, a violent chemical reaction releases a tremendous volume of hot gases which propel the rocket. Most of our space shots have been made with liquid-fuel rockets, such as this Atlas launch vehicle, right, shown as it was fired with a Mercury space capsule as its payload.

ZELL (Zero Length Launch) of F-104 Starfighter by solid fuel rocket.

The life of a rocket is very short. Solid-fuel rockets usually last only about 15 seconds. Liquid-fuel types may last several times as long. But once they are fired, our present rocket engines are doomed to be consumed by the heat of the combustion of their own fuel. However, progress has been made on a rocket engine which can be started and stopped repeatedly in manned space flight.

THE AIRPLANE

Every airplane, whether it is powered by a gas engine, jet engine, or rocket engine is acted upon by four forces — *lift, thrust, gravity,* and *drag.*

Lift. The pressure of a fluid decreases as the speed of flow of the fluid increases. This physical law is the basic principle of the airplane. The upper surfaces of the plane's *airfoils* — that is, the wing and tail surfaces — are slightly curved, but the lower surfaces are flat. As the plane pushes forward, the air which passes over the wing and tail is forced to travel farther and faster than the air which passes under them. Both parcels of air arrive at the back edge of the wing or tail at the same instant. The air pressure from below, therefore, is greater than the air pressure from above. This difference in air pressure between the upper and lower surfaces creates the lift, or upward push, that keeps the plane in the air.

The airfoils of a helicopter are the blades of its horizontal rotor. A helicopter develops lift by twirling the airfoils round and round, rather than by forcing them straight forward through the air. The vertical tail rotor controls the direction the helicopter points and prevents the body from revolving beneath the main rotor.

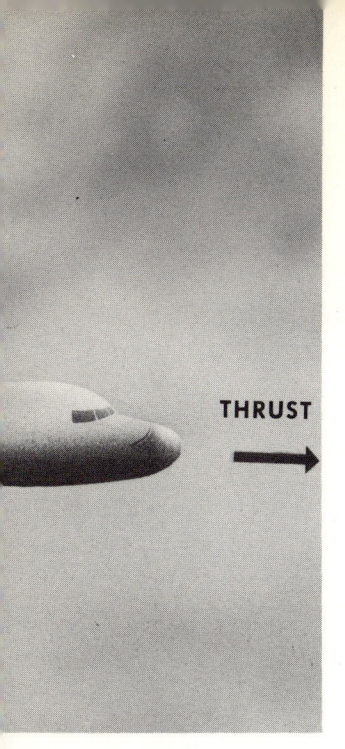

Thrust acts to speed the plane on its way. In cross-section an airplane propeller is shaped much like a wing. Its leading surface is curved and its back surface is flat. When the propeller is rotated by the engine, air pressure is greater against the back of the propeller than against the front. As a result, the propeller and the plane to which it is attached, are pushed forward. This forward push is the thrust. The thrust of a jet airplane is the reaction to a backward push caused by the gases issuing from the engine's tailpipe. A helicopter develops forward, backward, or sideways thrust by tilting its rotor slightly downward in the direction the pilot wishes to travel.

Gravity. The earth's gravitational attraction works against lift, and tends to pull the plane toward the ground (see page 72).

Drag tends to retard a plane's progress. Like all other matter, air has substance. An airplane must push the air aside as it moves forward. Air resistance causes a loss of forward speed. Eddy currents form in the air behind each exposed part of the airplane, causing a further resistance to forward motion. The total effect of air resistance at the front, and of eddies at the back of each exposed part constitutes the drag.

When a plane is in level flight and traveling at a constant speed, the four forces are in balance—lift equals gravity, and thrust equals drag.

SOUND

THROUGHOUT LIFE we are surrounded by sounds—sounds of human voices, sounds of the city, sounds of the farm. We learn to identify sounds and to communicate our desires, opinions, passions, and knowledge by them.

But what are sounds? They are series of compressions in an elastic medium, such as air, water, wood, or steel, produced by a vibrating body. The vibrating body may be the vocal cords of a human throat, the tight skin of a drum, a column of air in an organ pipe, or any one of many other objects.

In the horn at the left of this picture, the vibrating body is a small metal diaphragm. As the diaphragm flexes outward, it pushes the molecules of the air closer together, forming an area of compression. As it flexes in-

New acoustics laboratory at Trane Company in La Crosse, Wisconsin, will allow engineers to study sounds of air conditioners and other machines with no outside interference. The test room floats on huge, rubber-mounted springs and is lined with a maze of sound-absorbing panels.

ward, it momentarily reduces pressure and the air molecules move farther apart. The energy transmitted from the vibrating diaphragm to adjacent air molecules is transferred from molecule to molecule by billions of collisions. In this way, compression waves separated by bands of low pressure are beamed out from the loudspeaker. A special device was used to change these sound waves to ribbons of light. The bright lines are compressions. In the darker areas between these lines the air molecules have spread apart farther than normal.

You have undoubtedly noticed that a flash of lightning is always seen before thunder is heard, and smoke is seen discharged from a distant gun before the shot is heard. These observations indicate that sound travels at a speed slower than that of light (186,321 miles per second). Careful measurements have shown that the speed of sound is only 1,090 feet per second or 741.3 miles per hour in air at the freezing point of water (32° F or 0° Celsius). Its speed increases by about 2 feet per second (1.4 miles per hour) for each degree Celsius (or 1.8° F) rise in air temperature and decreases by 2 feet per second with every degree Celsius drop in air temperature.

BENDING LIGHT

LIGHT RAYS which strike a piece of glass obliquely are bent as they pass through the glass. This bending, which also occurs when light passes through water, plastic, or other transparent substances, is known as refraction.

Our knowledge of refraction has led to the development of lenses. A lens is essentially a transparent object with two opposite, smooth surfaces. These surfaces may both be curved, or one may be curved and the other flat.

There are two classes of lenses: *Converging lenses* have convex surfaces. They are thicker at the center than at their edges. When parallel rays of light pass through a lens of this type they are bent inward. Therefore, the rays converge at a point beyond the lens, the principal focus. The distance between the lens and this focus point is known as the focal length of the lens. It decreases as the lens becomes more convex. An inverted image of the object from which the light was reflected or emitted is produced behind the principal focus point. Such an image, which can be seen on a sheet of paper held in the proper position, is termed a real image.

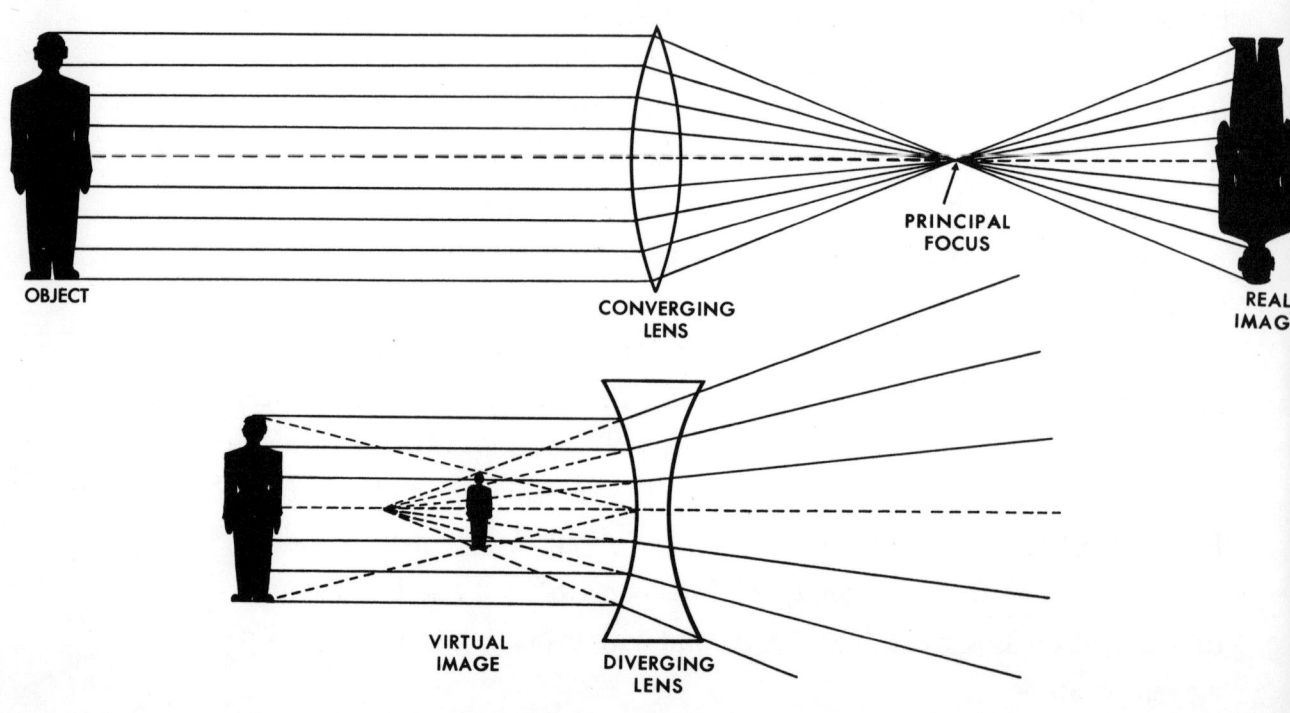

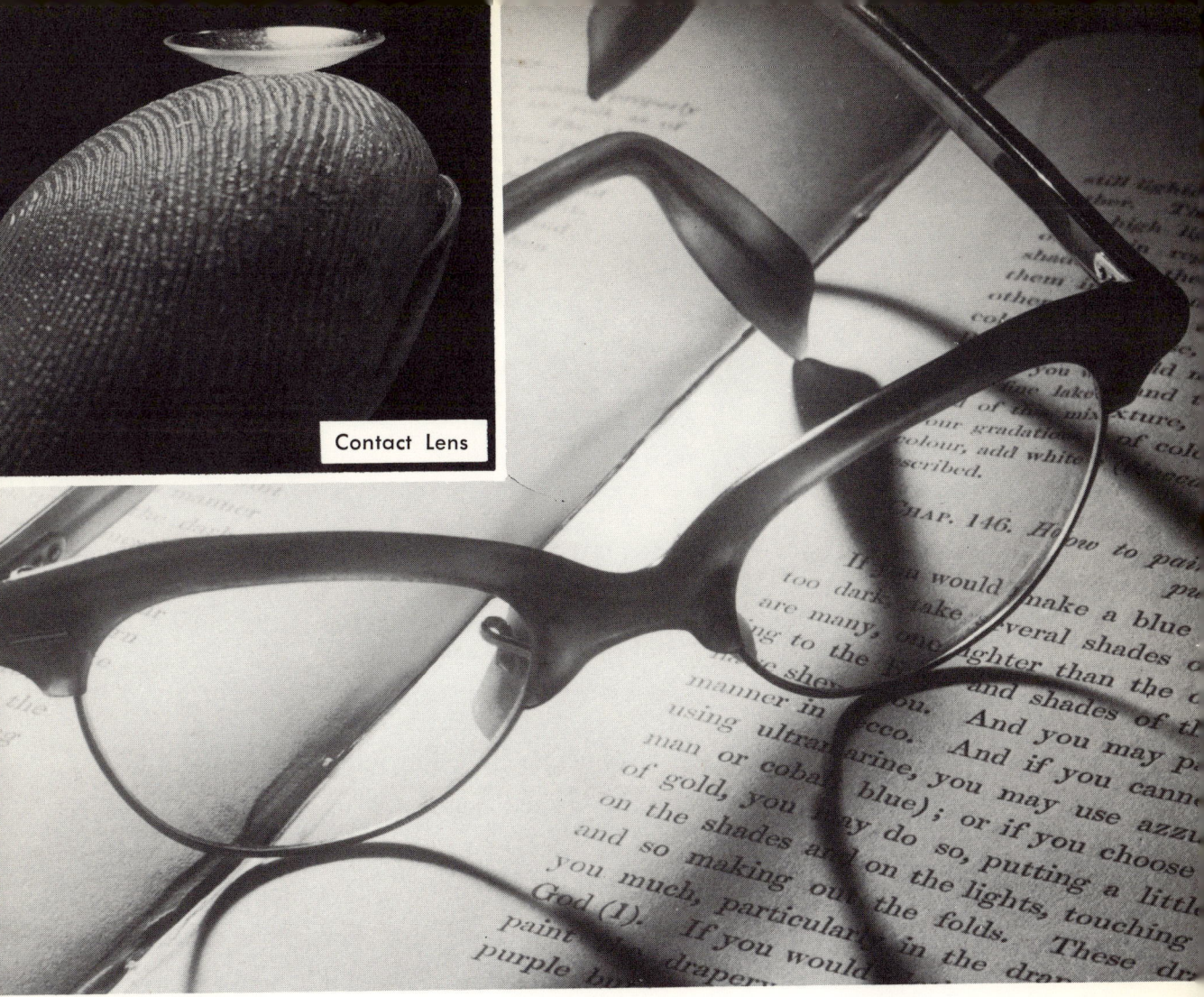

Contact Lens

Diverging lenses are concave. Their edges are thicker than their centers. When parallel rays of light pass through a lens of this kind, they are bent outward. Because the rays diverge, no real image is formed by this type of lens. However, if the axes of the diverging rays are extended back through the lens, they meet at an imaginary principal focus point which is located on the same side of the lens as the light source. The upright image that appears to be produced between the object and the lens is known as a virtual image. It cannot be projected onto a sheet of paper.

Lenses are found in the eyes of nearly every animal, in eyeglasses, telescopes, microscopes, binoculars, magnifying glasses, cameras, motion picture projectors, and many other optical instruments.

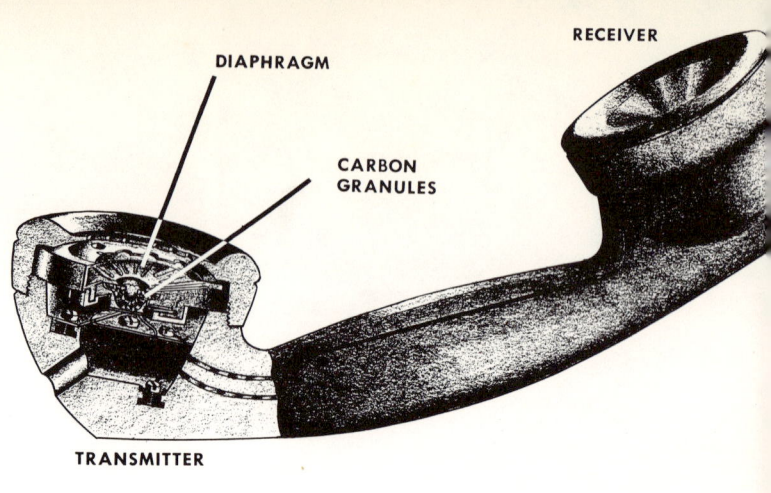

THE TELEPHONE

For business, for pleasure, in emergencies—the telephone is used 190 million times a day throughout the United States. Let us see what makes a telephone work.

The transmitter is the part of the instrument into which you speak. Sound waves from your voice cause a thin metal diaphragm in the transmitter to vibrate. These vibrations are carried to a small box of carbon granules located behind the diaphragm. If your telephone is off the hook, an electrical current is continuously flowing through this carbon. When a vibration squeezes the box, the carbon granules are pushed more tightly together, permitting a stronger current to pass through them. In this way,

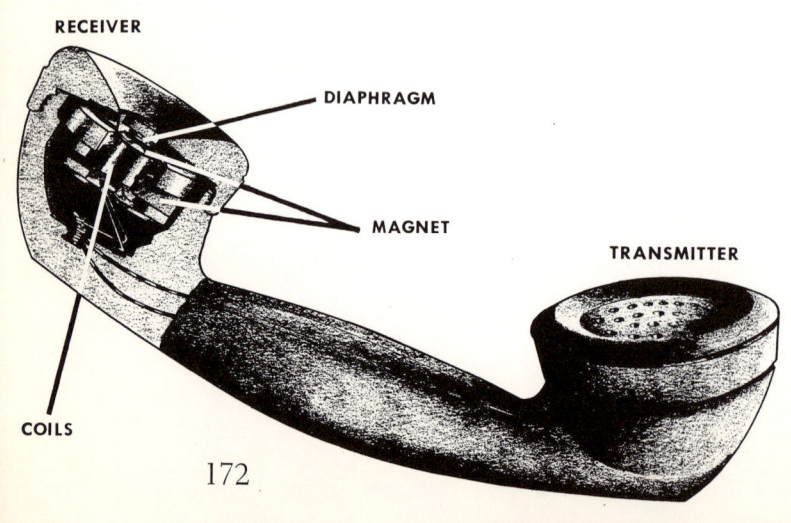

a varying electrical current whose pulsations correspond to the vibrations caused by your voice, is sent out from the transmitter.

The pulsating electrical current is carried over wires, through a central telephone office, and finally to another telephone. There, in the receiver (the part of the instrument that you hold against your ear) the current passes into wires coiled around a small magnet. In front of this magnet is a thin iron diaphragm. When an electric current flows through the wire

coils, the magnet becomes stronger and pulls the diaphragm toward it. As the current ebbs, the diaphragm snaps away again.

The motion of the diaphragm in the receiver duplicates that of the diaphragm in the transmitter. The receiver, therefore, produces sound waves similar to those you produced by speaking. When these waves strike the ear of the person at the other end of the line, he hears your words.

RADIO

Newscaster John Facenda keeps radio listeners up to date.

WHEN AN ANNOUNCER speaks into a microphone (a type of telephone transmitter), the sound of his voice is changed to a fluctuating electric current. This current is used to shape or modulate a uniform series of high-frequency electromagnetic carrier waves. The modulated waves are broadcast from a tall antenna.

An alternating current is induced in the antenna or circuits of your radio set by waves broadcast from the station. In the radio set, this current is strengthened and changed to a fluctuating direct current. It then flows to an electromagnet in the loudspeaker. As the electromagnet alternately strengthens and weakens, it causes a diaphragm to vibrate, converting the electric current back to sound waves.

Radio circuits employ a number of vacuum tubes. When a piece of metal is heated in a vacuum, electrons "boil off." If a positively-charged metallic plate is introduced near the heated metal, the electrons flow toward it. A *diode* is a vacuum tube which contains a plate and a metal filament that can be heated by an electric current. These tubes can change an alternating current to direct current, because electrons will flow from the filament to the plate, but not in the opposite direction.

In a *triode,* a metallic screen or grid is inserted between the filament and plate, as shown in the diagram. The stream of electrons will pass readily through the uncharged grid. If the grid is negatively charged, the electrons will be repelled. The flow can be increased by placing a positive charge on the grid. Thus, if the weak current from the antenna is fed to the grid and allowed to modify the current from the filament, the current which reaches the plate will be similar to, but stronger than the original antenna current. The current from the plate of one tube can be fed to the grid of another and further strengthened. This process can be repeated several times. In this way, very weak signals are amplified until they are strong enough to operate the loud speaker.

TELEVISION

Action in a television studio is "photographed" by a special kind of camera. In this camera, an image of the scene is focused on a metal plate rather than on film. The plate, the screen of an electronic tube, is covered with flecks of cesium. This metal releases electrons when it is exposed to light. A fleck, upon which a bright portion of the image falls, releases many electrons. A fleck receiving less light emits fewer electrons.

The electrons released by the cesium flow to the target, a metal plate behind the screen, where they produce variations in its normally-uniform positive charge. The original light image is changed to a pattern of strong charges corresponding to dark areas, and weak charges corresponding to lighter areas.

Only a scramble would result if the entire electric pattern were transmitted simultaneously. Therefore, before it is dispatched, the pattern is systematically divided by scanning it with a pinpoint beam of electrons from an "electron gun" at the rear of the tube. The beam is moved back and forth across each of 525 lines on the target 30 times a second. Areas with a strong positive charge absorb many electrons. Those with weak positive charges reflect many electrons. The picture consequently is changed to a fluctuating electric current which is used to modulate the carrier wave sent out by the station.

The carrier waves induce a current in the antenna of your television set. This current is amplified and it finally enters the picture tube of the set where it controls the flow of electrons from an electron gun. As the electron beam sweeps back and forth across the screen of the picture tube, it causes a fluorescent substance on the screen to glow. The intensity of light depends upon the number of electrons which strike a given point. The screen's 525 lines are scanned so quickly that the entire picture seems to be illuminated at once. The image seems to move because the picture changes thirty times each second, just as a series of still pictures projected in rapid succession on a screen gives the impression of motion.

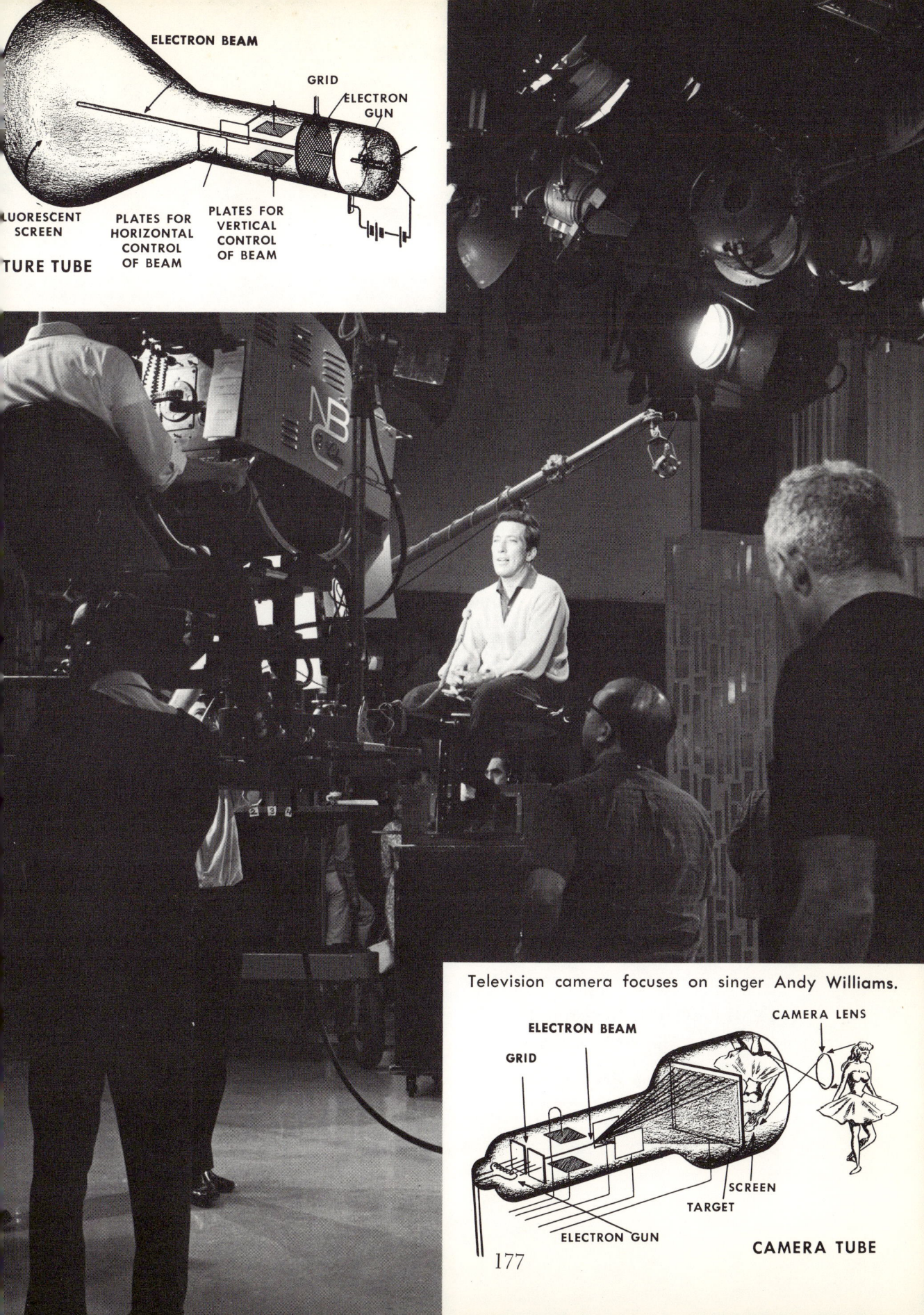

Television camera focuses on singer Andy Williams.

REFRIGERATION

Temperature is made to order by your refrigerator, freezer, and room air-conditioner. The same fundamental principles underlie the operation of each of these devices. An evaporating liquid absorbs heat from its surroundings (see page 38), and heat may be transferred from one body or place to another. The working parts of the three devices also are similar.

In an electric refrigerator, a compressor driven by a small motor subjects a gaseous refrigerant, sulfur dioxide (SO_2), freon (CCl_2F_2) or methyl chloride (CH_3Cl), to high pressure. The compressed refrigerant then passes into thin metal condenser coils where, after losing heat to the surrounding air, it liquefies. These coils are usually mounted on the back of refrigerators and freezers. They are the outermost element in a window-type air-conditioner.

The liquid refrigerant next flows into evaporator coils. These surround the freezing compartment of your refrigerator, and are built into the shelves of a freezer. In an air-conditioner they are covered by vanes and placed just behind the grill. In these coils, the pressure is reduced and the refrigerant is allowed to expand into a gas. As this change occurs, the refrigerant absorbs heat from the coils. In turn, the coils absorb heat from the air around them. The cooled air, which is more dense than the warmer air around it, settles to the lower portion of the box. The food in the refrigerator or freezer is chilled when it loses heat to the air or directly to the metal coils. In the air-conditioner, air is chilled when it is blown across the coils by a fan. The refrigerant passes from the evaporator coils back to the compressor where it begins its journey again.

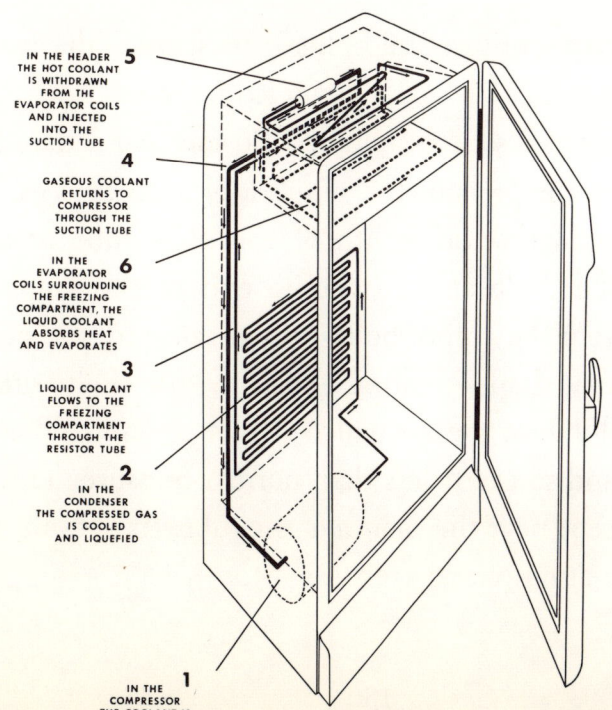

REFRIGERATION DIAGRAM WITH EXPLANATION OF PHYSICAL CHANGES EMPLOYED IN COOLING.

PUTTING AIR PRESSURE TO WORK

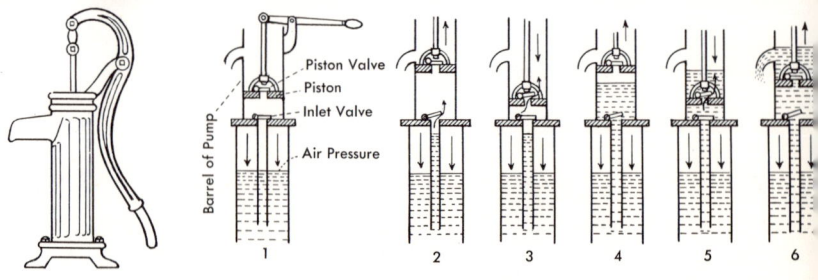

A LIFT PUMP PRODUCES UNBALANCED AIR PRESSURE

A NUMBER OF DEVICES utilize atmospheric pressure — the weight of the air resting upon the earth's surface — to do work. At sea level this pressure is about 14.7 pounds per square inch or 1.06 tons per square foot.

A medicine dropper is perhaps the simplest of such devices. To operate the dropper, you submerge the mouth of the glass tube in a liquid. A squeeze on the rubber bulb at the opposite end of the dropper forces a portion of the air from the empty bulb. When released, the bulb tends to flex back to its original shape, creating a space within itself with a capacity greater than the volume of the air which it still contains. This air, therefore, must expand and so exerts less than normal pressure. The liquid is at normal pressure except near the mouth of the tube. As a result, it is pushed up into the tube by atmospheric pressure.

Fountain pens and rubber syringes operate in the same way. When you use a drinking straw, your mouth takes the place of the rubber bulb of the dropper. A vacuum cleaner utilizes a motor-driven fan to produce a partial vacuum at the sweeper intake. Air pressure pushes air and dust into the machine and the fan forces it out into the dust bag. Air can pass through the bag, but the dirt is filtered out and kept inside the bag.

Hand-operated water pumps, once a common household fixture, are still found in some rural areas. These pumps are more complicated than a medicine dropper, but they operate on the same principle. The workings of a standard pump are shown in the diagram. As the handle is pushed down, the piston inside the pump rises, creating a partial vacuum below it. The water in the ground is subjected to normal atmospheric pressure, except at the well pipe. Therefore, the water is pushed up into the pipe and through the inlet valve of the pump. Clearly, such a pump cannot raise water higher than atmospheric pressure can push water up into a tube with a perfect vacuum — about 34 feet.

When the pump handle is raised, the piston moves downward, forcing the inlet valve to close and pushing the water trapped in the pump cylinder up through the piston valve. On the next upward stroke of the piston, the water rises and spills out through the pump spout.

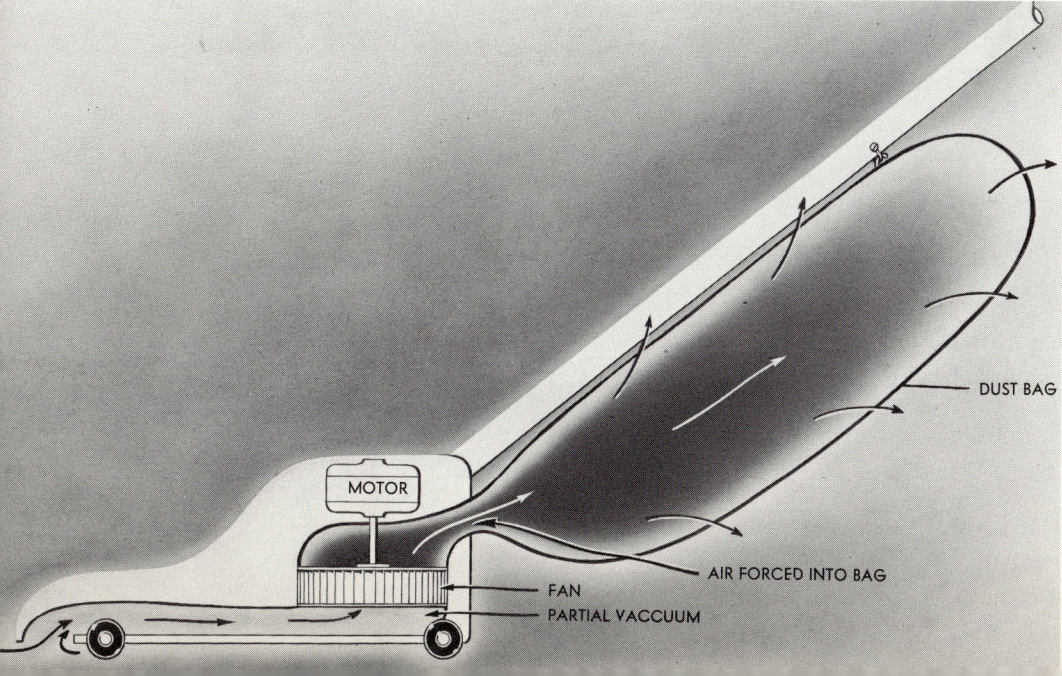

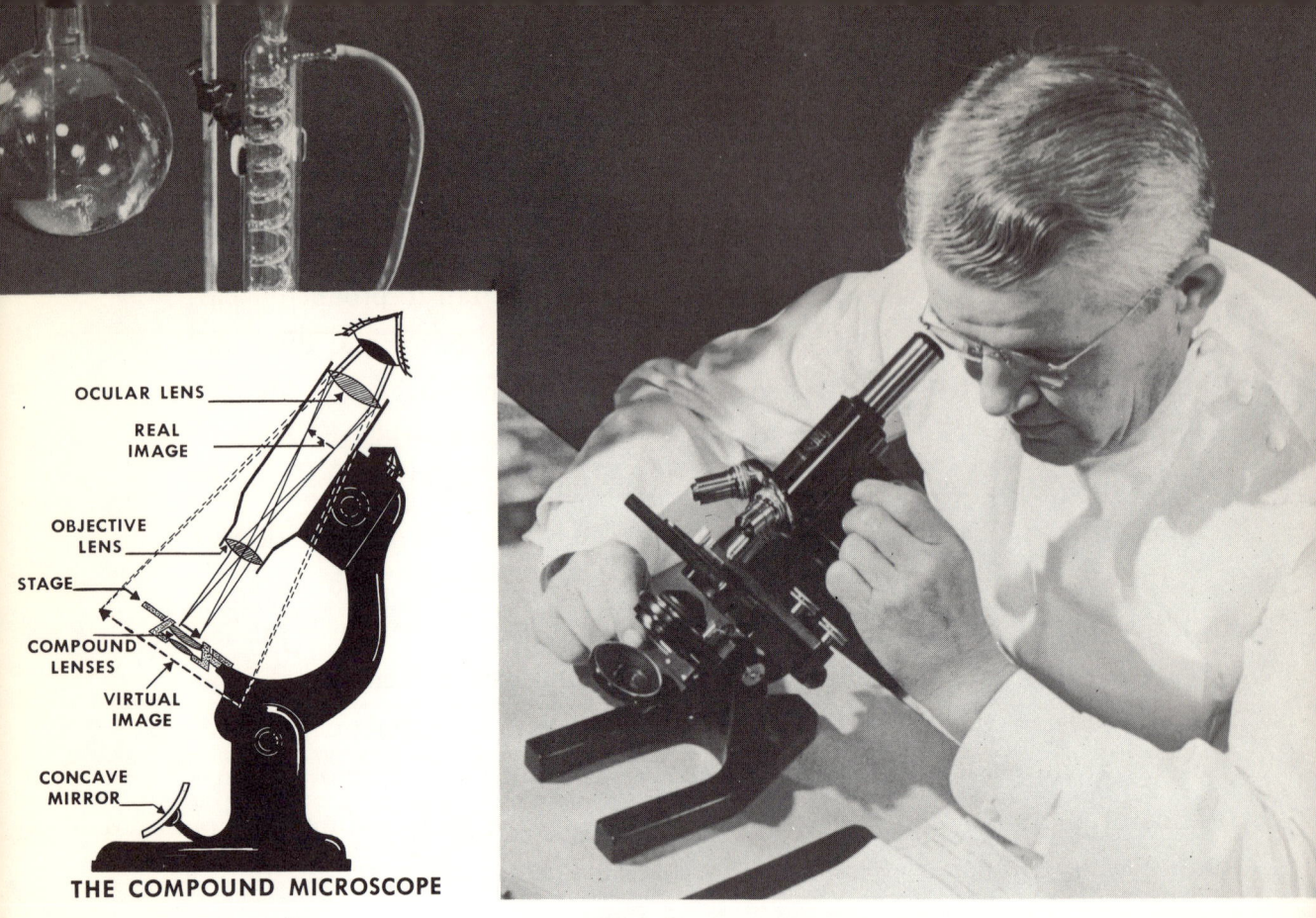

THE COMPOUND MICROSCOPE

MICROSCOPES AND TELESCOPES

LENSES HAVE EXTENDED man's vision into the infinitesimally small world of the microbe, as well as to the infinitely large world of outer space. The microscope is the tool which has allowed scientists to probe the realm of the minute. The telescope has allowed them to investigate the mysteries of the distant.

A microscope contains at least two converging lenses (see page 170). The lens nearest the object to be viewed is the *objective lens*. It has a very short focal length. The other lens, into which you look, is called the *ocular lens* or *eyepiece*. It is a lens of intermediate focal length.

When an object is placed beneath the objective lens, an inverted real image, larger than the object, is formed inside the microscope. The ocular lens then forms an enlarged, virtual image of the real image. This virtual image seems to be outside and below the microscope, and is still inverted with respect to the object. Finally, the eye of the viewer transforms the virtual image to a real image on the retina.

The simple sky telescope, like the microscope, contains two converging lenses. In the telescope, however, the objective is a lens of long focal length, while the ocular lens has a short focal length. The two lenses are separated by distance slightly less than their combined focal lengths. At this distance the inverted, real image of the distant object is formed by the objective lens inside of the focal point of the ocular lens. The ocular lens then produces an enlarged virtual image of the object, still inverted.

Even though an inverted image does not distract one gazing at a star, it would be very confusing to a person observing the movement of a ship or other object here on earth. Spyglasses, or terrestrial telescopes, therefore employ a third lens between the objective and the ocular lenses to re-invert the real image before it is enlarged by the eyepiece. Terrestrial telescopes are extensively used by land surveyors, military men, seamen, and others.

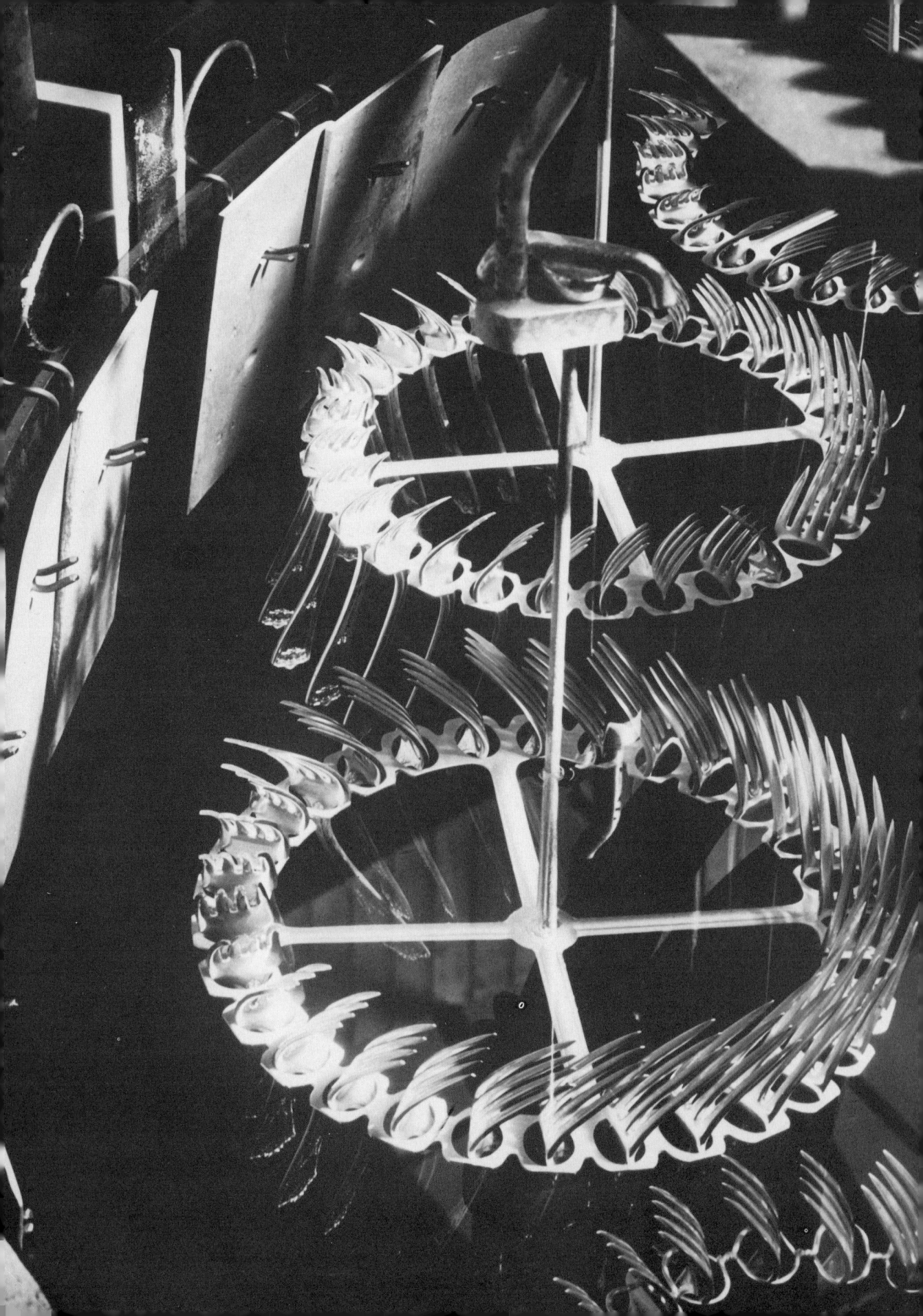

ELECTROLYSIS

AND

ELECTROPLATING

THESE BRASS FORKS are being coated with a thin plate of silver which will protect and beautify them. Many other items, such as pieces of jewelry, automobile bumpers, and electrical appliances may also be plated with silver, chromium, or some other metal. This plating is deposited from a liquid solution by an electric current.

Only solutions which contain positively and negatively-charged ions (see page 66) will conduct electricity. Such solutions, usually water solutions of an acid, base or salt, are called *electrolytes*. The passage of an electric current through an electrolyte is accompanied by a series of chemical reactions collectively known as *electrolysis*.

The electrolyte used in plating is a solution of a salt of the plate metal. In silver plating, for example, it is a solution of potassium argentous cyanide ($KAg(CN)_2$) which dissociates into potassium, silver, and cyanide ions. Thin blocks of silver, which are submerged in the solution, are connected to a battery or other source of direct-current electricity and become positive electrodes (anodes). The pieces to be plated are connected to the negative pole of the battery and become negative electrodes (cathodes). The entire unit—solution, container, and electrodes—is called an *electrolytic cell*.

Electricity enters the cell through the silver blocks and passes out through the forks. Positively-charged potassium and silver ions migrate to the forks (negative electrodes) where the silver ions are neutralized and the metal is deposited in a thin, even coating. The potassium, due to its greater resistance to de-ionization, remains in solution.

CHAPTER VII

CHEMISTRY

IN EVERYDAY LIFE

The alchemists of medieval times attempted to combine substances, but they did not have a basic understanding of the reactions which occurred. They sought to create potions that would prolong life, or to transform common metals to precious gold and silver. They worked in scientific darkness and failed to comprehend the fundamental laws of chemistry.

Modern chemists bear slight resemblance to the alchemists of old. Modern chemists work in well-ordered laboratories, stocked with purified chemicals, and provided with many forms of complicated equipment.

In these pages are some of the modern miracles they have accomplished, illustrations from the vast industries built on their discoveries — iron, steel, aluminum, petroleum, plastics. Even now, the findings of some unknown scientist may be destined to give rise to tomorrow's greatest industry or most powerful medicine.

THE CHEMISTRY OF IRON AND STEEL

Each year over 100 millions tons of iron and steel are used by American industries. These metals are manufactured into home appliances, automobiles, food containers, ships, and trains, and are used in the construction of bridges, buildings, and reinforced highways.

Hematite (Fe_2O_3) and limonite ($2Fe_2O_3 \cdot 3H_2O$) are the most important sources of iron. Our supply of these ores is obtained chiefly from the Mesabi Range in Minnesota. After excavation, the ore is shipped to steel-producing centers, such as Chicago, Cleveland, Detroit, and Pittsburgh.

At the steel mill, the ore is mixed with coke and limestone ($CaCO_3$), and fed into tall blast furnaces like those shown in the photograph below. As

the mixture settles through the furnace, at least 20 chemical reactions occur at various temperatures. The most important are the several reduction reactions by which carbon (coke) separates oxygen from the iron. For every ton of pig iron, the furnace also produces 2,050 pounds of slag ($CaSiO_3$) and 160,000 cubic feet of gas (CO, CO_2, N_2). The gas is used in the four stoves next to each furnace to preheat air for the furnace.

Pig iron contains from six to eight percent of impurities. It may be used directly for cast iron and wrought iron, or it may be further purified and used for steel.

Most American steel is produced by the open-hearth process. This steel is of great purity and is used to make machinery, girders, rails, armament, and other products. The hearth, which is about the size of a private swimming pool, is contained within a large furnace, like the one shown in the photograph above. A charge, consisting of about 100 tons of scrap iron, limestone, iron ore, and molten pig iron is heated in the hearth for about 10 hours. During this time, impurities are removed by various chemical reactions. Exact amounts of carbon and other elements are added to the molten iron to produce steel of the quality and properties desired.

THE CHEMISTRY

Aluminum products are all around you: in airplanes, trucks, trains, toothpaste tubes, metal foil, and many other things. But a century ago, aluminum was so precious that Emperor Napoleon III of France set aluminum utensils only before his most honored guests. The fantastic change in aluminum prices was brought about by the development, in 1886, of the relatively inexpensive Hall process for refining the metal from its ores.

Aluminum occurs in compounds with other elements, primarily oxygen. Bauxite, the most important ore, contains about 60 percent alumina (Al_2O_3), 30 percent water and 10 percent silicon dioxide (SiO_2).

The Hall process requires pure alumina. Purification is accomplished by crushing the bauxite ore with pneumatic drills (shown, right) and heating the finely divided bauxite in a solution of sodium hydroxide (NaOH). After a series of reactions, the impurities settle out, leaving aluminum hydroxide ($Al(OH)_3$) as a residue. The aluminum hydroxide is then heated to change it to alumina, a white powder which resembles granulated sugar.

The alumina is dissolved in molten cryolite (Na_3AlF_6). The solution is made in a large steel tank like the one shown, left. A strong current of electricity is fed into large carbon blocks suspended in the solution. The current passes through the solution to the carbon lining of the tank, making the tank an electrolytic cell. The electricity decomposes the alumina to aluminum and oxygen ions. Aluminum settles to the bottom of the tank. The oxygen migrates to the carbon blocks, where it combines with carbon to form carbon dioxide gas.

Molten pig aluminum is cast into molds. Later, the pig metal is remelted and the remaining impurities are skimmed off. If the aluminum is to be alloyed to modify its characteristics, other elements are added to it during the remelting step. Finally, the aluminum may be made into tubes, ingots, or thin sheets rolled on spools, such as those shown in the picture below.

OF ALUMINUM

THE CHEMISTRY OF PETROLEUM

Petroleum, the "black gold" that gushes from oil wells throughout the world, is a mixture of hydrocarbons (compounds of carbon and hydrogen). From the oil field the petroleum is transported to the refinery, where impurities are removed by a series of chemical treatments and the various hydrocarbons are separated by physical processes.

Closely related hydrocarbons, called petroleum fractions, have very similar boiling points. This characteristic is used to separate the hydrocarbons by a process called fractional distillation. After petroleum has been heated to about 300° C. (572° F.), it is pumped into a 100-foot-tall fractioning tower, seen at the left of the photograph. Heavy oils, which do not boil at this temperature, flow immediately to the bottom of the tower. They may contain lubricating oils, paraffin or asphalt, depending upon the source of the petroleum. The remaining hydrocarbons, all vaporized, gradually cool as they rise through the tower. Gasoline liquefies first; then kerosene liquefies at a slightly higher temperature; then naphtha.

Each fraction is caught as it liquefies, and is led off through a complicated system of pipes to huge tanks where it is stored temporarily. The gaseous fraction which contains gasoline vapor is led off through a tube at the top of the tower. The gasoline is subsequently liquefied when the gas is cooled. The remaining portion of the fraction, a gas at normal pressure, is compressed and sold as "bottled gas" which is widely used for cooking.

Gasoline is not a single compound, but a mixture of several hydrocarbons, including hexane (C_6H_{14}), heptane (C_7H_{16}), and octane (C_8H_{18}). Due to its widespread use as a fuel for engines, gasoline is one of the most important petroleum products. Chemists, therefore, have developed methods to produce additional gasoline molecules by linking together several molecules of simpler hydrocarbons (polymerization) and by splitting up the more complex molecules of heavy oils and gas oils (cracking). The large tower in the upper right of the photograph is a cracking tower.

PLASTICS

A PLASTIC is a resinous organic compound which can be molded or cast into any shape by the application of moderate heat or pressure, or both, and which will maintain this shape after cooling. Certain natural resins, such as pitch, rosin, and shellac are considered to be plastics under this restricted definition. But the great majority of plastics — more than 5,000 kinds — are synthetic substances developed in the chemical laboratory. Some of the best known are cellulose plastics, bakelite, saran, vinylite, lucite, polystyrene, and polyethylene.

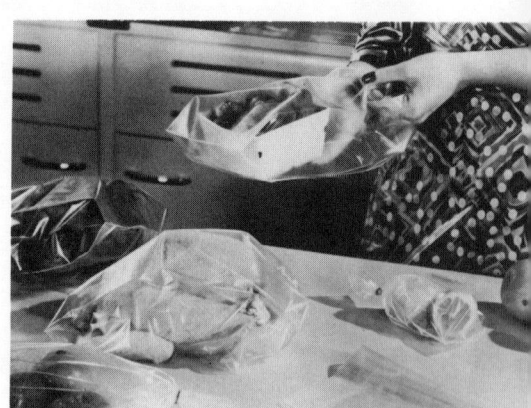

There are two general classes of plastic resins, thermosetting and thermoplastic. Thermoplastic materials can be repeatedly softened by heat and remolded to the desired shape. Thermosetting materials can be softened during the original casting, but cannot be resoftened after cooling. Chem-

ists suspect that the molecular structure of the materials is responsible for the differences in their behavior. Thermoplastic resins, such as lucite and polyethylene, are composed of long-chain molecules with few side linkages. Molecules with numerous side linkages, in the form of complex networks, are characteristic of thermosetting resins, such as bakelite.

Polyethylene is rapidly becoming the most popular plastic. You may have several squeeze-bottles made of this material in your kitchen, workshop, or medicine cabinet. The plastic is also made into transparent bags, weather balloons, toys, electrical insulation, garden hose, irrigation pipe, and a thousand other items.

Like all synthetic plastics, polyethylene is produced by *polymerization*, that is, by causing small organic molecules to join together into long chains or complex networks. In its production, molecules of ethylene gas ($H_2C = CH_2$) are linked together to form seemingly endless polyethylene chains ($..CH_2CH_2CH_2CH_2...$).

Another polymerized plastic, *Mylar*, was coated with a thin film of aluminum and used to build the Echo I satellite shown above right. The plastic skin of this 100-foot diameter balloon satellite is only 5 ten-thousandths inch thick. Deflated, the giant balloon was packed in the small nose cone, shown above left, and carried aloft by a rocket.

Glass Furnace

Annealing Lehr

GLASS

GLASS IS HARD, but it lacks a crystalline structure and does not have a definite melting point. Therefore, it is not a true solid, but an extremely viscous, or *super-cooled liquid*. And glass is not a compound, but a mixture, because its composition can be varied through a considerable range. More than 50,000 different formulas are used to produce glasses that possess greatly diverse characteristics.

Lime glass is used to make window glass, plate glass (polished window glass), bottles, light bulbs, tableware, and a host of other products. It is manufactured by heating a mixture of sodium carbonate (Na_2CO_3), calcium carbonate ($CaCO_3$), and silicon dioxide (SiO_2). Simultaneous reactions occur which produce lime glass, which is a mixture of water glass (Na_2SiO_3) and a cement ($CaSiO_3$), and release carbon dioxide gas (CO_2).

$$Na_2CO_3 \xrightarrow{\text{heat}} Na_2O + SiO_2 \longrightarrow Na_2SiO_3$$
$$CO_2 \text{ (released)}$$
$$CaCO_3 \longrightarrow CaO + SiO_2 \longrightarrow CaSiO_3$$

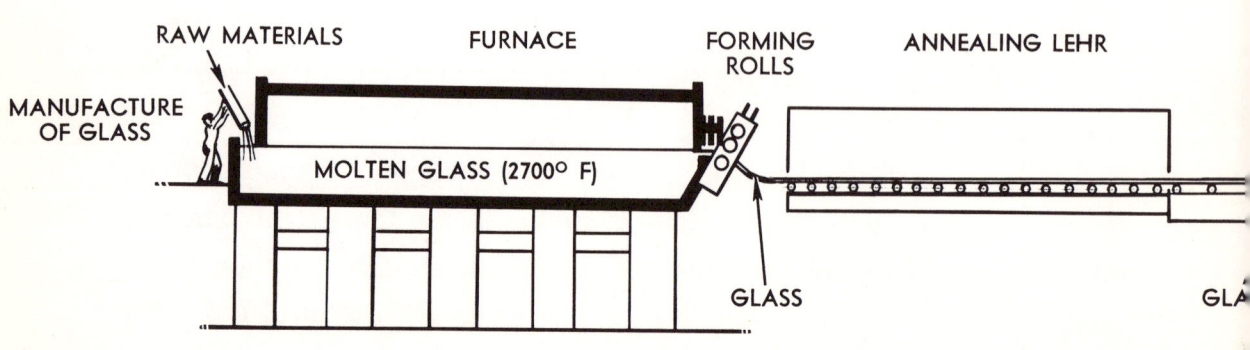

MANUFACTURE OF GLASS

MATERIALS MELTED, MIXED → GLASS COOLED SLIGHTLY, FORMED → GLASS COOLED SLOWLY MADE MORE STABLE, LESS BRITTLE, EASIER CUT

Twin Grinder — 880 feet long

Polishing Machines

Silicon dioxide and sodium carbonate are used to manufacture all kinds of glass. Other chemicals are added to give glass special properties. Lead oxide (PbO), used in place of calcium carbonate, produces lead glass, which is more difficult to melt and shape than lime glass. *Lead glass* is used for radio, radar, television, and neon tubes, and crystal glass tableware.

Boric oxide (B_2O_3) and aluminum oxide (Al_2O_3) are used in the manufacture of borosilicate glass. This glass, which is extremely resistant to chemical attack and rapid temperature change, is ideal for chemical laboratory equipment, ovenware, and many industrial uses. Optical glasses are of various compositions, including all the foregoing types. They are, however, very carefully processed and must be free from imperfections.

Glass of almost any color can be made by mixing very small amounts of various metal oxides to a normal formula for clear glass. Nickel or cobalt produces purple glass; cobalt and copper, blue; copper or chromium or both, green; iron or carbon, yellow; gold, copper or selenium, red; and tin, white.

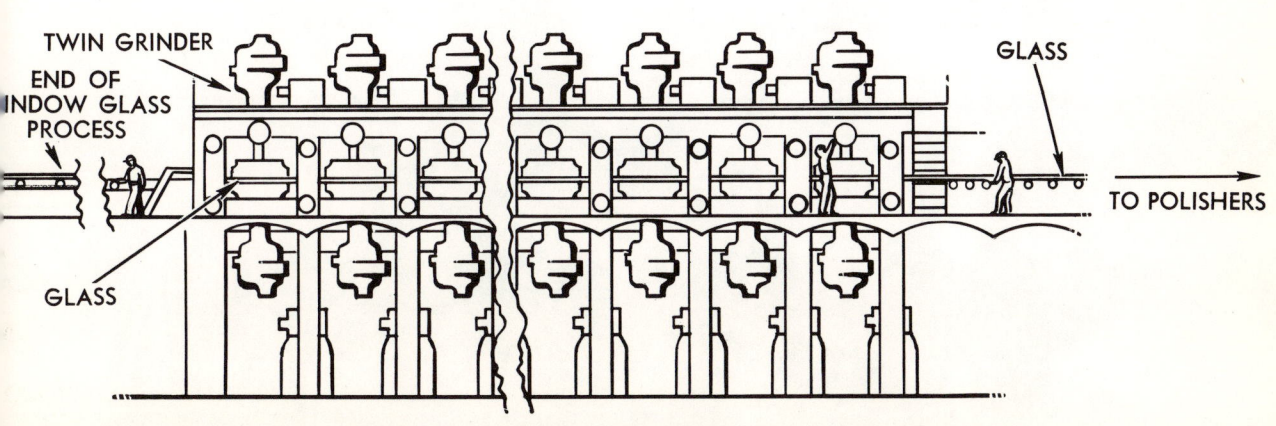

EXTINGUISHING FIRES

When you turn off your gas range you are extinguishing a fire by removing its fuel. You may have put out a camp fire by covering it with soil, thereby cutting off its oxygen. And, each time you blow out a match you are extinguishing a fire by cooling the fuel below its kindling temperature.

Water, the most familiar fire fighter, works in two ways. It blankets the fuel—shutting out oxygen—and as it changes to steam, it absorbs heat and cools the fuel.

Soda-acid Extinguisher

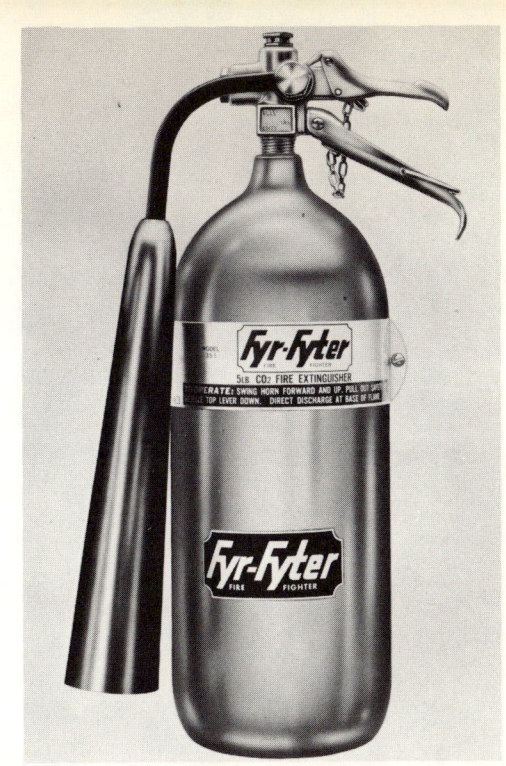

Liquid carbon dioxide Extinguisher

Soda-acid extinguishers contain a solution of baking soda ($NaHCO_3$) and water. When the extinguisher is inverted, a bottleful of sulfuric acid spills into the solution, resulting in a reaction which liberates carbon dioxide. The pressure forces carbon dioxide and water through a small hose onto the fire.

In foamite extinguishers, carbon dioxide is generated by a reaction between alum ($Al_2(SO_4)_3$) and soda. As the pressure increases, the gas mixes with aluminum hydroxide ($Al(OH)_3$), a gelatinous substance also produced by the reaction, forming a foam. When sprayed over a fire, the foam, stabilized by the addition of a licorice extract, shuts out the oxygen.

Liquid carbon dioxide under high pressure is used in another kind of extinguisher. When released, part of the carbon dioxide expands into a gas, thereby cooling the other portion into solid, snow-like flakes. The expanding gas blows the snow over the fire. As it melts, the snow absorbs heat, cooling the fuel, and forms carbon dioxide gas which smothers the fire.

Pyrene extinguishers, the smallest in common use, contain pyrene or carbon tetrachloride (CCl_4). When the liquid is pumped onto a fire it boils readily, forming a heavy, non-inflammable gas that shuts off the supply of oxygen to the fuel and cools the area as it evaporates.

Each kettle produces enough soap for 629,500 bars.

SOAPS AND DETERGENTS

Soap is a champion dirt chaser. It lowers the surface tension of water, thereby allowing the water to soak into the materials more readily. It greatly increases the power of water to dissolve oil and grease. It lubricates dirt particles, facilitating their removal by water. And soap acts as an emulsifier, causing substances to mix so thoroughly with water that they do not settle rapidly.

In pioneer America, soap-making was a kitchen chore. Wood ashes were soaked to secure lye (NaOH). When waste cooking fats ($C_3H_5(C_{17}H_{35}COO)_3$) were mixed with the lye, a slow chemical reaction took place which produced soap ($C_{17}H_{35}COONa$) and glycerine ($C_3H_5(OH)_3$).

The chemistry of soap production is virtually the same today. The small bucket on the kitchen stove, however, has given way to huge kettles which stretch up through two or three stories of a modern factory.

Soap is made by running a dilute solution of lye into a kettle filled with melted animal greases, tallow, or vegetable oils. The mixture is heated and stirred by steam which continually bubbles through it. When the reaction is complete, in perhaps four or five days, several tons of table salt are shoveled into the kettles. Glycerine and other impurities dissolve in the brine, but the soap floats on the salty solution as a "curd." By purification, the curd is transformed to "neat." If a fine toilet soap is to be made, perfume is added to the neat.

After receiving any additives, the soap is stored in large steel boxes until it hardens. The huge soap blocks are then cut into small bars which eventually reach your grocer's shelves. Soap is also sold in the form of powders, flakes, creams, pastes, jellies, liquids, and chips.

During World War II, a large proportion of the inedible fats and oils which had been used to make soap was used instead to produce explosives. Soap manufacturers experimented with other cleaning compounds and developed synthetic detergents from petroleum by-products. The commercial manufacture of these detergents began on a small scale about 1944 and by 1960, the annual production of detergents had risen to more than a million tons per year.

Detergents, unlike soaps, do not form insoluble curds, or "bathtub rings." These curds are produced by the interaction of soaps and water impurities, such as calcium and magnesium. In addition, many soaps develop insoluble precipitates in acid water, whereas detergents do not. By varying the formula of the detergent, other valuable characteristics can be added, such as special fabric-softening and germicidal properties.

900 pound slab is cut into regular bar size by piano wires.

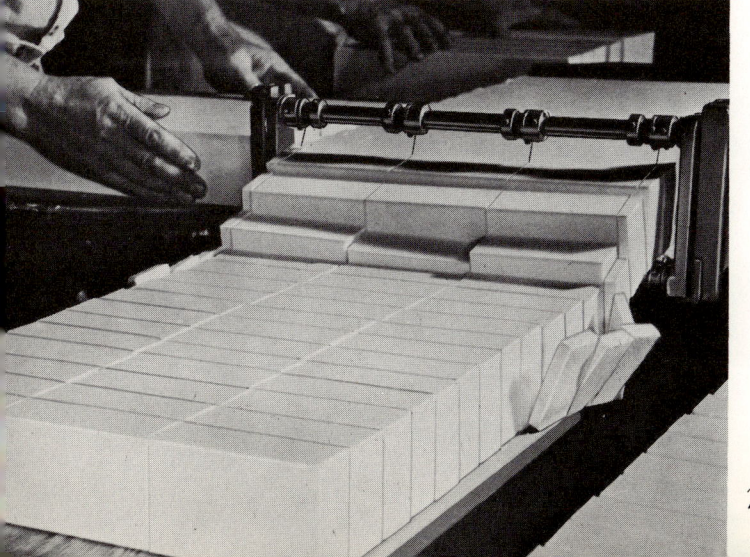

Detergent display at modern store.

PAINT

Indians and other primitive people used plant juices and other natural substances for decorating themselves and their homes. Today, however, chemistry gives us an artificial rainbow of thousands of colors of paints to beautify and protect our homes, our automobiles, and a vast number of other things. Most of these paints contain three principal ingredients: pigments, binders, and thinners.

Pigments are finely-powdered solids used to impart color to the paint and to hide the surface. White lead $(2PbCO_3 \cdot Pb(OH)_2)$ is the most common paint pigment. It is inexpensive and covers well. However, it has two important disadvantages. It often makes painters ill, and it becomes gray when exposed to sulfur compounds which are often present in the air in industrialized areas. Zinc oxide, another pigment, is added to prevent this discoloration.

Shellacs and varnishes are pigment-free paints which afford protection without hiding the surface.

Freshly painted cars move past banks of infra-red lamps in huge drying oven.

River of paint flowing from a roller mill.

Manufacturing of paint.

Binders serve to carry the pigment and to cause it to adhere to the surface being painted. Linseed oil, obtained from flax seed, is the most commonly used binder. "Plastic" paints employ as a binder a synthetic resin, such as bakelite or nylon. These binders dry, not by evaporation, but by combining with atmospheric oxygen. The oxidation reaction produces a hard, glossy film over the painted surface. Lacquers are paints which employ highly volatile organic solvents as binders. These paints, which are primarily used on automobiles, dry rapidly by evaporation.

Thinners are used to dilute the binder so that the paint can be spread easily. Once its task has been performed, the thinner evaporates, leaving only pigment and binder on the painted surface. Turpentine is the thinner most often used in paints. Water-soluble paints employ glue as a binder and water as a thinner. Evaporation of the water leaves the pigment suspended in a film of dried glue.

CHEMISTRY ON THE FARM

John Burkholder is typical of thousands of modern farmers who use chemicals to increase the amount of food grown on their land. On his 80-acre farm in Pennsylvania, Mr. Burkholder grows corn, hay, wheat, potatoes, and tobacco. He also raises cattle and chickens. In the course of an average year, he uses this huge mound of chemicals to fertilize or improve the soil on his farm, to supplement animal feeds, to prevent or correct plant and animal diseases, and to kill insect pests.

Fertilizers, the most important farm chemicals, are primarily used to replace elements removed from the soil by harvested crops. A tobacco crop, for example, requires approximately 166 pounds of potassium, 76 pounds of nitrogen, and 7 pounds of phosphorus from each acre. Commercial fertilizers contain these three elements in varying proportions. The choice of the fertilizer to be used on a field depends upon the requirements of the crop to be raised, and upon the condition of the soil, as revealed by chemical analyses.

About 7,000 kinds of insects are known to attack crop plants in the United States. These pests cause losses calculated in billions of dollars each year.

Chemicals used to combat insects are of three sorts: *Stomach poisons*, such as arsenic compounds ($Ca_3(AsO_4)_2$), must be eaten to be effective. *Contact poisons*, such as pyrethrin ($C_{22}H_{30}O_5$) and nicotine ($C_{10}H_{14}N_2$), kill after they fall upon an insect's body. *Fumigants* kill after being taken into the respiratory system. Fumigants must be gases [hydrocyanic acid (HCN)], highly volatile liquids [carbon disulfide (CS_2)], or solids which sublime or change directly to the gaseous state [paradichlorobenzene ($C_6H_4Cl_2$)]. Rotenone ($C_{23}H_{22}O_6$) and dichloro-diphenyl-trichloro-ethane, better known as D.D.T. ($C_{14}H_9Cl_5$), act as both stomach and contact poisons.

PHOTOGRAPHY

The film in your camera is a long, thin strip of cellulose acetate, a transparent plastic coated with a cream-colored suspension of silver bromide (AgBr) in gelatin. When you snap the camera's shutter, light strikes the film for a split second. Due to a reaction not yet completely understood, silver bromide is more easily reduced after it has been exposed to light.

When the film is developed, an alkaline solution reacts with the light-struck silver bromide to form metallic silver and a soluble compound of bromine. The blackish deposits of silver form a "pictorial memory" of the scene you photographed. In this picture, shown on the left below, the bright objects of the original scene appear dark, and the dark objects appear light. Because of this reversal of tones, the picture is called a *negative*.

Comedian Woody Allen takes no chances with his snapshots.

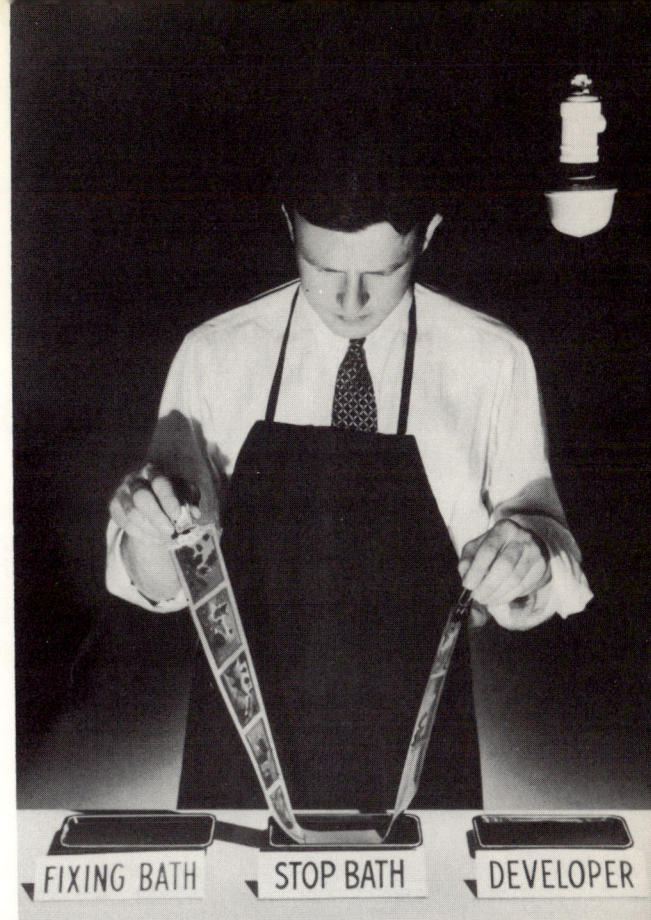

FIXING BATH   STOP BATH   DEVELOPER

The action of the developer is halted by the stop bath. However, the lighter portions of the negative still contain unreduced silver bromine. To remove it, the film is placed in the fixing bath, which is an acid solution of sodium thiosulfate ($NaHS_2O_3$). The fixer reacts with the silver bromide to produce compounds which are later washed away, leaving portions of the negative transparent.

To make a photograph, the negative is laid on a sheet of paper sensitized with a silver bromide suspension. When light is flashed on the negative, the paper beneath the transparent parts is illuminated, and that beneath the dark parts is shaded. In the developer, the silver bromine that was struck by light is reduced to metallic silver, creating the dark areas of the finished photograph. Thus, the photograph shown at the right on the opposite page is a negative of the negative, or a *positive*. The dark areas of the original scene are reproduced as tones of black, and the light areas look white because the paper shows through its gelatin coating. After development, the positive is fixed, washed, and dried.

TOMORROW'S WORLD: POWER FROM THE ATOM

MANY OF US JUDGE the progress of science by the effects that scientific discoveries have on our own lives. Often, the application of basic research findings lags behind discovery by many decades or even centuries. A notable exception was the discovery of a means to "split the atom." In just six years, this discovery evolved from a laboratory curiosity to a bomb that killed thousands of people, brought World War II to an abrupt end, and changed the future of the earth. Fortunately, most nations have realized that the tremendous force unleashed from the atom must be used wisely and for peaceful purposes rather than thoughtlessly and for war. Today

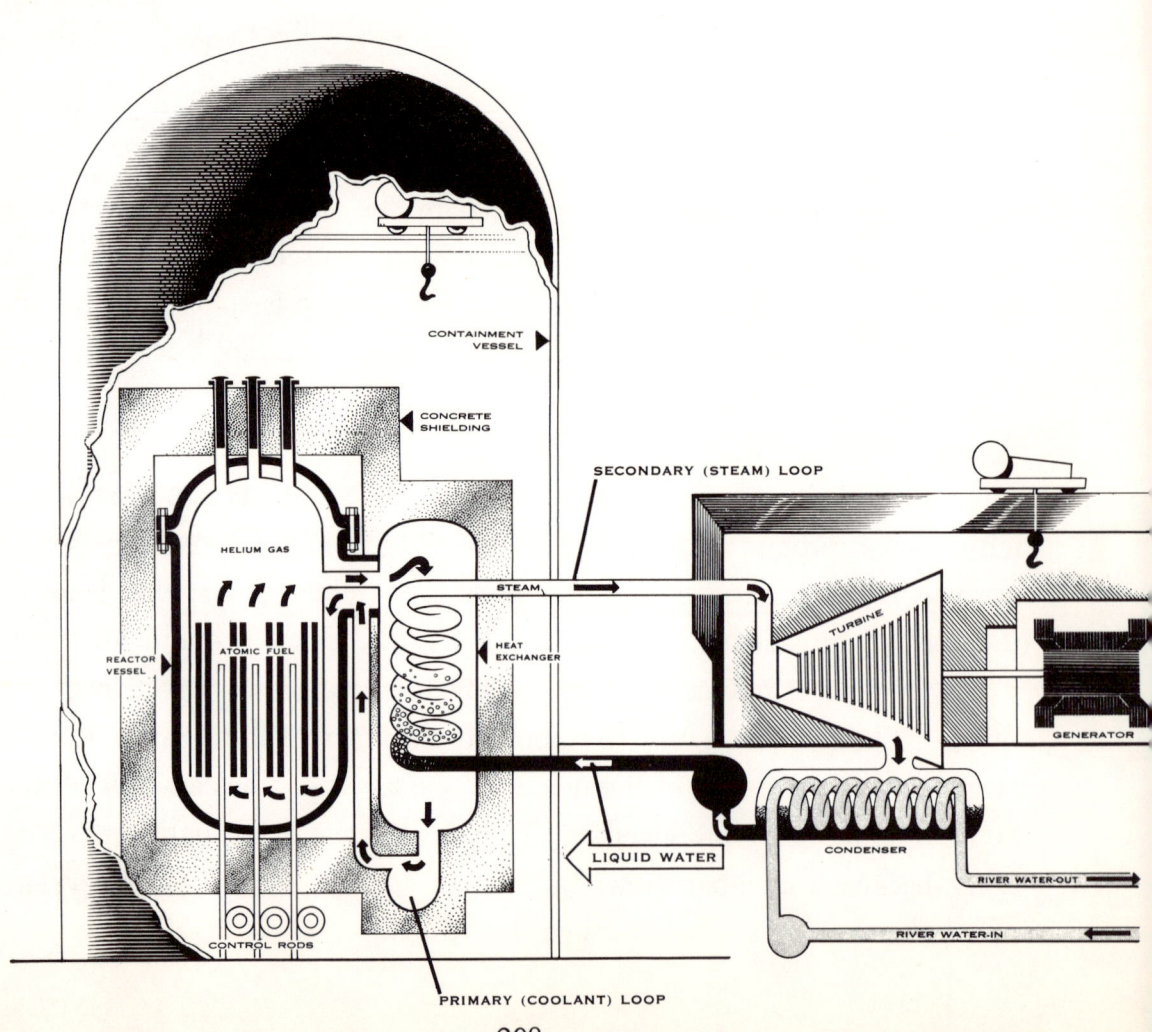

we are on the brink of the greatest breakthrough of all times in the application of scientific knowledge to everyday life.

Our buildings now are heated by a chemical reaction known as oxidation, or burning. This kind of reaction also powers our automobiles, airplanes, trains, rockets, and drives giant generators which produce most of the electricity that powers still other machines, and lights our homes, streets, offices, and factories. But oxidation releases only a tiny fraction of the energy present in matter.

For years, physicists have been trying to utilize more of the potential energy of matter. Finally, in 1939 — a moment ago in the history of man — two German scientists, Otto Hahn and Fritz Strassman, announced they had learned to split atoms, or to initiate *nuclear fission*. By this process we can obtain many millions of times the amount of energy released by a chemical reaction! Three years later, on 2 December 1942, at the University of Chicago, a group of scientists led by Enrico Fermi set in operation the first nuclear reactor. This opened the exciting era of atomic energy development.

Here is an introduction to the field of nuclear energy. Although the subject is complex, it is based on a few, easily-grasped principles. Many of the problems of nuclear physics still are not solved. But we do know that the power of the atom can be harnessed for the benefit of mankind.

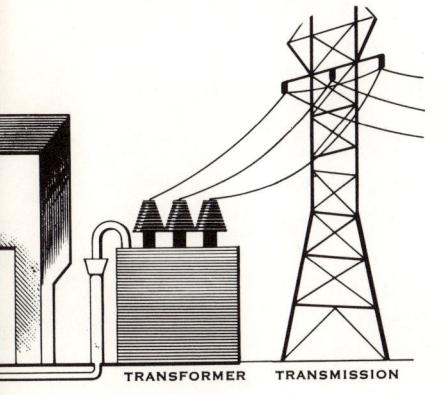

PEACH BOTTOM ATOMIC POWER STATION
on the Susquehanna River, Pennsylvania

The heart of this station is a high-temperature, gas-cooled reactor. As helium gas circulates through the reactor, it absorbs heat. In the exchanger, the heat is transferred to water, which changes to steam. The steam drives a turbine connected to the generator which produces electricity.

At Peach Bottom, as at most nuclear power stations, there is an information center with displays and lectures to explain the plant and its reactor. Visit the reactor nearest your home.

NUCLEAR FISSON, NUCLEAR FUSION

THE MASS OF THE NUCLEUS of an atom (except common hydrogen) is less than the total of the masses of its protons and neutrons. It is almost as if one were to add 5 to 5 and get an answer of 9. What happens to the missing atomic mass? In advanced physics, mass and energy are known to be different forms of the same thing — one can change into the other. Thus, the mass lost during the formation of an atomic nucleus changes to energy and this energy escapes from the atom. The quantity of energy lost is called the *binding energy* of the nucleus and equals the powerful force which holds protons and neutrons together in a nucleus.

The nature of binding energy is unknown. It is not electrical. Protons have positive electrical charges and repel one another. Neutrons have no charge and neither repel nor attract other particles. However, neutrons and protons are held tightly together in a nucleus, so the binding energy must be stronger than electrical forces which would cause the protons to fly apart. Actually, it is more than 40 times as strong.

Careful studies have shown that the binding energy per *nucleon* (page 13) increases as the atomic mass approaches 80, then decreases. Apparently, nuclear binding energy acts over a distance about equal to the diameter of a nucleon. The binding force is greater when a nucleon is attracted by several other particles in a large nucleus than when it is attracted by only one or two other particles in a small nucleus. When the nucleus becomes too large, nuclear forces between more distant nucleons are less than the electrical forces which cause protons to repel one another. Nucleons in elements with atomic masses greater than 208, and those in many isotopes with smaller masses, are bound so loosely that they are unstable and literally fall apart. As the nuclei of these atoms emit protons, neutrons, electrons, and radiant energy they change to other, more stable elements.

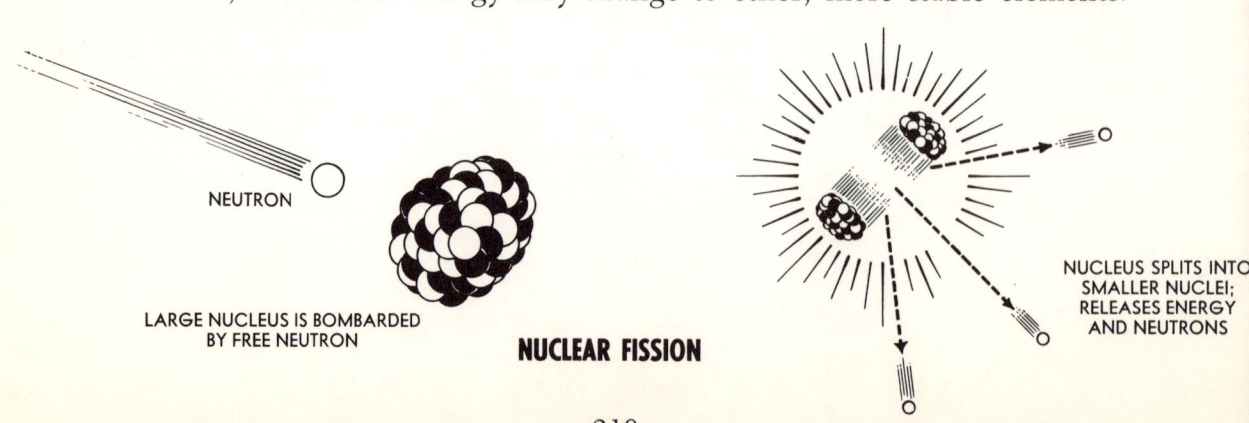

NEUTRON

LARGE NUCLEUS IS BOMBARDED BY FREE NEUTRON

NUCLEAR FISSION

NUCLEUS SPLITS INTO SMALLER NUCLEI; RELEASES ENERGY AND NEUTRONS

AND NUCLEAR REACTORS

This information was treated as a scientific curiosity until we realized that great amounts of energy could be obtained if we could "split atoms" or make them fuse. Now we have developed both methods which release some of the binding energy of the nucleus.

Nuclear fission is a process by which a heavy nucleus is penetrated by a free neutron which causes it to split, or *fission*, into two parts. The two smaller nuclei have a greater total binding energy and, thus, a smaller total mass (about one tenth of one percent less) than the heavy nucleus. The lost mass changes to energy, which escapes from the nucleus. Two or three neutrons also are released by each fission event.

Nuclear fusion occurs when two light nuclei combine, or *fuse*, and form one nucleus of greater mass. The larger nucleus has a stronger binding energy and a mass about one half of one percent less than the total mass of the two small nuclei. Thus, a fusion reaction releases several times as much energy as a fission reaction.

Nuclear fission is used many ways, but nuclear fusion reactions cannot be controlled well enough to be of practical use. An uncontrolled fusion process is used in hydrogen bombs. Each nucleus bears a positive electrical charge and repels other nuclei at ordinary temperatures. However, when heated to a high temperature, nuclei no longer repel one another and are able to fuse. Because they require temperatures of several million degrees Fahrenheit, fusion reactions also are called *thermonuclear* reactions. (*Therme* is Greek for heat.) Although these temperatures are extreme, the energy of the fusioning material is too little to damage a containing vessel. However, particles of a fusioning material move in all directions at several thousand miles per second. All particles would collide with the walls of a container in less than a millionth of a second and lose their kinetic energy

2 DEUTERIUM (H^2)
NUCLEI COLLIDE

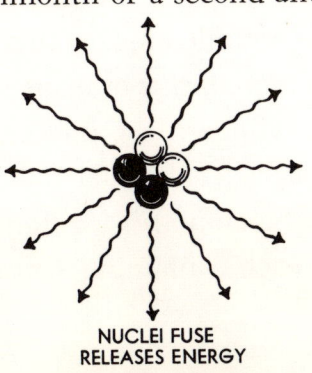

NUCLEI FUSE
RELEASES ENERGY

NUCLEAR FUSION

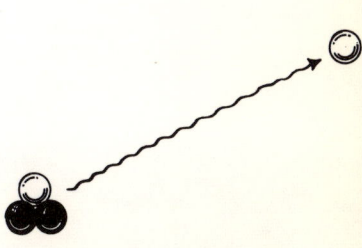

FORMS HELIUM (He^3) NUCLEUS
AND RELEASES NEUTRON

— that is, the material would cool so rapidly that little fusion would occur. Research is in progress to develop a method to hold fusion materials inside magnetic fields, rather than material containers, to avoid this cooling.

Neutrons freed by a fission event are important. Other fissionable nuclei may be penetrated by the neutrons and new fissions may occur. These will release other neutrons which may trigger still more fissions. If less than one neutron per fission event strikes another nucleus and causes it to fission, there will be fewer and fewer fission events in each *generation,* or series of fissions. Finally, the reaction will stop. In this case, the amount of fissionable material present is said to be *sub-critical* and the reaction is not *self-sustaining* (Diagram, #1). When enough material is present so that at least one neutron from each fission strikes another nucleus and causes a new fission, the reaction is *self-sustaining* — it continues without an outside source of neutrons — and is called a *chain reaction* (Diagram, #2). The amount of fissionable material needed to support a chain reaction is known as the *critical mass.* For pure uranium the critical mass is only a few pounds. If an average of more than one neutron released by each fission produces new fission events, the number of events in each new generation increases rapidly and the reaction may become explosive. Enormous amounts of energy may be released in an instant (Diagram, #3). An intentional explosive chain reaction occurs when an atom bomb is triggered.

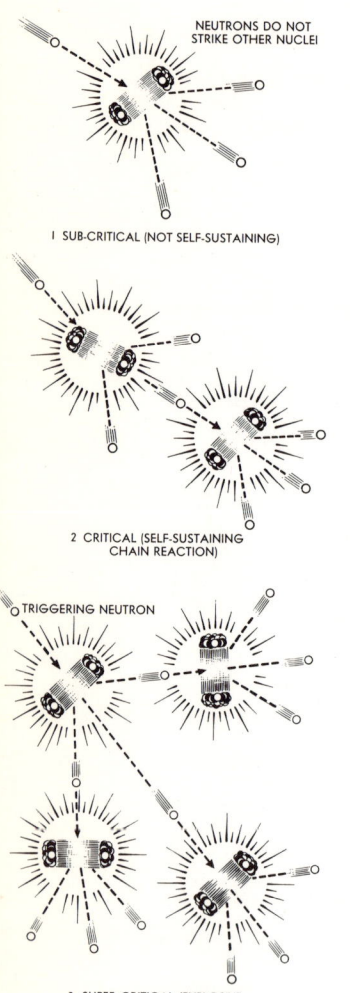

1 SUB-CRITICAL (NOT SELF-SUSTAINING)

2 CRITICAL (SELF-SUSTAINING CHAIN REACTION)

3 SUPER CRITICAL (EXPLOSIVE CHAIN REACTION)

A *nuclear reactor* is a furnace in which heat energy is produced by a controlled fission chain reaction. The heart, or *core,* of most reactors consists of many stainless steel, zirconium alloy, or graphite cylinders, the *fuel rods,* which are packed with fissionable material. The fuel rods are bundled into *fuel assemblies.* In the San Onofre (California) reactor, there are 157 fuel assemblies, each containing 180 rods — a total of 28,260 rods.

Laid end to end, these rods would extend 55 miles. The fuel weighs 72 tons, will last about 3½ years, and will produce as much heat as 3 million tons of coal.

Various fuels are used in reactors, but uranium dioxide (UO_2) and thorium dioxide (ThO_2) are most common. Thorium does not fission, but when penetrated by neutrons it changes to uranium-233 which is fissionable. Thorium and uranium-238 which form fissionable material when exposed to neutron bombardment are called *fertile materials*. The addition of fertile materials to the reactor fuel helps to conserve uranium-235, the only naturally-occurring fissionable material. Less than 1% of the uranium present in the earth's crust is ^{235}U, but nearly all of the remainder is the fertile isotope ^{238}U which forms fissionable plutonium-239 when struck by neutrons. Some reactors are designed to produce slightly more fissionable material than is used to operate them. This is called *breeding*, and such reactors are known as *breeders*. Reactors that produce almost as much fissionable material as they use are termed *near-breeders*. Most of the present power reactors use more fissionable material than they produce and are referred to as *converters*.

Slow-moving neutrons are more effective in triggering fission than fast-moving neutrons. When released from a fissionable nucleus, neutrons travel at very high speeds. As they collide with the reactor core, they are slowed and become more effective. However, as more collisions occur, the chance increases that any particular neutron will collide with an atom that will absorb it. To reduce the chance of such neutron losses, a *moderator* is included in the reactor. This is a material that slows, but absorbs relatively few neutrons. Most commonly used are ordinary water, heavy (deuterated) water, graphite, beryllium, and some organic compounds. In some reactors, the moderator circulates between the fuel rods; in others, the moderator is mixed with or surrounds the fuel.

A few reactors, known as *fast reactors*, do not utilize moderators and their fuel is more highly *enriched* (the concentration of fissionable ^{235}U is greater than that in natural uranium. In moderated reactors, ^{235}U makes up 6% or less of the total uranium. In breeders it forms 25-50%). Fast neutrons are very effective in initiating fission in such enriched fuels.

Each fission releases two or three neutrons. From the time they are released to the time they trigger another fission event or are absorbed, these neutrons exist in a free state only about one ten-thousandth of a second. Most neutrons are released at the instant of fission, but some are released a few seconds or minutes later. If all the neutrons were released immediately, a slight increase in the *population* (numbers) of neutrons from one generation of fusions to the next would result in a several-hundredfold increase in the rate of fission. It would be nearly impossible to control the rate of fission closely. However, if the neutron population in the core is kept to a point at which delayed neutrons are needed to keep the fission chain reaction operating, the rate of fission increases slowly enough that the reactor can be controlled easily.

The rate of fission is controlled with *poisons* — such substances as cadmium and boron, which have a large capacity to absorb neutrons. These poisons "blot up" neutrons from the core and thereby reduce the neutron population. Usually poisons are contained in cylinders inserted into the reactor or withdrawn by means of adjustable rods, known as *control rods.* Most reactors have two sets of control rods. One set, the *safety rods,* is used in emergencies to shut down the reactor quickly. The second set, the *regulating rods,* is used for regular control purposes.

When the core is being loaded with fuel, the control rods are placed in the "in" position. After the reactor is loaded, it is started up by drawing out the safety rods. The regulating rods are pulled out slowly while the rate of fission in the core is measured with neutron-counting instruments. Once the reactor "goes critical," that is, once the fission chain reaction has become self-sustaining, the regulating rods are moved only to maintain a constant fission rate. The regulating rods are drawn farther out to increase the reactor power level — to increase the rate of fission — and are pushed in to reduce the power level. The reactor is "shut down" — the fission reaction is stopped — by fully inserting all control rods.

Several hundred nuclear reactors now are in operation in the United States. Most are small reactors used in research, teaching, and materials testing. We also have equipped submarines and surface ships with reactors and are experimenting with others, to be used in airplanes and space satellites. One of the most important applications of reactors, however, is to produce electricity. (See map inside front cover.)

During the next 20 years, the United States will use as much fossil fuel — coal, petroleum, and natural gas — as it has used in its whole history. Although our reserves of these fuels are large, they could be exhausted by the year 2100. Much of this fuel is burned to produce electricity. If nuclear reactors are installed at electric generating stations, fossil fuels — especially coal — could be conserved for other uses, such as the production of gasoline and as raw materials for plastics and other chemicals. America's first large-scale nuclear electric station began operation in 1957 at Slippingport, Pennsylvania. Electricity now can be produced in nuclear stations at costs about equal to those in conventional stations. As our experience grows, nuclear power costs will become less than those for power from fossil fuels.

Electric generating stations are of two basic types. In hydroelectric plants (page 75), moving water rotates huge turbines, connected to electric generators. In steam electric plants, heat is produced to change water into steam. The steam, under pressure, is directed against the blades of a turbine. The turbine is connected to an electric generator. In *conventional steam electric plants,* heat is produced by burning coal. In a *nuclear electric plant,* heat is produced in a nuclear reactor. The electric generating system of a nuclear plant is the same as that in a conventional plant and, of course, the electricity produced is identical.

Nearly 90% of the energy released by fission in a reactor is represented by kinetic energy of fission products and, to a much smaller extent, of free neutrons. These particles fly apart with tremendous speed and, as they bump into surrounding reactor parts, their kinetic energy is converted to heat. This heat must be removed continuously or the reactor might experience a *nuclear excursion* — that is, it may become so hot that the core would melt if the reactor were not shut down. In power reactors, which operate with core temperatures of 500°F. or higher, heat is the chief product. It is removed by a heat-transfer fluid, known as the *coolant*. Coolants used in power reactors include ordinary water, heavy (deuterated) water, air, helium gas, carbon dioxide gas, fused salts, and liquid metals (as sodium, lithium, potassium, or molten bismuth). The reactor core is enclosed within a massive steel tank called the *reactor vessel*. The coolant is circulated through the reactor vessel and then flows out to a heat exchanger, or steam generator.

In theory, a nuclear reactor could operate at any power level. They are limited, however, by the rate at which heat can be removed from the core. For this reason, the coolant selected for use largely determines the design of a power reactor. It is common to describe the kind of reactor by naming its coolant and moderating substances. Water is used for both purposes in many present reactors.

When a reactor is planned, people living near the proposed site often wonder if the reactor could cause an atomic blast. This is not possible because the fuel in a reactor is not as highly enriched as fissionable materials must be in a bomb. However, a reactor could overheat. This could cause a non-nuclear explosion if the pressure of the coolant fluid became too great. Such an explosion might scatter solid radioactive materials and release radioactive gases and liquids. But such an accident is made almost impossible by the many "fail-safe" devices. Automatic systems constantly monitor the rate of activity and temperatures in the reactor and other portions of the plant. These systems are connected to switches which are set to shut down the reactor immediately if a potentially dangerous condition is detected. In addition, there are temperature fuses in the control rods which melt at a temperature lower than that which would cause damage to the nuclear fuel elements. If these fuses melt, the control rods drop into the core and shut down the reactor. The final safety device is the huge *containment vessel* which is strong enough to withstand the greatest pressure which could be exerted by the reactor materials in the event of an explosion. The outline of the containment vessel is the most conspicuous feature of most nuclear power stations. Often, it is a huge, hollow steel ball.

PLANTS, ANIMALS AND THE ATOM

Plants in experimental garden are exposed to radiation which produces unusual changes.

For many years, scientists have known which elements occur in living things and the proportion of their tissues composed of each. But they were not certain how the various elements entered, nor did they understand the action of the elements within the bodies of the plants and animals. Recently, however, we have learned to trace "tagged" atoms — radioactive isotopes which release small amounts of radiation — by the use of radiation-detecting devices, such as geiger counters. When a few tagged atoms are mixed with normal ones, the movement of an element can be followed from the instant it enters the body of a living thing until it leaves the body.

Crude model represents tagged atom in organic molecule.

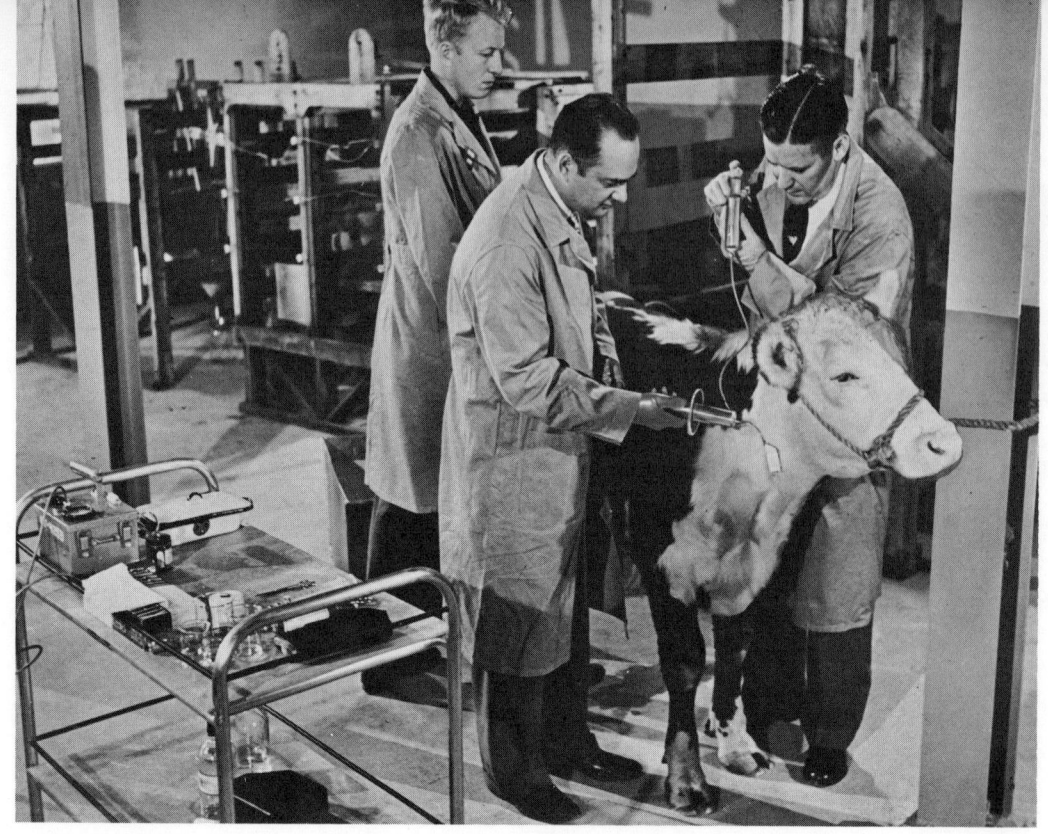

Radioisotopes are used to learn how milk is formed in the body of a cow.

Radioactive isotopes have been added to animals' food and injected into various parts of their bodies to study how cows make milk and how eggs form in hens.

Tagged atoms have proved valuable in medicine, too. The discovery that iodine always collects in the thyroid gland led to the development of a new method of treating thyroid cancer. Radioactive iodine administered to a patient accumulates in the thyroid and its radiations kill the cancer cells. Scientists now are searching for chemicals that accumulate in other organs of the body. The photograph showing a patient in an operating room illustrates the use of krypton-85, a harmless radioactive gas that is inhaled by the patient. From the lungs, the gas passes into the blood and is carried to the left side of the heart. If radioactivity is detected immediately in blood samples drawn from an artery supplied by the right side of the heart, surgeons know that there is a leak between the two chambers of the heart.

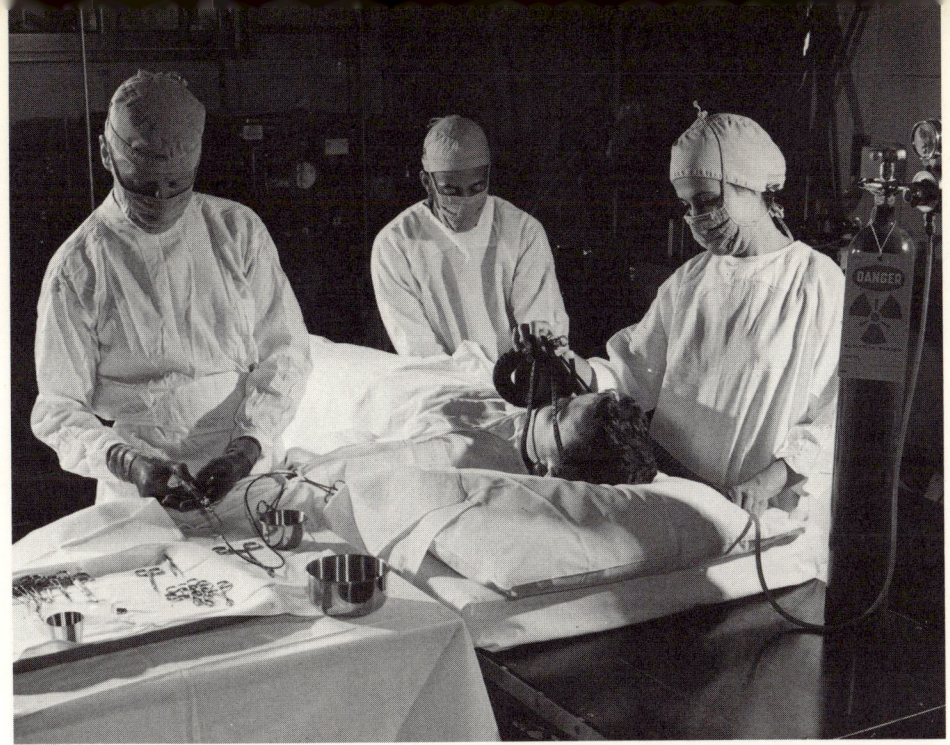

Research workers also are studying the harmful effect of radiation on the human body. Experiments which may cause malformations cannot be performed on humans. Therefore, scientists must study people who were irradiated during atomic blasts in World War II, or during accidental exposures since then. Much data valuable to medicine also is obtained by studying the effect of radiation upon other kinds of animals.

Technician observes rat treated with tagged drug. Isolation cage allows control of environment and analysis of all waste products.

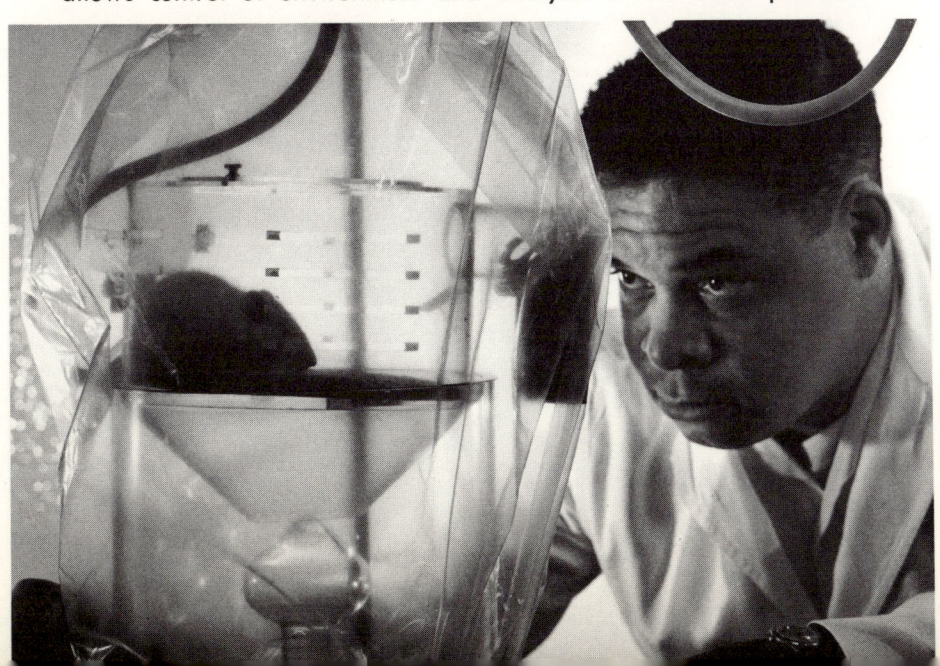

APPENDIX
ENGLISH AND METRIC MEASUREMENTS

LINEAR MEASURES — English System
1 inch (in.) = 2.54 centimeters
12 in. = 1 foot (ft.) = 30.48 centimeters
3 ft. = 1 yard (yd.) = 91.44 centimeters = 9.144 decimeters
16½ ft. = 1 rod = 5.0292 meters
5,280 ft. = 1 mile (mi.) = 1.6093 kilometers

LINEAR MEASURES — Metric System
1 millimeter (mm) = 0.03937 inch
10 mm = 1 centimeter (cm) = 0.3937 inch
100 cm = 1 meter (m) = 39.37008 inches = 3.2808 feet
1,000 m = 1 kilometer (km) = 3,280.83 feet = 0.62137 mile

SQUARE MEASURES — English System
```
              1 square inch (sq. in.)              = 6.4516 sq. cm
144 sq. in.  = 1 square foot (sq. ft.)             = 929.0304 sq. cm
  9 sq. ft.  = 1 square yard (sq. yd.)             = 0.8361 sq. m
4,840 sq. yd. = 1 acre (A.) = 43,560 sq. ft.       = 4,046.8564 sq. m
640 A.       = 1 square mile (sq. mi.)             = 2.5899 sq. km
```

SQUARE MEASURES — Metric System
```
               1 square millimeter (sq. mm or mm²) = 0.00155 sq. in.
  100 mm²    = 1 square centimeter (sq. cm or cm²) = 0.1550 sq. in.
  100 cm²    = 1 square decimeter (sq. dm or dm²)  = 15.5000 sq. in.
  100 dm²    = 1 square meter (sq. m or m²)        = 10.7639 sq. ft.
10,000 m²    = 1 hectare (ha)                      = 2.4710 acres
1,000,000 m² = 1 square kilometer (sq. km or km²)  = 0.3861 sq. mi. = 247.1040 acres
```

CUBIC MEASURE — English System
```
              1 cubic inch (cu. in.)                      = 16.3871 cu. cm
1728 cu. in. = 1 cubic foot (cu. ft.) = 7.4805 gallons    = 0.0283 cu. m
  27 cu. ft. = 1 cubic yard (cu. yd.)                     = 0.7645 cu. m
```

LIQUID CAPACITY — English System
```
              1 fluid ounce (fl. oz.) = 1.8047 cu. in.    = 0.02957 liter
16 fl. oz.  = 1 liquid pint (pt.)                        = 0.4732 liter
 2 pt.      = 1 liquid quart (qt.)                       = 0.9463 liter
 4 qt.      = 1 gallon (gal.) = 0.1337 cu. ft.           = 3.7853 liters
```

DRY CAPACITY — *English System*

$$\begin{aligned}
&& 1 \text{ dry pint (dry pt.)} &= 0.5506 \text{ liter} \\
2 \text{ dry pt.} &= 1 \text{ dry quart (dry qt.)} &&= 1.1012 \text{ liters} \\
32 \text{ dry pt.} &= 1 \text{ bushel (bu.)} &&= 35.2381 \text{ liters}
\end{aligned}$$

CUBIC MEASURE AND CAPACITY — *Metric System*

1 cubic centimeter (cc) = 1 (0.999972) millimeter (ml) = 0.0610 cu. in.
1 cubic decimeter (cu. dm) = 1,000 ml = 1 liter (l) = 61.024 cu. in. = 1.0567 qt.
1 cubic meter = 1,000 l = 1 kiloliter (kl) = 35.3147 cu. ft. = 264.17205 gal.

MASS — *English System*

1 grain = .0648 gram
437.5 grains = 1 ounce (oz.) = 28.3495 grams
16 oz. = 1 pound (lb.) = 453.59237 grams
2,000 lb. = 1 short ton (sh. t.) = 907.1847 kilograms = 0.907 metric ton

MASS — *Metric System*

1 gram (g) = 0.03527 oz.
1,000 g = 1 kilogram (kg) = 2.2046 lb.
1,000,000 g = 1,000 kg = 1 metric ton (t) = 2,204.6226 lb.

FORCE — *English System*

1 poundal = force that gives a 1 pound mass an acceleration
of 1 foot per second per second = 0.138 newton
1 pound = 32.17 poundals = 4.45 newtons

FORCE — *Metric System*

1 dyne = force that gives 1 gram mass an acceleration of
1 centimeter per second per second = 0.0007 poundal
100,000 dynes = 1 newton = 7.233 poundals

SPEED — *English System*

1 foot per second = 0.682 miles per hour = 0.305 meters
per second
1.467 feet per second = 1 mile per hour = 1.609 kilometers
per hour
1.15 miles per hour = 1 knot (1 nautical mile per hour) =
1.85 kilometers per hour

SPEED — *Metric System*

1 meter per second = 3.6 kilometers per hour = 2.237 miles
per hour
1 kilometer per hour = 0.278 meters per second = 0.621
miles per hour

Index

A

Absolute units, 69
Acids, 132
Acceleration, 72, 85, 91
Accelerator, 155
Action and reaction, 46, 47
Air, composition, 120
    foils, 166
    pressure, 122, 123, 180
    reactor coolant, 215
    weight, 121
Airplane, 161, 166, 214
Alternating current, 66, 175
Aluminum, 190
Amorphous carbon, 124
Ampere, 98
Animals and the atom, 217
Anodes, 185
Antenna, 175
Archimedes' principle, 150
Area, 80
Armature, 159
Atlas rocket, 165
Atmosphere, 120
Atom bomb, 212
Atomic energy, 209
    mass, 16, 17, 210
    numbers, 16, 17
    radiation, 217
    theory, 12
Atoms, 12-19
Axle, wheel and, 106

B

Ball bearings, 63
Balloons, 130, 150
    weather, 131
Bar magnet, 70
Bases, 133
Bauxite, 190
Beam balance, 84
Bending light, 170
Beryllium, 17, 213
Binders, paint, 203
Binding energy, 210
Biochemistry, biophysics, 119
Biological science, 9
Bismuth, 17, 216
Blast furnace, 188
Blimps, 151
Boats, 150
Body composition, 140
Boiler, steam, 152
Boiling point, 38
Boron, 17, 214
Borosilicate glass, 197
Bottled gas, 192
Breeding, 213
British measure, 78
British thermal unit (B.t.u.), 97
Broadcasting, 175
Brushes, 159
Burning, 129

C

Cadmium, 17, 214
Calorie, 97
Calorimeter, 97
Camera, 206
    TV, 176
Cancer research, 218
Carbohydrates, 141
Carbon, 124
    compounds, 125, 146
    cycle, 127
Carbon dioxide extinguishers, 199
Carbon dioxide gas, 120, 126, 127, 144, 154, 215
Cathodes, 185
Caustics, 133
Celsius, centigrade scales, 95
Centrifugal force, 43, 44, 83
Centripetal force, 43, 44
Cesium, 176
Chain reaction, 212
Change, of phase, 36
    physical, chemical, 24, 25
Charges, electrical, 66
Chemical change, 24
    energy, 64, 75
    reactions, 26
Chemistry, 9
Chlorophyll, 144
Clocks, 89
Coal, 125, 215
Colloidal dispersions, 22
Colors, glass, 197
    paints, 202
Combination reaction, 26
Combustion, 129
Commutator, 159
Compounds, 20
Compression stroke, 154
Compressor, 179
Concave lenses, 171
Condensation, 24, 134
Conduction, 58
Conductor, electrical, 66
Conservation of energy, 75
Containment vessel, 216
Contact poisons, 205
Control rods, 208, 214
Convection, 59
Converging lenses, 170, 182, 183
Conversion of energy, 75
Convex lenses, 170
Coolant, 215-216
Core, reactor, 212
Courier satellite, 57
Covalence, 19
Cracking tower, 192
Crank, 106
Crankshaft, 153, 155
Critical mass, 212
Crystalline carbon, 124
    solids, 34
Currents, electric, 66, 175
Cycle, electric, 66
Cylinder, 152, 155

D

Dalton, John, 12
Day, solar, 89
Decomposition reaction, 26
Definite proportions, law of, 12
Density, 86
Detergents, 201
Deuterated water, see Heavy water
Diaphragm, telephone, 172
Diesel engine, 156
Diet, balanced, 146
Diode, 175
Direct current, 66
Dirigible, 130
Dispersion, types of, 22, 23
Diverging lenses, 171
Double replacement reaction, 26, 133
Drag, 166
Ductility, 35
Dyne, 69, 82, 93

E

Echo satellite, 43, 195
Effort, 101
Electric currents, 66, 175
    meter, 98
    motor, 159
Electric plant
    hydroelectric, 75, 215
    steam, conventional, 215
    steam, nuclear, 215
Electrical charges, 66
    energy, 66, 75, 159
Electricity, 98
    static, 66
Electrodes, 185
Electrolysis, 185
Electromagnetic waves, 56
Electromagnets, 71, 159
Electromotive force (e.m.f.), 99
Electron gun, 176
    shells, 18
Electrons, 13, 129, 175, 176
Electroplating, 185
Electrovalence, 18
Elements, 12, 14
    in the air, 120
    in the body, 140
    in plants, 142, 143
    table of, 17
Emulsion, 23
Endothermic reaction, 26, 65
Energy, 51, 75
    atomic, 209
    chemical, 64
    conservation of, 75
    conversion of, 75
    electrical, 66, 159
    heat, 58, 60, 65, 212
    kinetic, 53, 55, 75, 160, 215
    levels, 18
    light, 144
    mechanical, 60, 159
    motion, 53-55
    potential, 52, 53, 75
    radiant, 56
    rotational, 75
    stored, 52
Energy from food, 65, 140
    from sun, 65, 145
Engines, 152-159
English system, 78
Erg, 193
Evaporation, 38, 135, 137
Excursion, nuclear, 215
Exhaust stroke, 155
Exothermic reaction, 26, 65
Extinguishers, fire, 198
Eyepiece, 182

F

Fahrenheit scale, 95
Fail-safe devices, 216

Index (continued)

Farm chemistry, 205
Fats, 141
Fermi, Enrico, 209
Fertite material, 213
Fertilizer, 205
Film, 206
Fire extinguishers, 198
Fission, nuclear, 209-215
Fissionable material, 212, 213
Floating, 150
Fluid friction, 60
Flying chair, 164
Flywheel, 155
Foamite extinguisher, 199
Focal length, 170, 182, 183
Focus, 170
Foot-pound, 93
Force, 68, 101
Fractional distillation, 192
Friction, 41, 60, 68
Fuel assembly, 212
Fuel, enriched, 213
Fuel, fossil, 215
Fuel rods, 212
Fulcrum, 102
Fusion, nuclear, 211

G

Gamma globulin, 138
Gas engine, 154
Gas, natural, 215
Gas turbine engine, 163
Gases, 29-31
Gasoline, 192
Gears, 109
Geiger counter, 217
Generator, 66, 75
Glass, 196
Glassy solids, 35
Graphite, 125, 212, 213
Gravitation, 72
Gravitational units, 69
Gravity, 68, 72, 82-85, 166
    specific, 86, 150
Grid, radio, 175

H

Hahn, Otto, 209
Hall process, 190
Hardness, 35
Heat, 58, 97
    energy, 58, 65, 75, 212
    mechanical equivalent of, 60
    specific, 97
    total, 97
Heavy water, 16, 213, 215
Helicopter, 166
Helium, 131, 209, 215
Hematite, 188
Hindenburg, 130
Horsepower, 93
Hydrocarbons, 192
Hydrogen, 15, 120, 130
Hydrogen isotopes, 16
Hydroxides, 133

I

Ice, 38, 39
Image, real, 170
    virtual, 171

Incandescent substances, 57
Inclined plane, 112
Industry and the atom, 214
Inertia, 40, 160
Insecticides, 205
Insulators, 66
Intake stroke, 154
Internal combustion engine, 154
Inverted image, 170, 182, 183
Ions, 18
Iron, 188
Isotopes, 16, 210, 213, 217, 218

J

Jet engines, 160, 161
Joule, 93

K

Kerosene, 192
Kilowatt hours, 98, 99
Kilowatts, 93
Kinetic energy, 53-55, 75, 160, 215
    of molecules, 58
Krypton, 17, 79, 218

L

Latent heat of evaporation, 38
    of fusion, 37
Laws of motion, 40-45, 68, 161
Lead glass, 197
Lenses, 170, 177, 182, 183
Levers, 102
    three classes, 104
Lift, 166
    pump, 180
Light, speed of, 56
Light energy, 75, 144
Lightning, 169
Lime glass, 196
Limonite, 188
Liquid-fuel rockets, 164
Liquids, 28, 32, 61
Lithium 17, 215
Load, 102
Lodestone, 70
Lubrication, 63

M

Mach number, 91
Machines, 100-117
Magnets, magnesium, 70, 159
Malleability, 35
Mass, 68, 69, 82, 84, 85
Matter, 28
Mean solar day, 89
Measurements, 77-79
Mechanical advantage (M.A.), 101
    energy, 60, 75, 159
    equivalent of heat, 60
Melting point, 37
Mercury space capsule, 165
Metric system, 78
Microphone, 175
Microscope, 182
Mixtures, 21
Moderator, 213, 216
Molecules, 18
Motion, energy of, 53-55
    laws of, 40-45, 68, 161

Multiple proportions, law of, 13
Mylar plastic, 195

N

National Bureau of Standards, 79, 97
Negative electric charge, 66
    electrode, 185
    photograph, 206
Neutrons, 13, 210, 215
Newton, 69, 82
Newton, Sir Isaac, 40
Newton's Laws, 40-45
Nitrifying bacteria, 138, 139
Nitrogen, 138
Nitrogen cycle, 139
North pole, 70
Nuclear excursion, 215
Nuclear fission, 209-215
    electric plant, 215
    fusion, 211
    reactors, 208, 209, 212, 216
Nucleons, 13, 210
Nucleus, 13, 210

O

Objective lens, 182, 183
Ocular lens, 182, 183
Ohm, 99
Oil, 192
Open hearth furnace, 189
Optical glass, 197
Organic chemistry, 125
Oxidation, 64, 129, 209
Oxygen, 120, 128

P

Paint, 202
Parachute, 30
Peach Bottom Atomic Power
    Station, 208-209
Petroleum, 192, 215
Phases of matter, 28
Photography, 206
Photosynthesis, 65, 135, 144
Physical change, 24
Physical science, physics, 9
Picture tube, 176
Pigments, 202
Pioneer V, 91
Pistons, 155
Pitch, screw, 116
Plant chemistry, 65, 142, 217
Plastic paints, 203
    resins, 194
    solids, 35
Plastics, 194
Plate, radio tube, 175
Poison, neutron, 214
Polyethylene, 195
Polymerization, 192, 195
Positive electric charge, 66
    electrode, 185
    photograph, 207
Potassium, 17, 215
Potential energy, 52, 53, 75
Pound, 69
Poundal, 69
Power, 93
Power arm, 102
    stroke, 155

Index (continued)

Precipitation, 135, 136
Pressure, air, 122, 123, 180
Principal focus, 170
Properties, 49
Proteins, 138, 141
Protoplasm, 138
Proton, 13
Prototypes, 79
Pulley, 110
Pumps, 181
Pyrene extinguisher, 199

Q

Quantum, 56

R

Radiant energy, 56
Radiation, 59
Radio, 175
Radioactive isotopes, 217, 218
Ramjet, 163
Reaction, 45, 161, 164
Reactions, chemical, 26
Reactor, breeder, 213
Reactor, converter, 213
Reactor, fast, 213
Reactions, nuclear, 212
Reactor, gas-cooled, 208-209
Reactor, near-breeder, 213
Reactor, nuclear, 208, 209, 212, 216
Reactor vessel, 216
Real image, 170, 183
Receiver, 173
Reciprocating engines, 160
Reducing agent, 129, 131
Reduction reaction, 129, 189
Refraction, 170
Refrigeration, 178
Refrigerator, 179
Regulating rods, 214
Replacement reaction, 26
Resistance, 101
　electrical, 99
Rockets, 164
Roller bearings, 63
Rolling friction, 60, 63
Rotary motion, 160
Rotor, 160, 166

S

Safety rods, 214
Salts, 133
San Onofre reactor, 212
Satellites, artificial, 43, 44, 195, 214
Screen, TV, 176
Screw, 116
Self-sustaining reaction, 212

Shipping port reactor, 215
Simple machines, 100-117
Sliding fraction, 60, 63
Soaps, 200
Soda-acid extinguisher, 199
Sodium, 17, 215
Solar cells, 57
Solar noon, 89
Solenoid, 71
Solid-fuel rockets, 164
Solids, 28, 34
Solutions, 22, 23, 185
Sound, 168, 173, 175
South pole, 70
Space shots, 165
Specific gravity, 86, 150
　heat, 97
　properties, 49
Speed, 91
　of light, 56
　of sound, 91, 169
Spring scale, 84
Spyglass, 183
Standards of measurements, 78
States of matter, 28
Static electricity, 66
Steam, 134
Steam engine, 152
Steel production, 188
Stomach poisons, 205
Stored energy, 52
Strassman, Fritz, 209
Submarine, 151, 214
Sub-critical reaction, 212
Subsonic speed, 91
Sun, energy from, 65, 145
Super-cooled liquid, 196
Supersonic speed, 91
Surface tension, 33
Suspension, 23
Symbols, atomic, 16, 17, 138

T

Target, TV, 177
Telephone, 172
Telescopes, 183
Television, 176
Temperature, 36, 94, 178
Temperature scales, 95
Tenacity, 35
Thermal expansion, 94
Thermometers, 94
Thermonuclear reactions, 211
Thermoplastic resins, 194
Thermosetting resins, 194
Thiamine, 146
Thinners, paint, 203
Thompson, Sir Joseph J., 13

Thorium, fissionable, 214
Thorium dioxide, 212
Thrust, 166
Thunder, 169
Time, 88
　measuring, 89
Tools as machines, 114-117
Total heat, 97
Transmitter, 172
Transpiration, 135
Triode, 175
Turbines, 75, 160, 163
Turbojet, 162
Turboprop, 162

U

Uranium, 15, 212, 214
Uranium dioxide, 212

V

Vacuum cleaner, 184
Vacuum tube, 175
Valence, 18, 129
Van Helmot, 142
Velocity, 41, 68, 73, 91
Virtual image, 171, 182, 183
Viscosity, 61
Vitamins, 146
Vitreous solids, 35
Volt, 99
Volume, 80
Von Guericke, Otto, 123

W

Water, 32, 38, 134, 213, 215
Water cycle, 135-137
　density, 134
　pumps, 181
　turbine, 75
　vapor, 38, 120, 135
Water-soluble paints, 203
Watts, 93, 99
Wave lengths, radiant energy, 56
Weather balloons, 131
Wedge, 114
Weight, 82, 84, 85
Weightlessness, 83
Wheel and axle, 106
Woodward, John, 142
Work, 93, 101

Z

Zirconium, 212